SanFrancisco™
Design Patterns

SanFrancisco™ Design Patterns
Blueprints for Business Software

James Carey
Brent Carlson
Tim Graser

ADDISON–WESLEY

An Imprint of Addison Wesley Longman, Inc.

Reading, Massachusetts • Harlow, England • Menlo Park, California
Berkeley, California • Don Mills, Ontario • Sydney
Bonn • Amsterdam • Tokyo • Mexico City

Many of the designations used by manufacturers and sellers to distinguish their products are claimed as trademarks. Where those designations appear in this book, and Addison Wesley Longman Inc. was aware of a trademark claim, the designations have been printed with initial capital letters or in all capitals.

The authors and publisher have taken care in the preparation of this book, but make no expressed or implied warranty of any kind and assume no responsibility for errors or omissions. No liability is assumed for incidental or consequential damages in connection with or arising out of the use of the information or programs contained herein.

The publisher offers discounts on this book when ordered in quantity for special sales. For more information, please contact:

AWL Direct Sales
Addison Wesley Longman, Inc.
One Jacob Way
Reading, Massachusetts 01867
(781) 944-3700

Visit AW on the Web: www.awl.com/cseng/

Library of Congress Cataloging-in-Publication Data
Carey, James, 1962–
   SanFranciso design patterns : blueprints for business software / James Carey, Brent Carlson, Tim Graser.
      p. cm.
   Includes bibliographical references and index.
   ISBN 0-201-61644-0
   1. Object-oriented methods (Computer science) 2. IBM SanFrancisco. 3. Application software—Development. I. Carlson, Brent, 1961– II. Graser, Tim, 1965– III. Title.

QA76.9.O35 C365 2000
005.1'17—dc21   99-089298

ISBN 0-201-61644-0
Text printed on recycled paper
1 2 3 4 5 6 7 8 9 10—CRS—0403020100
First printing, March 2000

Contents

v

Part II   Behavioral Patterns   59

Chapter 7   Simple Policy   61

Chapter 8   Chain of Responsibility-Driven Policy   75

Chapter 9   Token-Driven Policy   91

Part III   Structural Patterns   101

Part IV   Process Patterns   191

Chapter 13   Cached Aggregate   193

Chapter 14   Keyed Attribute Retrieval   221

Chapter 15   List Generation   235

Part V   Dynamic Behavioral Patterns   247

Chapter 16   Extensible Item   249

Chapter 17   Hierarchical Extensible Item   269

Chapter 18   Business Entity Lifecycle   285

Foreword

Human beings learn in different ways for different purposes. Software, in my view, is an engineering profession—engineers are builders, and for builders to learn they need to look at buildings. They need to see how the buildings are constructed, to find what worked, to understand problems—whether or not they were solved.

But software's buildings are hidden things, with design decisions masked behind compilation and discussions and principles lost to fading memories. If we want to advance, we need to see more of these designs. We need to learn more about the hardest part of software development—that little-understood skill of design.

Back when I began working with objects, we were offered an alluring glimpse of the future: standard business objects, bought with the same ease that a hardware engineer buys chips. Armed with these components—an account here, a customer there—we could assemble new software systems with much of the difficult detail work already completed. What a false promise this has been! Business systems are fiendishly complicated, more so even than operating systems and graphics frameworks. Building such a library of reusable objects has been software's El Dorado.

IBM's SanFrancisco project has tried to reach this El Dorado. It's developed a framework of business components that aims to realize the promise of those early dreams. In doing so it's faced head-on the complexities of building frameworks for business software. It's also faced the primary challenge of doing this on a global scale: providing components that will work just as well in Peking as in Peoria.

Although this book is essential to anyone who wants to use SanFrancisco, the concepts it captures go beyond SanFrancisco the product. This book is priceless because it explains why the developers of SanFrancisco designed things the way they did. As such it takes a good hard look at the problems involved in writing flexible business software, and the patterns inherent in the solutions this team came up with.

If you are at all involved in large framework or business application development, you should study this book. It doesn't present academic theories about how software *should* work; instead it shows you the techniques used in one of the largest, most complex framework developments ever. Its lessons are there for all of us to learn.

—Martin Fowler

Preface

One of the core forces behind object-oriented development is the need to manage increasing application complexity. Object-oriented techniques are not a magic bullet in this regard; however, a well-executed object-oriented design will result in well-partitioned assignment of responsibility across the objects within the design—a major step toward isolating complex pieces of an application.

Many of you have already discovered the power of object-oriented design patterns when defining and implementing complex applications. IBM's SanFrancisco Application Business Components is a set of frameworks that have been built around design patterns, both those that are well known throughout the software industry and new patterns described in this book. Why new design patterns? As we analyzed the requirements of typical business applications, we discovered many recurring situations whose needs were not adequately met by existing patterns. Often those needs could be met by extensions of well-known patterns; sometimes new patterns arose directly out of specific business application requirements. This book covers both the extended and the new patterns of IBM SanFrancisco, describing them within the context of a typical business application's requirements.

So what should you expect to get out of this book? The design patterns documented here capture the experiences we have gained from developing business components across multiple business domains. Every pattern in this book has been refined through multiple uses within SanFrancisco and has been validated by users of the frameworks as they build and deploy applications based on SanFrancisco. In particular, we have found these patterns very useful in helping us "think outside of the box" when confronted with complex business application requirements.

Regardless of your level of design experience, we encourage you to read this book with an eye toward the design problems you have come across in your past and toward opportunities to apply these patterns (or extensions of them) to your current projects.

About This Book

This book follows the format established by Gamma, Vlissides, Johnson, and Helm (the "Gang of Four") in their groundbreaking book *Design Patterns: Elements of Reusable Object-Oriented Software* (Addison-Wesley, 1995). Beginning in Chapter 2 with a case study describing a typical set of business requirements for a hypothetical food distribution enterprise, the book continues with chapters that address each design pattern in turn. Each pattern is defined along the lines of the standard design pattern template used by the *Design Patterns* book, typically incorporating an aspect of the case study to provide a concrete example that motivates the pattern.

Introduction

Over the course of IBM SanFrancisco development, our belief in design patterns as a core component of effective object-oriented development has been strongly reinforced. Chapter 1 distills some of the key reasons for this belief. Those of you who are already sold on design patterns won't find any great revelations here, but we hope you will find the consolidation of these points in one place to be useful. Those of you who are new to design patterns will find some strong arguments for using them in all your object-oriented development projects.

Case Study

Design patterns don't exist in a vacuum. Each design pattern described in this book was developed as a result of meeting real-life business application requirements. What we have attempted to do in the case study (Chapter 2) is provide a business context for many of the patterns in this book. (Although not all patterns are used in the case study, we provide a detailed business motivation in each pattern chapter of this book.) If your background is oriented toward business analysis, the case study will help justify these patterns and will help you make the leap from business domain analysis to object-oriented design. If your background is primarily technical, the case study will help you communicate with business experts as you jointly explore the right solutions for specific application requirements.

Design Patterns

Design patterns, as you would expect, are the core of this book. Many of the design patterns we describe build on or are extensions of patterns defined in *Design Patterns,* and you will find it helpful to have previously read about and used those patterns. However, each pattern in this book is described in enough detail for you to understand its purpose, design, and implementation without a detailed knowledge of any underlying design patterns.

This book divides the patterns into five major categories:

- **Part I: Foundational Patterns.** SanFrancisco's foundational patterns provide an underlying structure for all SanFrancisco-based business objects. The foundational patterns provide mechanisms for business object creation, changing behavior, and construction of business processes. Many of these patterns are incorporated into higher-level patterns described in the remaining parts of the book.

- **Part II: Behavioral Patterns.** SanFrancisco's behavioral patterns describe various methods of incorporating flexible algorithms throughout a business application. Each of the behavioral object patterns described in this book defines a variation or extension of the Strategy pattern defined by *Design Patterns.*

- **Part III: Structural Patterns.** SanFrancisco's structural patterns are concerned with how business information is organized and accessed. Structural class patterns deal with the issue of business information access through inheritance. Structural object patterns define how business information (in the form of business objects) is organized within the scope of a complex business environment.

- **Part IV: Process Patterns.** SanFrancisco's process patterns are concerned with how businesses organize and process information. The process patterns do not identify the information involved, but rather define *how* businesses work with that information. Process patterns can be applied in many business situations. The use of these patterns provides consistency for the same types of processes, allowing the user to grasp more quickly the mode of information processing and the flexibility provided as part of that processing.

- **Part V: Dynamic Behavioral Patterns.** SanFrancisco's dynamic behavioral patterns describe object-oriented approaches for modeling entities in the business domain that exhibit behavioral changes throughout their existence— not only changes to existing behavior, but also changes to the set of behaviors (responsibilities) supported by the business entity at any given time. The dynamic behavioral patterns described in this book build on the general concepts described in the State pattern of *Design Patterns* and on one another.

Acknowledgments

Many people have been involved in the development of this book and the ideas behind it, and it's impossible for us to list them all, but we'll give it a shot.

First, we would like to thank Paul Monday and Robert Schmidt, who established the "Publish" pattern for books on IBM SanFrancisco and grappled with the numerous (and often tedious) details to build a long-term working relationship between Addison-Wesley and members of the SanFrancisco development team. Thanks also go to Tyrrell Albaugh, Paul Becker, Julie DeBaggis, Mike Hendrickson, and Ross Venables of Addison-Wesley for being patient with us as we struggled to keep a collective balance among work, personal lives, and meeting publishing deadlines; we have to admit that there were times when those deadlines got the short end of the stick.

The patterns described in this book resulted from a team effort across the entire SanFrancisco development organization. Unfortunately, we can't list everyone who played a part, but we do want to mention some key individuals who played major roles in the process of building something that stands up to real-life business needs. Thanks go to Steve Salk for providing the continuing product vision for SanFrancisco from its inception through the present; to Robert Schmidt for providing crucial project management to the Germany-based development team as it developed the first release of SanFrancisco; and to Kathy Bohrer, the first chief architect of the SanFrancisco project, for establishing a strong foundation on which we could build and for trusting us enough to let us work through the hard problems of building a truly flexible and robust business framework. Thanks also go to Anders Nilsson, the business domain architect of SanFrancisco throughout much of its life; and to Tore Dahl, Finn Ganz, Jesper Lindblom, Tor Michalsen, Helge Ødegaard, Torbjörn Pernbeck, Stephen Porter, and the many other domain experts involved in the SanFrancisco project for continually stretching our initial design solutions to their business requirements until they broke, and then working with us to rebuild those designs into something better. Special thanks go to Tor Michalsen's second cousin, who helped us decide when to stop.

LindaMay Patterson and Clark Scholten worked closely with us throughout the development of this book, ultimately providing some of its contents. Thanks go to them for their significant contribution, and particularly for their patience with our perfectionist tendencies.

Our reviewers—Gary Alexander, Thomas Bishop, Michele Chilanti, Joshua Engel, Martin Fowler, and Edwin Jaufmann Jr.—were often opinionated and helped us crystallize thoughts about many of these patterns that otherwise would have gone unwritten. Nothing is quite so painful to an author as a seemingly innocuous review comment that ultimately forces the rewriting of a major section of the book. Although we may not have enjoyed receiving such comments, we (and this book) certainly benefited from them. Thanks go to our reviewers for their diligent efforts.

Finally, thanks go to our copy editor, Stephanie Hiebert, who tidied up after our somewhat messy efforts at the English language.

Now for the mushy stuff . . .

Brent would like to thank his wife Lisa for keeping "alles in Ordnung" during the hectic early days of the project in Germany, and for continually nudging him out of the rut that he would otherwise wear in life's path.

Tim would like to thank his wife Shirl and children Jaimee and Christopher for their love, patience, and understanding, and his parents Sid and Margaret for believing in him.

And finally, Jim would like to thank his wife Anne and children Joseph and Marinda for putting up with a second book so soon after the first. It wouldn't have happened without their patience and support. Also, he would like to thank his parents, Barbara and John, for teaching him to see patterns in the world around him.

1

Introduction

Designing a business application is difficult, designing reusable components for a business application is more difficult, and designing a reusable framework on which multiple business applications can be built is still more difficult. Under the auspices of the SanFrancisco development team, IBM, with the help of various application providers, set about building application frameworks for specific business domains. The resulting application frameworks aid application providers in creating highly flexible business applications within those domains and allow them to create these applications more rapidly than by starting from scratch.

By using object-oriented technology, the SanFrancisco team was able to provide the basis for these next-generation business applications. Object technology is all about managing complexity and being receptive to change. The complexity of frameworks is an order of magnitude higher than the complexity of applications focused on a specific implementation of a business domain. Frameworks have the resulting payback in flexibility. Design patterns are key to managing and organizing complex concepts into an understandable form.

The SanFrancisco effort to build application frameworks provided many challenges for the development team. The frameworks needed to be extremely flexible because they were to be used to build various applications, each with its own specific set of requirements. Each of us as authors were directly involved in developing these frameworks from the ground up, and we have found through the experience of building application frameworks five key benefits from using patterns:

1. **Thinking out of the box** to solve difficult application problems
2. **Providing a higher-level language** for designers to use when solving design problems, and for developers and domain experts to use for communication
3. **Dealing with complexity** by using consistent approaches throughout framework or application design
4. **Creating flexible solutions** for varying circumstances
5. **Increasing maintainability** for dynamic business problems

Let's explore these five benefits in more detail.

Thinking Out of the Box

By providing a library of potential design solutions to consider, design patterns help developers think about application problems in ways they might not have previously considered. In other words, the patterns documented in this book allowed us to quickly explore alternative solutions to the design problems we encountered when augmenting the frameworks. Often we found that an existing pattern solved a problem directly or with a simple variation. By performing this mapping process, we resolved most problems with minimal effort.

Historically there has never been enough time to create software, so by drawing from the pattern catalog to solve a majority of the problems, our team could focus its time on the unique problems that arose. In some situations these basic patterns were used as building blocks to devise a solution to the more unique problems. Often these solutions to unique business problems turned out to be not quite as unique as we originally thought, and we captured the common aspects of these solutions as additional design patterns building on top of previously defined patterns.

Providing a Higher-Level Language

Design patterns can be thought of as providing a higher-level language for developers to work with, much as compiled languages simplified the development of software when compared with writing programs in assembly languages. These patterns allowed us to communicate key design principles to the developers without discussing each aspect of the model in detail. Once each developer learned how a particular pattern operated, he or she knew what mechanisms to apply to the design and thus could work effectively. We used this language to communicate to the domain experts as well. With the motivation behind the pattern articulated, the domain experts could understand how the pattern was being used to solve the problem and could validate the solution.

Dealing with Complexity

Enterprise-strength business applications provide support for complex business functions. One of the most important jobs of a business application framework developer is to deal with the complex tasks and processes occurring within the domain. Patterns allowed us to break up these complex problems into smaller, graspable units, making the problems easier to think about and resolve. Breaking up application problems into smaller units had two benefits: The smaller units increased the flexibility of the solution, and they made the problems manageable.

Creating Flexible Solutions

A business application that can't be adapted to the needs of a particular user is not very useful. This truth becomes even more apparent in the building of an application framework. We used patterns to capture the essence of key business problems in a more abstract way. This approach allowed us to deal with the possible variations in the problem without necessarily having to implement them.

Increasing Maintainability

One of the major driving forces behind object-oriented development is its promise of improved application maintainability when compared to the "spaghetti code" that often results during the maintenance of existing applications developed using procedural languages. Proper use of design patterns helps accomplish the goal of improved maintainability by assisting the designer in providing a well-defined set of responsibilities for each class. By assigning these responsibilities appropriately, the designer isolates changes to a small subset of the objects in the application. Unlike conventional application development, this approach minimizes the code that must change to implement modifications.

The values we found in using and creating design patterns bring to mind the attributes of good object-oriented design. Design patterns reinforced these attributes by helping us achieve the objectives of good object-oriented design and creating truly flexible frameworks. This book presents the design patterns defined during the creation of SanFrancisco. We used these design patterns to overcome many of the design issues encountered in building flexible and understandable application frameworks.

Frameworks by SanFrancisco

The book *Design Patterns* defines a framework as a set of cooperating classes that make up a reusable design for a specific class of software. SanFrancisco's mission is to create highly flexible application frameworks that service a wide variety of implementations within specific domains. To build highly flexible and understandable application frameworks, we used well-established object-oriented software engineering techniques, including the following:

- **Determining the core business processes of the selected domains.** Core business processes are the processes or business activities within a particular business domain (like distribution) that exist in the many variations of that domain. For example, a distributor manages the items (products) that a business sells, and a common activity within that management responsibility is to count those items on a cyclical basis. *→ re Entities*

- **Determining the business ~~objects~~ *Entities* within each domain.** Business objects represent entities in the business domains that are recognizable to all experts within that domain. For example, products, orders, and warehouses are business ~~objects~~ *Entities* that occur within the distribution domain. Once these business ~~objects~~ *Entities* have been identified, they are scrutinized for the common content and analyzed to determine the true essences of the classes.

Then a corresponding Business Object is created (during OO Design & never before).

- **Using design patterns.** When designing the resulting frameworks, we consistently used design patterns to aid in the understandability of the frameworks. As we have already stated, design patterns aid by making the application frameworks understandable while maintaining sufficient flexibility to meet the needs of a specific application.

The SanFrancisco project began in March 1995. Since that time we have produced four releases of the product. Each release hardened the capabilities provided in the previous release while extending the product to new business domains. The product currently provides frameworks to support Warehouse Management, Order Management, General Ledger and Accounts Payable/Accounts Receivable domains. At present, we are teaming with other groups to provide frameworks in the Call Management and Customer Relationship Management domains. In addition, numerous application developers are building other industry-specific applications and frameworks using SanFrancisco. The design patterns discussed in this book have been used and continue to be used effectively across all these domains.

Why Business Frameworks?

Application frameworks form the foundation for application developers to create commercial, mission-critical business management systems that meet the needs of a wide variety of customers and satisfy both their current and future needs.

Business environments are becoming more dynamic with the increase of worldwide competition and changes in the way businesses market, sell, and manage their products (e.g., using Internet, extranet, and intranet). Distributed object technology is being recognized as a key means of building solutions that satisfy customer needs. However, using object technology requires sophisticated skills that are limited in many application provider environments. An application framework provides much of the architecture and design "out of the box," allowing the application designer to focus on critical aspects of the application and greatly enhance its capabilities. By using the framework, the application provider can implement a business application much more quickly, because a large portion of the development work already has been done and the results have been tested.

The SanFrancisco project is attempting both to fill the skill gap (lack of object-oriented expertise) and to minimize the amount of effort an application provider must expend to build an application that supports this dynamic business environment. By building an infrastructure for developing business applications and by creating the application frameworks, SanFrancisco has improved the prospect of application providers venturing into the complexities of object-oriented development.

Book Structure

Each pattern documented in this book is defined along the lines of the pattern definition template from the book *Design Patterns,* since this template has become a de facto standard. The sections that follow describe each part of the template.

Pattern Name

This section gives the name used for the pattern. It should convey the essence of the pattern so that it can be used naturally when talking about the pattern.

Intent

This section briefly describes the pattern at a high level. This description should encompass the heart of the pattern in such a way that someone familiar with it can be reminded of the essence of the pattern.

Motivation

This section gives the business motivation for the pattern—that is, the problem in the domain space that led to this solution. The motivation also introduces the general solution provided by the pattern. Some business motivations are extracted directly or indirectly from the case study presented in Chapter 2. In such instances, a paragraph summarizing the case study requirement(s) leading to the pattern is highlighted within the "Motivation" section.

Applicability

This section describes when and where a pattern should be used.

Structure

This section is a graphical representation of the structure of the design pattern. We use the Unified Modeling Language (UML), the highlights of which are covered in Appendix A, as the means to express this structure.

Participants

This section describes the classes in the structure diagram and their roles in the pattern.

Collaborations

This section describes the main interactions between the participants.

Consequences

This section describes the tradeoffs involved in using this pattern, as well as its benefits and drawbacks.

Implementation

This section discusses issues you will encounter when you apply this pattern in a particular situation.

Sample Code

This section consists of Java code snippets that demonstrate the application of the pattern.

Known Uses

This section identifies places where this pattern is currently used.

Related Patterns

This section describes how other patterns are related to and used by this pattern.

What's Next

The rest of this book focuses on explaining the SanFrancisco design patterns. We recommend that every reader start with the case study (Chapter 2) because it provides a context for the patterns and at a high level explains how the patterns can be used to resolve concrete business application design issues. Following the case study are the design patterns (Chapters 3 through 20). We have grouped these patterns in a fashion similar to the grouping in *Design Patterns:* by the types of capabilities they provide. Here we list the patterns by group.

Foundational Patterns

Foundational patterns provide an underlying structure for all SanFrancisco-based business objects: mechanisms for creating business objects, changing behavior, and constructing business processes.

- The **Class Replacement** pattern (Chapter 3) provides the means to change the behavior consistently for a provided class without changing the provided class or application logic that already uses that class.

- The **Special Class Factory** pattern (Chapter 4) provides a way of creating a class that supports customization of how and where the instances are created.

- The **Property Container** pattern (Chapter 5) provides a flexible means to dynamically extend an instance of a business object with attributes or relationships to other business objects.

- The **Business Process Command** (Chapter 6) pattern provides an extensible mechanism for encapsulating a business process supported by a logical business object or subsystem that is implemented as multiple physical objects.

Behavioral Patterns

Behavioral patterns describe various methods of incorporating flexible algorithms throughout a business framework or application.

- The **Simple Policy** pattern (Chapter 7) defines a family of algorithms, encapsulates each one, and makes them interchangeable. This pattern is similar to the Strategy pattern in the book *Design Patterns.* It lets the algorithm vary independently from the business objects affected by it.

- The **Chain of Responsibility–Driven Policy** pattern (Chapter 8) defines a family of encapsulated domain algorithms and associated chains of responsibility to locate the correct algorithm to be used and makes the family members interchangeable so that either a domain algorithm or a chain of responsibility can be configured into a business object. Encapsulated chains of responsibility search for the correct domain algorithm based on business objects involved in the processing being done by the domain algorithm.

- The **Token-Driven Policy** pattern (Chapter 9) defines a family of encapsulated domain algorithms for a behavior and makes them interchangeable, establishes groupings of these algorithms and configures these groupings into business objects responsible for the behavior, and controls which algorithm is used, on the basis of the client (represented by token) using the behavior.

Structural Patterns

Structural patterns deal with how business information is organized and accessed throughout a business framework or application.

- The **Controller** pattern (Chapter 10) provides a composite view of objects of a specific type across a hierarchical context. Users of this view are not aware of which context provides a particular object. Objects within the view may be aggregated (retrieved) from a higher-level context or provided locally at the current context. Locally defined objects either are newly introduced or override an aggregated object. The pattern also provides a way to hide objects that would otherwise be aggregated.
- The **Key/Keyable** pattern (Chapter 11) encapsulates a set of diverse business information in such a way that the set can be used as an independent whole for processing information. These uses include mapping, combining, filtering, and caching information.
- The **Generic Interface** pattern (Chapter 12) provides an enforceable object-oriented way of working with another subsystem without coupling this use with the particular implementation of that subsystem.

Process Patterns

Process patterns define how business information participates in various business situations.

- The **Cached Aggregate** pattern (Chapter 13) provides an encapsulated way of storing, updating, and retrieving the results of an aggregation, or a derivative of the aggregation, for a set of criteria, and it does so in a manner that provides a configurable means of effectively maintaining and using a cache of aggregations that require fast access.
- The **Keyed Attribute Retrieval** pattern (Chapter 14) provides a way of retrieving values of an attribute on the basis of a set of criteria. How the criteria are used is encapsulated in a policy to allow easy customization.
- The **List Generation** pattern (Chapter 15) defines a consistent way of generating a list from a set of input items and working with the list and its

entries. List entries are composed of one or more input items with common characteristics that are selected by policy.

Dynamic Behavioral Patterns

Dynamic behavioral patterns support the structural and behavioral transformation of business objects throughout their lifecycles. These transformations include the addition and removal of attributes and capabilities (methods).

- The **Extensible Item** pattern (Chapter 16) allows an object to support dynamic changes in behavior and data, simulating dynamic inheritance. The mechanisms defined by this pattern include adding, removing, or overriding supported methods and adding or removing data attributes as necessary to model a business object correctly at different stages of its existence.

- The **Hierarchical Extensible Item** pattern (Chapter 17) provides a flexible, loosely coupled mechanism for arranging business objects in a tree structure that naturally reflects the structure and behavior of hierarchies of entities found in many business domains, and allows those entities to emulate dynamic inheritance.

- The **Business Entity Lifecycle** pattern (Chapter 18) allows a business object to accurately model the various lifecycle paths of the business entity it represents through a decoupled and configurable state management mechanism. State and behavioral changes in the modeled business entity that occur at each stage of its lifecycle are reflected in the associated business object by runtime changes to the object's behavior and data.

- The **Hierarchy Information** pattern (Chapter 19) provides a mechanism for capturing and defining hierarchical process structure and common lifecycle behavior for instances of a business entity that share a specific usage type.

- The **Decoupled Processes** pattern (Chapter 20) represents applicable business processes for a given business entity in a self-contained and reusable form, allowing the processes to be arranged in arbitrary orderings for specific types and uses of the business entity.

Summing Up

In this introduction we discussed why we created the design patterns presented in this book and how they were used to make the SanFrancisco product a reality. Creating and using our design patterns played a major role in the success of the SanFrancisco project. The fact that these design patterns have been used across various domains shows that they are well tested, very flexible, and highly reusable. We hope you find them as valuable to your development as we have found them to ours.

Chapter 2 discusses some of the business requirements that initiated the need for our design patterns. The case study provides a business context and sample use of many of the patterns included in the book.

2

Case Study

In Chapter 1 we discussed the SanFrancisco project and the reasons for creating our design patterns. The case study we present in this chapter is intended to give you a concrete example and context for the patterns, looking at some of the business requirements that drive application design and pointing out how our design patterns can be used to resolve the related application design issues.

Business Problem

Food Warehouse (FW), a bulk distributor of food products to restaurants and repackagers, is used as the basis for this case study. This fictitious company requires a business application to support both its order management and warehouse management business processes—that is, an application that provides *constrain ti* business processes to support the creation, maintenance, and deletion of orders and order-related information. This application must also support the day-to-day activities required to run the warehouse environment and support information about the products, inventory, and warehouse(s). Along with providing applications to manage its warehouses and orders, FW wants to enhance the application support for its financial application. Revamping its General Ledger application will improve its ability to support the needs of the business managers and the financial team.

An application provider, Wondrous Functions, will be developing the application for FW. This application will also be used as the basis for an application sold by Wondrous Functions to other businesses within the distribution and warehousing industry. The goal of Wondrous Functions is to create an application that is highly flexible and easily customizable for other clients, while providing the functions required by FW such that FW can easily make changes in the future as its business needs change.

General Application Requirements

For purposes of the case study, we have selected FW's order management application requirements to show the need for some of our design patterns. Here are some of those requirements:

- **Expand existing data as necessary.** New data or capabilities are required as FW expands its businesses by attracting new customers, suppliers, and products. For example, new information is required to support the relationship between FW and its new customers and suppliers. Frequently, new information is required to define, manage, or handle new products. This new data is usually associated with existing data and provides specific or unique details required by the business.

- **Manage core business data.** FW must manage its business data in order to have an effective business environment. Managing this data entails creating, maintaining, and controlling access to that information.

- **Establish business policies that affect the operation of the business.** FW has established a set of business policies that define how the company and its employees conduct business. Specific aspects of these policies must be implemented within the application, to provide consistent behavior across all users of the application and to assist FW in customizing the application to conform to its business processes.

- **Provide timely and accurate totals (balance) data.** FW is a business within a dynamic, fast-paced industry. This environment requires many day-to-day decisions relying on up-to-date summary data in the form of totals or balances.

- **Manage order processing.** FW is committed to providing exceptional service to its customers. One way to accomplish this goal is by tracking, managing, and satisfying customer orders in an efficient manner. FW has taken the time to establish the necessary processes and expects its application to help it accomplish these objectives.

- **Maximize operations efficiency.** FW must provide an efficient working environment for its employees. The majority of the activity within the warehouse focuses on storing and retrieving products from the coolers and bins. To make the picking (retrieval) process better, FW needs a flexible way to structure the pick lists so that the products being picked can be grouped in a variety of ways.

In the following sections we will review these requirements specifically from the design perspective and identify the various patterns used to solve design problems.

Expand Existing Data

The information base of Food Warehouse has changed over time as new products or ways of doing business have been adopted by the company. These changes sometimes require new data to be collected and added to the existing pool of information. For example, FW recently decided to venture into a new product line: organic foods. With the organic food line, FW needed to track new data, such as grower certification level and grower location. This new data does not apply to any other products being offered. FW needed this information for specific business processes, such as order entry, and it required this information to be added without disturbing the existing product data or the supporting application.

All the data in the application, including this new data, is represented by business objects. In particular, product data is represented in the form of Product objects. As stated earlier, business objects often need to be extended to include information that does not apply to every instance of a class. Sometimes the additional information has many of the same characteristics as optional attributes; however, they may need to be added on the fly. In this case, Product objects need to be flexible enough to allow additional information to be included with some instances but not with others. Specifically, FW wants to place grower information on organic food Product objects, whereas its other products do not require this information. During order creation, if the product being ordered is an organic food, this grower information is used.

Wondrous Functions knows that the need to add new information to the existing data used by a business is common. By determining how to do this effectively, Wondrous Functions could solve a problem that has plagued application developers for a long time. The Class Replacement and Property Container patterns (discussed in Chapters 3 and 5) allow the developer to do just this—easily add attributes to a business object.

Manage Core Business Data

Various types of business data are vital to FW's operation. For the order management application, the vital data includes customers, customer orders, products and product lines, and inventory levels. FW requires its business application to provide a means to collect and manage its business data from differing business perspectives.

The FW business environment is composed of five distribution centers, three trucking units, a sales force within each of its five regions, and a corporate office. FW also maintains a subsidiary in Belgium that it uses to import European goods to the United States. This complicated organizational structure affects the way FW's business data is used. Much of this data needs to be shared in various ways among the departments and their different levels of organization. By sharing this information, FW increases the consistency and accuracy of the data used and eliminates both redundancy of data and duplication of effort in maintaining that data. For example, the corporate office can elect to share only specific types of data across the organization and allow other data to be maintained by the individual units of the organization.

All this data needs to be managed in a flexible way. An application must have access to all the business data and, where necessary, provide the ability to distribute the data across the corporation. Object technology provides multiple types of collections as a means to manage objects. However, Wondrous Functions feels that these collections of business objects should be available within a corporate structure. It needs the flexibility to do the following:

- Share the entire collection of business objects provided by the higher-level organization
- Create an entirely new collection of business objects at any level, including the lowest, of the organization
- Share some of the "corporate"[1] business objects while having its own subset
- Share some of the corporate business objects but hide others
- Partially share the corporate business objects by sharing some of the data in the business objects but maintaining other data on a unit basis

These requirements taxed the capabilities of standard collections. The Controller pattern defined by SanFrancisco (discussed in Chapter 10) overcame the limitations of collections and fulfilled the application needs specified here.

Establish Business Policy

FW has established a set of business policies to provide a consistent working environment for its employees and to establish the terms for working with its customers. Business applications are developed to aid a company in performing its business activity by collecting and maintaining business data and by supporting its day-to-day business activities. Often these business activities rely on business policies to carry out their objectives. FW expects its business application to integrate aspects of these business policies into the processes.

By their nature, business policies require special considerations. To implement business policies successfully, the application must consider the following needs:

---

1. Note that "corporate" in this list means any higher level within the corporate structure—not just the corporate office.

[handwritten: ⌐⌐ "re'requirements"!]

- **Flexibility.** Business policies change as business needs change. The degree of volatility can depend on a variety of factors both internal and external to the business. For example, competitors may offer special discounts on products that FW sells. One way for FW to react is to change its discount policy to be either equal to or better than its competitors' discount policies. *[handwritten: ⌐ wh? really mean "different"]*

- **Applicability.** Various <u>versions of</u> a business policy may exist that apply to particular business information. For example, a particular discount policy may apply to specific products, while the product line discount policy may apply to other products, and a company-wide discount policy may apply to all the rest of the products that do not fall under the other two categories.

[handwritten left margin: ∴ not a version of a policy, but a new one.]

- **Specialization.** Business policies may vary on the basis of specific business circumstances. For example, FW establishes various product availability checking policies that apply at different times in the processing of an order. At order entry, product availability checking takes into account stock available and expected future receptions when determining if the company can accept the order. When actually processing the order and allocating the inventory to particular orders (order lines), FW uses a different product availability checking algorithm to determine the stock location(s) to be used for picking the product.

As stated earlier, business rules *[handwritten: describe]* govern the manner in which a company does business or directs the flow of a given business process. Wondrous Functions knows that the application must embody the steps to be followed to support a business process. It understands that the business rules implemented as application logic must be implemented so that they provide the right level of flexibility, applicability, and specialization. The Policy patterns (discussed in Chapters 7 through 9) provide the following:

- **Flexibility.** Policies make it easy to change existing business logic without affecting the overall business activity or business application. Policies also allow the application to support variations of the business rules for particular business objects.

- **Applicability.** Policies can be broadly applied across various situations— for example, when a business rule is applicable to different types of business objects.[2] Such broad applicability is possible in this instance because different object types have one of a family of policies applied to it. In addition, a separate business rule can be used to select or find a business object with

---

2. An example of this type of applicability is determining the time increments to use when calculating order delivery times, sequencing pick lists, and performing other business operations related to a distribution enterprise.

the business rule to be used. The key enhancement here is the use of the selection algorithm.

- **Specialization.** Sometimes a business rule needs to vary for a particular business object, depending on the current business process. For example, stock availability for a specific product when an order is placed can search all the FW warehouses; however, when an order is being filled inside of a specific warehouse, the stock availability algorithm will need to be different, searching only the warehouse where the order is being filled.

Refer to Part II, "Behavioral Patterns," to understand how extensions to the well-known strategy pattern were used to solve these various requirements.

Provide Balance Information

Detailed business data (like customer and customer order information) is vital to Food Warehouse. This business data is used in various processes within the business. FW frequently needs summary (balance) information, based on the detailed data, as input to making rapid business decisions. For example, when an FW customer places an order on credit, FW needs to determine immediately if the customer is creditworthy. For FW to make this determination, it needs the customer's outstanding balance. This balance information needs to be quickly and easily accessible.

Using this example of credit checking, the FW does the following:

- Establishes a credit limit for each customer—in other words, a maximum amount against which the customer can apply unpaid orders.
- Maintains the customer's outstanding balance, consisting of all the customer's accepted and unpaid orders (FW excludes taxes and shipping and handling charges from this balance).
- Adds the new order total to the existing outstanding balance, creating a current total.
- Compares the current total to the credit limit. If the limit is exceeded, a credit manager works with the customer to solve the problem; if not, the order is accepted.

Let's focus on the customer's outstanding balance. This balance is derived from all the customer orders that have been accepted but are still unpaid. Because taxes and shipping and handling charges must be excluded, the overall order total is not appropriate. We must create the balance by looking at each order line total amount for all the customer's orders that have been accepted but are unpaid. A customer can change the content of an order (the order lines) frequently, thus complicating the maintenance of accurate balances. FW demands the ability to respond rapidly to customer requests for information. Waiting for the computer to dynamically calculate totals information—for example, the customer's outstanding balance—is unacceptable.

Wondrous Functions knows that to maintain this information, two things are necessary:

1. A method of organizing and identifying the information that needs to be tracked and later accessed

2. A mechanism to summarize and collect the information from different sources into useful results

We can determine a customer's credit balance by performing a query over all the orders from this customer, selecting those that apply (accepted but not yet paid), and summing or aggregating (caching) these numbers to determine the current outstanding balance. Alternatively, the application can maintain these aggregates separately and update them as the information changes. The Key/ Keyable pattern (discussed in Chapter 11) is a natural fit for identifying the information of interest. An approach to support caching, the mechanism for storing these sums for fast access, is described in the Cached Aggregate design pattern (discussed in Chapter 13).

Manage Order Processing

Being a customer-centered company, Food Warehouse applies extra effort to managing customer orders. This heightened attention to order management puts a high demand on FW's business application:

1. Both the order and an order detail (request for particular product) go through various processing activities to satisfy (complete) the order:

    *   An order header reflects the status of the overall order. For example, an order may be accepted, on hold, in process, staged, packaged, shipped, or canceled.

    *   An order detail must reflect the specific handling of each particular product request. For example, an order detail can go through various processes, including planning, picking, staging, shipping, and invoicing.

2. Each processing activity has entry and exit criteria. That is, for an order or an order detail to go to the next activity, all the prerequisite activity must have been performed. While an order is in a particular stage, all associated activities must occur to satisfy the definition or rules of that stage, and any resulting information must be recorded.

3. As an order detail is processed, it may be subdivided into units. For example, during planning of an order detail (determining which warehouse

and bin or cooler will provide the stock to satisfy a detail), it may be determined that the stock must come from multiple locations. Each unit (in this case, the planning information) adds new information to the order detail, including the warehouse, stock location, and the quantity to be taken from a specific stock location. If only part of the order detail can be satisfied, that information must be kept as well. Two things happen when the order line is being processed:

a. It may change status.

b. Information may be added to the existing order detail.

4. Not all orders require exactly the same process or processing activities. A company may operate in a way that makes certain steps unnecessary. For example, a company may take orders from customers via phone or fax and prepare those orders for the customer. Customers are given either the option to have the order shipped to them (remote sales order) or to pick up the order (direct sales order). Customers who elect to pick up their orders must pay for the goods at that time, but they receive a discount and pay no shipping and handling charges.

Table 2.1 shows how the two different types of orders must be processed, specifying at a high level the order-handling business processes. These business processes are made up of subprocesses or activities. To improve its control of the processing flow, FW needs to relate these more granular activities to specific order types. The abilities to mix, match, and sequence at the activity level create a more flexible environment for supporting customer needs: The company can define a wider range of order types while still maintaining the control required to manage its orders consistently.

Several different patterns will be necessary to fulfill this requirement for the business application. Each of the four business problems that have been described in this section will be solved by a different design pattern. However, these four patterns can be combined to solve the larger problem of managing

Table 2.1. Processes Required for Remote and Direct Sales Orders

Process	Remote Sales Order	Direct Sales Order
Create	X	X
Plan	X	
Pick	X	X
Ship	X	
Invoice customer	X	
Record customer payment	X	X

order processing. Part V discusses each of these dynamic behavioral patterns. The Business Entity Lifecycle pattern, central to solving this problem, combines many of the lower-level design patterns discussed in Part V.

Maximize Operations Efficiency

Food Warehouse must provide an efficient working environment for its employees. The majority of the activity within each FW warehouse focuses on storing and retrieving products from the coolers and bins. To make the picking (retrieval) process more efficient, FW needs a flexible way to structure its pick lists so that the products can be grouped in a variety of ways.

By organizing the information about the location of the products, the product information and the quantity requested in a form that allows the pickers (the employees responsible for collecting the various products to fill a customer order) to work efficiently, FW can process its customer orders more expeditiously. Different criteria can be used to organize the information. For example, if all stock of a particular product is stored in a single location (bin or cooler) within the warehouse, all the requests for a particular product could be grouped together so that the picker needs to go to that location only once. Another pick list could be organized such that all the products for a particular order are grouped together (e.g., if the customer was at the warehouse waiting for the order). In a third scenario, the pick list could require a certain set of products to be picked last because they are perishable.

Another aspect of the picking process is ensuring that inventory is updated to reflect the removal of the product from its location within the warehouse. Each product or occurrence of a product on the list is given a unique pick list number. This number is used to a map a product's information (the warehouse location and quantity picked) to a particular inventory item for that product so that the inventory quantity can be decremented properly.

The List Generation design pattern, described in Chapter 15, was defined to provide a means both to organize lists from a set of products and to allow working with the list and the products included in that list. Business policies can be associated with the process used to determine the organization of the products on a list and the content of a list. List Generation also provides a means to map the information contained in the list to other uses—for example, updating the inventory quantity.

Putting Our Example in Context

In an introductory chapter such as this we can't begin to explore all the features that a business such as Food Warehouse requires for its order fulfillment application. Those of you who have business expertise are well aware of the many subtleties of the business requirements we have discussed briefly in this chapter. We do hope, however, that this chapter serves as a jumping-off point for further exploration of the design patterns documented in the remainder of this book. For those of you with limited business experience, we hope this introduction also gives you a feel for the types of problems that business applications must solve.

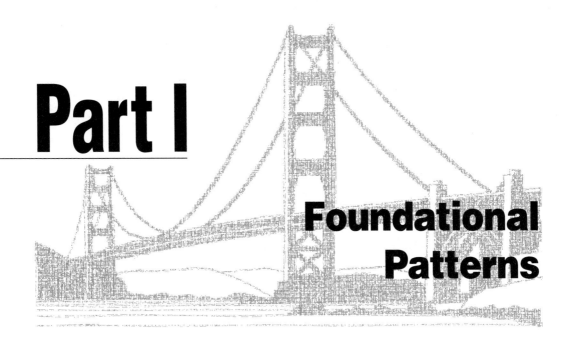

Part I

Foundational Patterns

SanFrancisco's foundational patterns provide the structure for all of SanFrancisco's business objects: mechanisms for creating business objects, changing behavior, and constructing business processes.

The Class Replacement pattern (Chapter 3) provides a way to alter the behavior for all business objects of a given type. It is a composite of the Abstract Factory and Factory Method patterns of *Design Patterns*, with the addition of a mechanism for flexible configuration.

The Special Class Factory pattern (Chapter 4) provides a way to customize the creation of business objects, including the determination of where a business object is to be stored and how it is to be identified. With this pattern, users of a business application can distribute business information efficiently and in a way that conforms to the existing infrastructure of data and processes for that business.

The Property Container pattern (Chapter 5) provides a way to dynamically attach additional information to a particular instance of a business object class.

The Business Process Command pattern (Chapter 6) provides a mechanism for building business processes that work with a single business object or a subsystem of cooperating business objects. This pattern allows business processes to be separated from a single business object class so that those processes may be more easily customized for changing business needs. The pattern can also be used to selectively expose business operations from a subsystem to users of that subsystem. Under these circumstances, the set of commands defined for a subsystem makes up the user interface, or API (application program interface), of the subsystem.

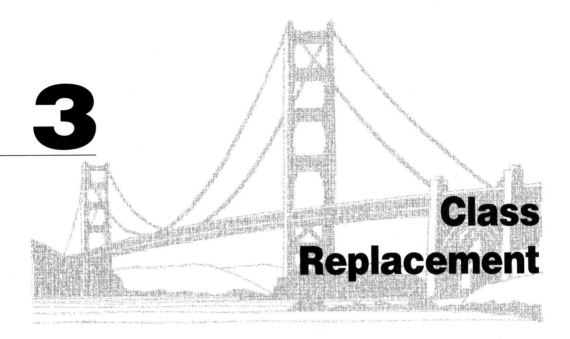

3

Class Replacement

Intent

Provide the means to change the behavior consistently for a provided class without changing the provided class or application logic that already uses that class.

Motivation

Application frameworks provide many useful business objects. A flexible application framework must provide a mechanism that allows implementers to replace some of these business objects with others that have been tailored for the particular implementation. This replacement mechanism should be flexible enough to allow the replacement during initial application development or as a modification during deployment of the application. The Abstract Factory pattern in *Design Patterns* defines a method for providing this mechanism.

The Food Warehouse application is complex, and as the application continues to grow, situations arise in which the application designers want to change existing information or behavior or add new information and behavior to a provided class. For example, the Product class may need to be changed to support new data (see Figure 3.1).

The data (or behavior) must be consistently changed for all instances of the relevant class. The Abstract Factory pattern (as implemented in SanFrancisco) defines how to add and create new subclasses.

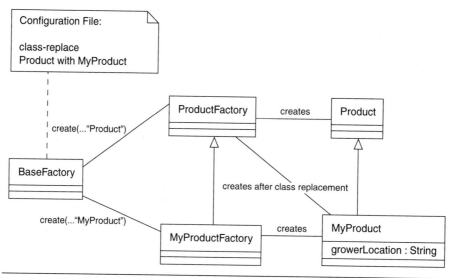

Figure 3.1. Replacing Product with MyProduct

Case Study Food Warehouse recently decided to venture into a new product line: organic foods. With the organic food line, FW needs to track new data, such as grower certification level and grower location. FW intends to expand into organic foods and replace most of its product line with organic foods, so this additional information will be required for the majority of its products. FW needs this information for specific business processes, such as order entry. The information must be added without the existing data or the supporting application being disturbed.

This pattern must be flexible enough to be used for initial application development, as well as for adding new function during deployment. Therefore, the pattern must be extended to allow the application code to make create calls for the class that was in the initial implementation (Product), while allowing a derived subclass (MyProduct in Figure 3.1) to be substituted later on the basis of the configuration information (set through BaseFactory). We do this by specifying a different token (a String) identifying each class to be created and mapping this token to the actual class to be created. This mechanism is called *class replacement*.

Food Warehouse can use class replacement to modify classes added as part of an application, or those provided by a framework, such as Product. Although class replacement is not essential in all situations, it does allow an application to change the behavior of an existing class for the entire application. Alternatively, if class replacement is not used, the application has to manage both the class and the replacing class. Thus, it has the flexibility of creating class instances of both the existing and the new classes. However, the specific class to be created must be specified in the application code, and the application must ensure that instances of the original class are never used where the application expects a new class instance.

Abstract Factory as Implemented in SanFrancisco (BaseFactory[1] Class)

Food Warehouse requires a flexible means to create its business objects. Implementation of the Abstract Factory design pattern fills this need. The Abstract Factory pattern is implemented in a single class, BaseFactory, in SanFrancisco. BaseFactory is an extensible abstract factory, having a single creation interface that takes as a parameter a token (a String) that identifies the particular class to create. This interface provides maximum flexibility because it is used to create all business objects. However, because of the single creation method in BaseFactory, all business objects are returned as a base Object and need to be cast as the correct type of business object and initialized.

For this reason the application designers of the Food Warehouse business application would need to weigh the need for flexibility and extensibility against concerns about type safety. These concerns can be alleviated by the combining of the Abstract Factory and Factory Method patterns of *Design Patterns*. As Figure 3.2 shows, in addition to the BaseFactory class, SanFrancisco has concrete factory classes. Each of these classes will return business objects of a specific type. Internally, these concrete factory classes call BaseFactory.

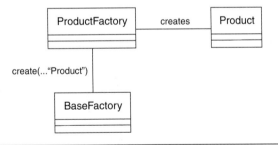

Figure 3.2. ProductFactory

---

1. BaseFactory performs a larger function than the Abstract Factory pattern. It contains the general-purpose creation method but also handles the function of allocating storage for the object being created. The business objects created by Food Warehouse need to persist beyond the current instance of the running application. BaseFactory, therefore, needs to allocate space in a persistent store. SanFrancisco allows the persistent storage mechanism to be configured, causing instances of a class to be persisted in a specific location (e.g., a relational database).

Applicability

Consider using the Class Replacement pattern when the ability to change or add new behavior to all instances of a class needs to be supported.

Structure

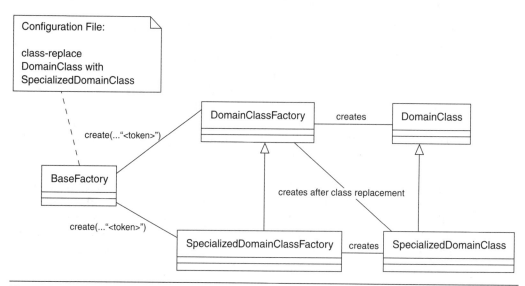

Figure 3.3.   Class Replacement Structure

Participants

- **BaseFactory.** A class that implements the Abstract Factory pattern. When one of the concrete factory classes calls the BaseFactory creation method, an identifying String, or token, is passed as a parameter, indicating which class should be created. Changing the configuration information for a given token will cause a different class to be instantiated.

- **DomainClass** (Product). The class that needs to be specialized. This class may be provided by a framework that is being used to build an application, or it may be part of an application.

- **DomainClassFactory** (ProductFactory). The factory class for the Domain-Class. This class contains the create methods that will return the specific type of business object (Product), eliminating the need for the user to cast the object as the correct type upon return. The object actually will be constructed in BaseFactory.

- **SpecializedDomainClass** (MyProduct). The specialized class with the new or changed behavior. This class will need to support all the existing interfaces of the parent class so that new and old instances can interoperate freely.
- **SpecializedDomainClassFactory** (MyProductFactory). The factory class for the SpecializedDomainClass.

Collaborations

- The application may have existing code that will call DomainClassFactory to create new instances of DomainClass objects. New application code can choose to call SpecializedDomainClassFactory to create instances of the SpecializedDomainClass type.
- Each of the factory classes will call BaseFactory to create the business object instances, passing in a token (String) to indicate the type of object to create.
- Because of the change in the configuration file, DomainClassFactory calling BaseFactory with the String "DomainClass" now creates instances of the SpecializedDomainClass specialized class.

Consequences

The Class Replacement pattern has the following tradeoffs, benefits, and drawbacks:

Tradeoffs

- **Type safety versus flexibility.** If the Abstract Factory pattern is being used, flexibility and extensibility must be weighed against code safety because this pattern can return objects of only a very basic type. Combining the Abstract Factory and Factory Method patterns eliminates the need for this tradeoff decision.
- **Explicit dealing with the subclass versus transparency.** A developer can create a subclass that uses the Abstract Factory and Factory Method patterns without using class replacement. In this circumstance the application can create objects of either the base or the specialized type. However, the application code will need to specifically call the corresponding base or specialized factory. The result may be changes to existing application code.

Benefits

- **Minimal impact to existing uses.** Class replacement provides the benefits of the Abstract Factory and Factory Method patterns: It simplifies the process of replacing business objects with specialized versions of the business object within an existing application, and it allows new code to take advantage of new enhancements without requiring changes in the existing application code. The existing code will continue to function as it has in the past. This is especially important to frameworks in which specialization is expected. Use of this pattern allows existing framework code, which uses the class, to continue operating without change.

Drawbacks

- **Only one replacement class.** Specialized classes that will class-replace their parent classes require careful consideration because they have the potential to affect other running applications. If the application that requires the class replacement is expected to operate freely with other applications, a problem could result if another application uses class replacement on the same class. For this reason, only core applications should use class replacement.

Implementation

Consider the following implementation issues for the Class Replacement pattern:

- **Configuring.** A large portion of the pattern is implemented in BaseFactory and the configuration file it uses. Most of the implementation work is in creating the subclass. Changing the configuration information will affect all applications that use BaseFactory for object creation. The behavior that is added or changed must be acceptable for all installed applications that will use this configuration.

  Alternatively, the tokens could be scoped to the specific applications that require them. For example, if we had two applications, A and B, we could use the token "ProductA" when creating the Product in application A and the token "ProductB" when creating the Product in application B. These tokens could then be configured to refer to the same class, such as Product, or to two separate classes.

- **Creating classes.** A factory class for the subclass will also need to be created. Because application code already exists that uses the create signature for the class being replaced, you must ensure that your application subclass can be successfully created by the create signature of the framework class being replaced. For example, additional attributes on the newly defined class may need to be derived from parameters passed in on the existing create signature or to be assigned a default value.

- **Changing methods.** If the subclass is only overriding methods in the parent class, subclass implementation is straightforward. Only those methods being overridden need to be implemented by the subclass. However, if the subclass changes the implementation of existing methods, take care that existing code will continue to function.

- **Adding methods.** If the subclass adds methods, you need to define a new interface, as well as implementation for both the new methods and existing methods that are modified. The new methods declared by the subclass will not be visible to the existing application code; however, you can use these new methods either by accessing an instance of the replaced class or by casting to the new type.

- **Changing attributes.** If the application subclass changes the implementation of existing class attributes, you will have to override the get and set methods associated with the attributes that the subclass is no longer using. Typically, you will implement the get and set methods to use the get and set methods associated with the new attributes introduced by the subclass.

- **Removing attributes.** If attributes are removed,[2] the get and set methods associated with the removed attributes must still be implemented. The application subclass will no longer be able to use the removed attribute in its implementation, but the subclass must continue to support the get and set methods so that the class contract is preserved.

Sample Code

The code samples in this section show class replacement of the Product class by the MyProduct class. We also give an example of using the factory classes to achieve type safety and an example of how use of the Class Replacement pattern allows existing code to remain unchanged when the class is replaced.

The Product class interface defines the methods supported by the Product class:

```
public interface Product extends Object {
    public  void setPrice(CurrencyValue);
    public CurrencyValue  getPrice();
    ...
```

---

2. When this pattern is being used in Java, the replacing class does not have to extend the replaced class. It only has to implement its interface.

```
public void initialize (String productNumber,
                        String name,
                        CurrencyValue price,
                        ProductGroup productGroup,
                        DescriptiveInformation description);
}
```

In this example, the get and set methods for the price are shown. The price is represented by a CurrencyValue object that combines a currency, such as USD for U.S. dollars, and a value, such as 42.00. This interface also includes the initialize method, which sets the initial values during creation of a Product instance.

Instances of Product are created by use of the ProductFactory:

```
public abstract class ProductFactory extends Object {
    public final static Product createProduct
                                (String productNumber,
                                 String name,
                                 CurrencyValue price,
                                 ProductGroup productGroup,
                                 DescriptiveInformation description) {
        Product newProduct = (Product)(BaseFactory.create("ProductToken"));
        newProduct.initialize(productNumber, name, price, productGroup,
                              description);
        return newProduct;
    }
}
```

This factory class calls the BaseFactory to create an instance of the class associated with the "Product" token and casts the result to Product. It then calls the initialize method on the new instance of Product to set the initial values. One way that this example would be extended is by the addition of exception handling. For example, if configuration of the tokens does not ensure that the replacing class can be cast to the replaced class, then the class cast exception should be handled here. In addition, any exceptions thrown by the initialize method may need to be handled here. Usually every factory class contains very similar processing and is thus a candidate for being generated.

An application creates a Product instance by calling the createProduct method on the ProductFactory:

```
Product product = ProductFactory.createProduct(productNumber,
                                               name,
                                               price,
                                               productGroup,
                                               description);
```

Given the Product and ProductFactory classes already presented, MyProduct is defined and used to replace Product. The MyProduct interface must be defined:

```
public interface MyProduct extends Product {
    public  void setGrower(Grower);
    public Grower  getGrower();
    …
    public void initialize (String ProductNumber,
                            String name,
                            CurrencyValue price,
                            ProductGroup productGroup,
                            DescriptiveInformation description,
                            Grower grower);
}
```

In this example, the replacement class adds the ability to associate a grower with the product, thereby allowing the organic certification level of the grower (and other attributes) to be checked. Thus, the interface adds the setGrower and getGrower methods. The interface also defines a new intialize method, which adds the Grower as a parameter.

The implementation of the MyProduct interface, called MyProductImpl, extends the ProductImpl class (not shown) and implements the MyProduct interface:

```
public class MyProductImpl extends ProductImpl implements MyProduct {
    …
}
```

MyProductImpl could have extended Object instead of ProductImpl. What to extend is a tradeoff between creating a dependency and reuse. In our example, extending the ProductImpl class created a dependency on the code in ProductImpl. Extending just Object would have made them completely independent, but it would have provided no reuse, requiring all methods be implemented in MyProductImpl.

Having defined the MyProduct interface and its associated implementation, we can configure the BaseFactory to create a MyProduct instance whenever the "ProductToken" token is passed. In this case, the ProductFactory class will get an instance of MyProduct from the BaseFactory, cast it to Product, and then call the initialize method on it. In this example, the initialize method that will be called will be the one inherited by MyProduct when its interface extended the Product interface.

Because a grower is not passed on this initialization call, the implementation of this initialize method (in MyProductImpl) has to determine how to fill in the grower attribute added by MyProduct. In this example, grower is optional, so the initialization will simply set it to null. Now when existing code calls createProduct, it will get back a MyProduct instance with grower set to null.

Why didn't we just create a new MyProductFactory and call createMyProduct, passing the grower? The code that is creating the product may be outside of your control or it may be created as one part of a more complex operation.

Instead of replacing or modifying this code, it is easier to take the returned Product, cast it to MyProduct, and call the setGrower method. However, creation does not have to be done in this way; for new code or code you are modifying for other reasons, the createMyProduct method on the MyProductFactory can be used.

Known Uses

All the SanFrancisco Core Business Processes, as well as the Common Business Objects, make use of the Class Replacement pattern. In addition to this general use, specific uses of the pattern, which were identified by domain experts as places likely to require specialization, are highlighted. An example is SanFrancisco's support for the euro, which allows choosing between a class that does not support the euro and a specialization that does, but has more performance overhead.

Related Patterns

- **Abstract Factory and Factory Method.** The Class Replacement pattern is a composite of the Abstract Factory and Factory Method patterns of *Design Patterns*.

4

Special Class Factory

Intent

Provide a way of creating a class that supports customization of how and where the instances are created.

Motivation

Businesses require fast access of their data. One way to facilitate faster access is to put similar data together. Grouping similar data may mean placing data with a common attribute in a common table or placing it on different servers in different locations. Regardless, a flexible business application must provide the means to customize how and where data is created and stored.

Food Warehouse, like many worldwide businesses, has many suppliers and requires ways of grouping suppliers together (i.e., physically locating objects that represent suppliers on different application servers as they are typically accessed) in order to provide faster retrieval. Because Food Warehouse typically accesses its suppliers according to the countries in which they are located, groupings according to a supplier's country would be beneficial.

Food Warehouse uses the BusinessPartner class to represent its suppliers. The BusinessPartner object has a BusinessPartnerSharedData object associated with it to keep track of common, shared data such as its primary address. Because of how it will use its supplier data, Food Warehouse plans to store this shared data under the country of the supplier. In addition, the application designers do not want the application code to have to be aware of these specializations.

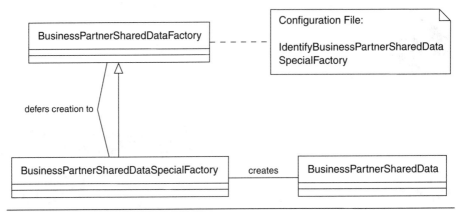

Figure 4.1. Special Factory Class for BusinessPartnerSharedData

Food Warehouse is using factory classes to create instances of all its business objects, including BusinessPartnerSharedData objects. These factory classes defer creation of the object to BaseFactory (see Chapter 3).

Customizations such as these require development of a subclass of the factory class. As Figure 4.1 shows, this kind of subclass is called a *special factory class*, in which these customizations and any others[1] can be implemented. The static methods of the factory class will delegate to this subclass; that is, the application code will not have to be changed for this customization to be used. The existence of this special factory class will be identified by information in a configuration file.

The application (and framework) code can continue to invoke the static creation methods of the BusinessPartnerSharedDataFactory class. These static methods are implemented to obtain an instance of any configured special factory class and delegate to that object's create method. In our example (see Figure 4.2), the special factory creates the BusinessPartnerSharedData instance and locates it with other objects containing the same country code in the primary address. If no special factory class is configured, the static create method will continue to create and initialize the new object.

Applicability

Consider using the Special Class Factory pattern when any of the following criteria apply:

- The application installation needs the class instances to be stored in groups according to defined criteria.

---

1. Another common use for the special factory class is to create primary keys (column values in a relational database table that are guaranteed to be unique across all rows in that table) that follow an implementation-specific algorithm.

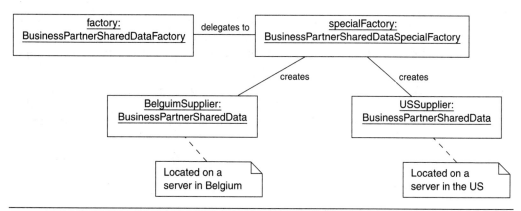

Figure 4.2.   Partitioning by Country

- The application has specific requirements for the database keys that are assigned to class instances.
- Other application-specific requirements are needed at object creation time that would not normally be handled by BaseFactory.

Structure

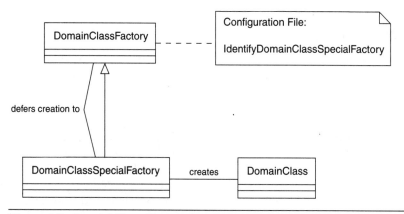

Figure 4.3. Special Class Factory Structure

Participants

- **DomainClass** (BusinessPartnerSharedData). The class that supports specialized creation. It may be provided by a framework that is being used, or it may be part of the existing application.

- **DomainClassFactory** (BusinessPartnerSharedDataFactory). The factory class for the DomainClass. This class contains the create methods that will be called by the application code. It will check for the existence of a special factory class and call it if one exists.

- **DomainClassSpecialFactory** (BusinessPartnerSharedDataSpecialFactory). The special factory class. It is a subclass of the DomainClassFactory that handles the specific requirements of object creation for the application installation.

Collaborations

- The application may have existing code that calls DomainClassFactory's create method to create new instances of DomainClass objects. No changes need be made to this code to use the new DomainClassSpecialFactory.

- Each of the factory classes will create the object or defer creation of the object to the create method on the DomainClassSpecialFactory by checking for its existence in configuration files.

- DomainClassSpecialFactory will perform the necessary additional creation logic. Of course, the object will actually be created through BaseFactory (which implements the Abstract Factory pattern of *Design Patterns*).

Consequences

The Special Class Factory pattern has the following tradeoffs, benefits, and drawbacks:

Tradeoffs

- **Flexibility versus performance.** Object creation can be specialized for a particular installation of an application according to the requirements of that location without the application code being affected. However, using the Special Class Factory pattern demands the performance overhead of calling through the existing class factory to reach the special factory class.

Benefits

- **Transparent customization.** This pattern simplifies customizing business object creation parameters to specialized versions without affecting the existing application code.

Drawbacks

- **Code duplication.** The only factory creation code that will be executed is the special factory class code. The business object creation code that exists in the class factory is no longer executed. Thus, any validation logic in the class factory must be duplicated in the special factory class code.

Implementation

Consider the following implementation issues for the Special Class Factory pattern:

- **Creating the special factory class.** Coding requires creating a subclass of the existing factory class, and overriding the nonstatic create method. Implementation of the create method should follow the same basic logic as the factory class (calling BaseFactory for object creation).

- **Customizing in the special factory class.** Arguments for key and location used in the createEntity call on BaseFactory should be determined according to the customization needed.

Sample Code

The existing factory class should always conform to the template that follows. This template allows a special factory class to be called if one is created and added to the configuration information for a particular installation location:

```
public static Class createClass(parameters) {
  ClassFactory factory =
          (ClassFactory)BaseFactory().getSpecialFactory("ClassToken");

  if (factory == null) {
    // Do the normal creation sequence
    ...
  } else {                  // Delegate to special factory class
    return factory.create(parameters);
  }
}
```

To use the template, you should replace Class (bold) with the class name (BusinessPartnerSharedData in this case), and the parameters (bold) with the parameters passed for this create method. Thus, the BusinessPartnerShared-DataFactory class would contain the following create method:

```
public static BusinessPartnerSharedData create BusinessPartnerSharedData (
                    String legalName,
                    Address primaryAddress,
                    String registrationId,
                    String shortName,
                    BusinessPartnerSharedData parentBusinessPartner,
                    DescriptiveInformation description) {
    BusinessPartnerSharedDataFactory factory =
            (BusinessPartnerSharedDataFactory)BaseFactory().getSpecialFactory(
            "BusinessPartnerSharedDataToken");
    BusinessPartnerSharedData bPSD = null;
    if (factory == null) {
      // Do the normal creation sequence
        bPSD = (BusinessPartnerSharedData)
                BaseFactory().create( "BusinessPartnerSharedDataToken");

        bPSD.initialize(legalName,primaryAddress,
                        registrationId,shortName,
                        parentBusinessPartner,
                        description);

    } else {  // Delegate to special factory class
        bPSD = factory.create(legalName,primaryAddress,
                        registrationId,shortName,
                        parentBusinessPartner,
                        description);
    }
    return (bPSD);
}
```

The special factory class code for the BusinessPartnerSharedData example is shown next. This class contains specialized logic to create a key. In this case the key for BusinessPartnerSharedData is the legal name of the business object. In addition, the Country object is selected as the object near which the BusinessPartnerSharedData object will be physically located when it is created. These parameters are then passed to BaseFactory, which will create the object using the additional parameters.

```
public class BusinessPartnerSharedDataSpecialFactory extends
                BusinessPartnerSharedDataFactory {

  public BusinessPartnerSharedData create(
                    String legalName,
                    Address primaryAddress,
                    String registrationId,
                    String shortName,
                    BusinessPartnerSharedData parentBusinessPartner,
                    DescriptiveInformation description) {

    // Provide a creation key that holds the business partner's legal name,
```

```
// which happens to be the primary key in the existing relational database
String creationKey = new String(legalName);

// Use the country of the primary address
// of this business partner as the location
Object location = primaryAddress.getCountry();

// Use the customized key and location to create the new business partner
BusinessPartnerSharedData bPSD =
                (BusinessPartnerSharedData)(BaseFactory().create(
                "BusinessPartnerSharedDataToken",
                location,creationKey));

    bPSD.initialize(legalName,primaryAddress,
                registrationId,shortName,
                parentBusinessPartner,
                description );
    return (bPSD);
  }
}
```

Known Uses

SanFrancisco classes built on the Foundation layer follow the Special Class Factory pattern.

Related Patterns

- **Class Replacement.** The Special Class Factory pattern uses many of the same classes as the Class Replacement pattern (see Chapter 3).
- **Controller.** The Special Class Factory pattern can be used to allow the location provided by the owning controller to be overridden, as described in Chapter 10.

5

Property Container

Intent

Provide a flexible means to dynamically extend an instance of a business object with attributes or relationships to other business objects.

Motivation

Business objects within an application must reflect the current data needs of the business. In many business situations new data or capabilities need to be added to specific instances of business objects. Let's take a look at our case study for an example.

Case Study

Food Warehouse recently decided to venture into a new product line: organic foods. With the organic food line, FW needs to track new data, such as grower certification level and grower location. This new data does not apply to any other products FW offers. FW needs this information for specific business processes, such as order entry. The information must be added without the existing data or the supporting application being disturbed.

In this case, newly introduced data applies to only selected objects of a specific type. Food Warehouse wants to associate this situational data with a Product object without affecting its general meaning or its interface. A standard rule of object-oriented design is that an object's interface must be as simple as possible; that is, it should reflect the attributes and methods that are common to all objects of a type.

We could have added these new attributes to the Product class by creating subclasses during application development; however, some situations require additional information to be added dynamically at runtime. By allowing the application code to dynamically add data (including attributes or relationships to other objects) to particular instances of a business object, we can localize the impacts on the application to only those portions that need this data.

In our example, specific pieces of information (e.g., grower certification level and grower location) need the ability to attach themselves to other objects (e.g., products) without requiring special client code or object code. These objects will either attach themselves to the target object when they are created or be attached to the target object by the application logic creating or maintaining the instance. The target object does not need to know that these attachments exist.

As Figure 5.1 shows, these new relationships may or may not be present for any given instance of the target object. In our example, only the new organic product line will require this additional information; other products will remain unaffected. Processes that operate on the new product line can check for the existence of this new data and operate on it if the data exists.

The grower certification level and grower location, and in general any new data that is added in this way, is referred to as a *property*. A class that supports the dynamic addition of properties is referred to as a *property container*. The property container implements an interface that resembles a keyed collection. The key to a property is a String that is the property name. We can retrieve a property from a property container by specifying its property name String. Property containers support most of the interfaces expected on any keyed collection. The properties held by a property container may consist of a mixture of types.

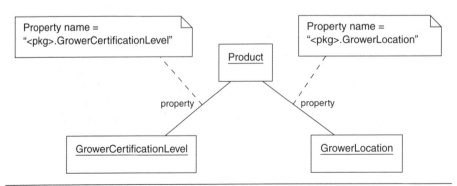

Figure 5.1. Adding Properties to Product

Let's expand on our example a bit further. Because grower certification level and grower location are unique to organic products, instances of these classes will exist only as properties of a product. Classes that will be used only as properties can be designed to add themselves to a property container upon creation. We could choose to take this approach for grower location (assuming that location is specific to each product type), but this approach doesn't make as much sense for certification level, since specific levels will be used on more than one product. Properties that exist only when attached to their property containers are referred to as *self-inserting properties.* Controllers are a good example of self-inserting properties (see Chapter 10).

In some cases business objects exist as part of a hierarchy. Often business hierarchies imply delegation of responsibility. For example, consider the holidays established by a business. In many cases, the corporate office will designate certain days as holidays (e.g., New Year's Day, Christmas) throughout the company but allow different locations within the company to designate holidays applicable to only those locations (e.g., Cinco de Mayo in Mexico).

We can take advantage of this natural characteristic of many business hierarchies by chaining each property container instance in the hierarchy to its parent. By chaining, we can automatically pass requests for a property that is not directly held by one object in the hierarchy to its parent (as in the Chain of Responsibility pattern of *Design Patterns*). In effect, a property can be attached to a single object or to a parent object and apply to all its children. In our case study, the company (Food Warehouse) is an example of such a hierarchy; it contains multiple subsidiary companies.

The company hierarchy is a key concept in the SanFrancisco architecture. In addition to allowing modeling of a company structure, Company objects can serve as focal points for common data needed by many business objects.[1]

Figure 5.2 shows how a company hierarchy can be created. In this example the parent company holds three subcompanies. ParentCompany holds a WorkingCalendar property, which contains standard U.S. holidays. The Nebraska and Boston subcompanies, by not introducing their own WorkingCalendar properties, inherit the WorkingCalendar of the parent company through property chaining. That is, if a client requests the property with the name "com.fw.WorkingCalendar" from either of these subcompanies, the parent company's WorkingCalendar will be returned. The Mexican subcompany, on the other hand, introduces its own WorkingCalendar property, with Mexican holidays. When a client requests the property with the name "com.fw.WorkingCalendar" from

---

1. Business object code within SanFrancisco can access the currently active Company object (referred to as the active Company). The active Company is a Company object from the company hierarchy that has been selected (usually at the start of the distributed process context) to be the active (or environment) Company for that process. In SanFrancisco, objects such as controllers are often accessed through the active Company.

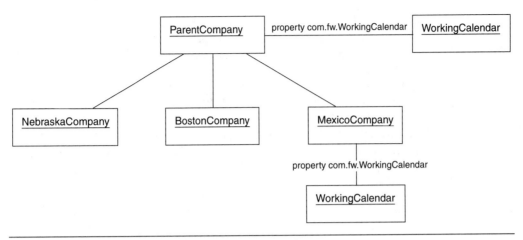

Figure 5.2. Finding a Calendar Using Chained Properties

the Mexican subcompany, the directly contained Mexico-specific WorkingCalendar will be returned.

Applicability

Consider using the Property Container pattern when any of the following criteria apply:

- Business objects are natural homes for related information.
- Loose coupling is an acceptable means of relating data to a business object.
- Data is associated with only specific instances of a class.
- Attributes must be dynamically added to business objects; for example, customer-defined fields need to be allowed.

Structure

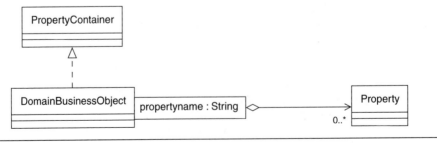

Figure 5.3.   Property Container Structure

Participants

- **PropertyContainer.** An interface that provides a keyed collection interface for holding business information in object form as values keyed by strings. PropertyContainer objects can be chained in a chain of responsibility that is followed during the retrieval of properties.
- **DomainBusinessObject** (Product). Any business object that implements the PropertyContainer interface, thereby obtaining the ability to have properties attached to particular instances of the class.
- **Property** (GrowerCertificationLevel). The object being held by the property container.

Collaborations

The property and property container have a loosely coupled relationship. "Loosely coupled" refers to the degree of coordination necessary between a using application or class (property container) and the used class (property). In particular, a property can be added to an object without the class for that object having any knowledge of the property or requiring any interface or code change to accommodate the addition of that property.

Consequences

The Property Container pattern has the following tradeoffs, benefits, and drawbacks:

Tradeoffs

- **Use of properties versus encapsulation.** By using the Property Container pattern as a means to extend a class, the client can easily add capabilities to a particular object of a given class. This approach supports a dynamic environment, allowing the client to manage additional functionality and data as needed. Because the class itself has no knowledge of these additions, subclassing is minimized, but this approach could be misused to add capabilities that should be encapsulated in a class. The developers must be vigilant to ensure that their overall application design is not jeopardized.

- **Use of properties versus use of subclasses.** The Property Container pattern allows us to add attributes to a business object dynamically. As such, it provides an alternative to subclassing. Creating subclasses for a business object would allow the information to be added to the class. However, if this data pertains to only a few specific instances of the class, it will cause more development effort than is warranted and may cause many variations of the same business object to fit specific needs.

- **Use of properties versus ease of persistence.** Business objects will most likely be persisted in a relational database. Creating a database schema for mapping a business object to one or more tables becomes more difficult when properties are being used.

Benefits

- **Lightweight business objects.** Business objects provide only essential attributes and methods.

- **Information added dynamically.** Dynamically adding attributes and relationships to other business objects to specific instances of a business object allows the application greater flexibility and acceptance to change.

- **Separation between subsystems.** Because of the loosely coupled relationship between properties and the property container, objects that are in separate subsystems can have a relationship without linkages being created between subsystems.

Drawbacks

- **Additional overhead for the call.** The client code must obtain the business object so that it can access the property, and each property must be accessed by its name. Finally, the retrieved object must be cast to its type before use (see also the final item in this list).

- **Less explicit interface.** The client must know the name of the property to access it. Simply examining the interface of the property container is no longer sufficient.

- **Loss of strong typing.** The client code may become more complex because it must manage accessing of the properties. Attributes are always returned from specific accessor methods, which return the appropriate type. Access of a property is general, and the client must cast the property to its type on its return.

Implementation

Consider the following implementation issues for the Property Container pattern:

- **Extension through aggregation.** A key alternative to properties is aggregation (i.e., containment of one or more class instances as attributes of a business object). Aggregation is one of the primary ways to extend an application. Some of the reasons for extending a business object through aggregation include the following:

- To ensure type safety in your application when the class is being used or passed as a parameter

- To control which attributes are exposed or hidden in the interface to a class

- **Standardized property names.** A standard for property naming is necessary to avoid name collisions across properties. We recommend that the package, the class to which the property should be cast, and, optionally, an identifier unique to the property usage, form the property name ("<pkg>.<classToCastTo>.<uniqueId>"). Two examples within SanFrancisco that follow this form are "cf.DDecimal.MaximumValue"and "cf.Natural-Calendar."

- **PropertyContainer base class.** Rather than forcing each class supporting the PropertyContainer class to implement separately the behavior specified by its interface, consider providing an abstract base class that implements this behavior. In the SanFrancisco framework the PropertyContainer interface is implemented in the DynamicEntity class.

- **Maintenance methods.** When PropertyContainer objects are used within a hierarchy, it may be necessary for the purpose of property configuration and maintenance to introduce methods on the PropertyContainer interface that access properties held directly by the target PropertyContainer object (i.e., without delegating retrieval to the parent object). This approach allows the maintainer of a given PropertyContainer object to view only the properties held on the target object itself. In the SanFrancisco framework, we name such methods using the phrase "directly contained." For example, we introduce a getDirectlyContainedPropertyBy method to retrieve a property directly held by the target object.

- **Muliple PropertyContainer hierarchies.** In our description of the PropertyContainer pattern, we limited our PropertyContainer objects (e.g., Company) to a single property retrieval hierarchy. In many cases, limiting a PropertyContainer to a single hierarchy is sufficient, but sometimes it is necessary to allow a PropertyContainer object to exist in multiple hierarchies simultaneously. For example, a Product object may exist in a manufacturing assembly hierarchy in which its hierarchical parent is another Product object, as well as in a locational hierarchy in which its parent is a StockZone object (see Figure 5.4). The Property Container pattern can be enhanced to support multiple property retrieval hierarchies in the following way:

  - Design the PropertyContainer interface to support a keyed collection of parents.

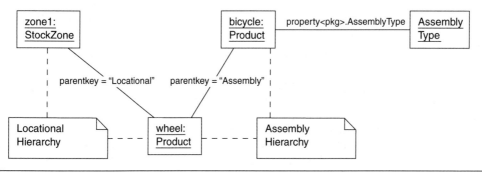

Figure 5.4. Supporting Multiple PropertyContainer Hierarchies

- Assign names to the different property retrieval hierarchies in which a PropertyContainer object may exist. Examples are "Assembly" and "Locational." These hierarchy name Strings will serve as the keys for different parent PropertyContainer objects.

- Enhance the property retrieval methods on the PropertyContainer interface to take not only a property name as a parameter, but also a hierarchy name (String). The hierarchy name parameter is used in the implementation of the property retrieval method; it is used to select the parent PropertyContainer object to which the property retrieval will be delegated (chained) when the specified property is not directly contained by the target object.

Using this approach, a client wishing to retrieve a property specifies both the property name and the name of the hierarchy to use in the retrieval. For example, a client interested in retrieving an AssemblyType property from a Product would specify "<pkg>.AssemblyType" as a property name and "Assembly" as a hierarchy name.

Sample Code

Each domain business object that supports the Property Container pattern must contain code (either directly or through inheritance) that implements the PropertyContainer interface. In SanFrancisco, all property containers inherit from a common base class called DynamicEntity, which implements the PropertyContainer interface.

In the example described earlier, the properties are the grower location and grower certification level. If the grower location were an attribute of the Product class, clients would get and set the grower location with a call to a specific accessor method for the grower location attribute:

```
// Set the grower location
theProduct.setGrowerLocation(growerLocation);

// Get the grower location
GrowerLocation growerLocation = theProduct.getGrowerLocation();
```

The client code that is needed to access the property looks a little different from a normal accessor method. Instead of calling a specific method (setGrowerLocation or getGrowerLocation), the client now calls a generalized method (addPropertyBy or getPropertyBy):

```
// Add the grower location property
theProduct.addPropertyBy(growerLocation,
                         "fw.GrowerLocation");

// Retrieve the grower location property
GrowerLocation growerLocation =
  (GrowerLocation)theProduct.getPropertyBy("fw.GrowerLocation");
```

These methods take as a parameter a property name that identifies the particular property to be added or retrieved. The property name is a String containing the package and class names. The other key point is that the generalized method getPropertyBy cannot return a specific object type, GrowerLocation. As a result, the returned Object needs to be cast to the correct type.

Properties can be retrieved from a property container that is part of a hierarchy. The Company object is the example we discussed earlier. Let's assume that the Product object is also part of a hierarchy. Each object needs to contain a method to retrieve the parent object. The getChainParent method is used for this purpose. As a result, the getPropertyBy method looks like this:

```
public Object getPropertyBy(String token) {
  // Check if the property is in this object's collection
  Object property = propertyCollection.getElementBy(token);

  // If property does not exist locally, attempt to retrieve it from
  // the parent in the property container hierarchy
  if (property == null) {
    return getChainParent().getPropertyBy(token);
  }

  // Return the property if it exists locally
  return property;
}
```

Because the Product class is a property container and is part of a hierarchy, it needs to have the ability to find its parent. The getChainParent method must be overriden for each class that is part of a hierarchy. As a result, the Product class must contain a parent Product attribute:

```
Product ivParentProduct;
```

The Product class also needs to override the getChainParent method to return the parent Product:

```
public Object getChainParent() {
  return (ivParentProduct);
}
```

Known Uses

Most SanFrancisco business objects implement the Property Container pattern. Specific examples of business objects that are property containers include BusinessPartner, Company, Country, and NumberSeries.

Related Patterns

- **Chain of Responsibility.** Properties that are accessed from within a hierarchy make use of the Chain of Responsibility pattern of *Design Patterns.*
- **Controller.** A class that is a property may be implemented as a self-inserting property such as a controller (see Chapter 10).

6

Business Process Command

Intent

Provide an extensible mechanism for encapsulating a business process supported by a logical business object or subsystem that is implemented as multiple physical objects.

Motivation

In certain situations in object-oriented design, a "logical" business object or subsystem may be modeled as multiple cooperating physical objects. This group of physical objects combines to provide the functionality of the represented business object or subsystem. Consider the following example: The company in our case study, Food Warehouse (see Chapter 2), has an Inventory System that handles movements of stock to and from warehouses that it owns. Within the FW application, the Inventory System consists of Warehouse objects that are associated with Product objects, which themselves contain collections of Balance and Cost objects.

Note that there is no one Inventory System object within the FW application; instead this logical business subsystem is represented as a structure of constituent objects—namely, the Warehouse, Product, Balance, and Cost objects. Now consider the business process known as a stock transaction—that is, a movement of stock (a quantity of a particular product) into, out of, or within the company's warehouses. A typical stock transaction consists of the following steps:

1. Creating a StockTransaction object to record the event
2. Increasing or decreasing the appropriate Balances for the given Product and the given Warehouse(s)
3. Updating the Cost information for the Product
4. Collecting the information necessary to create postings to the financial portion of the application

From a business standpoint, the Inventory System (a logical business object) has responsibility for stock transactions. Any one of the constituent objects that make up the Inventory System within the application provides only part of the functions necessary to complete a stock transaction.

In this situation, the stock transaction process is best modeled as a command (as defined by the Command pattern of *Design Patterns*) that works with the objects that make up FW's Inventory System (see Figure 6.1). Encapsulating the stock transaction process in a command provides the following benefits:

- Like a business object method, a command encapsulates the logic and ordering of the business process it represents. In this example, if a StockTransactionCommand object were not provided, the actions taken against the constituent objects of the Inventory System and the ordering of those actions to correctly execute a stock transaction would have to be made known to clients.

- Unlike a method, a command does not require a business object to play the role of responsible class. In our example, it eliminates the problem of having to introduce a method on one of the Inventory System constituent

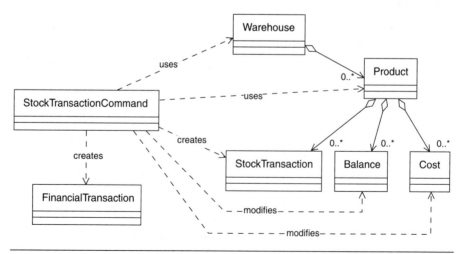

Figure 6.1. The Inventory System and the StockTransactionCommand

classes (such as Warehouse or Product) that would not represent a proper business responsibility of that class.

- Like a policy (see Chapter 7), the command generally represents a single business process and works well as an extension point for customization of the application. In many cases, it is useful to implement the command's do method as a Template Method (as defined by the Template Method pattern of *Design Patterns*), allowing subclasses to easily override distinct parts of the encapsulated business process without altering their overall order.

Given the preceding Inventory System example, here are some other processes of the Inventory System that could be implemented as commands:

- **Setup.** This is the initial setup and configuration of the constituent objects of the Inventory System. The following subprocesses are involved:
  - Building Warehouse objects
  - Building Product objects and associating them with Warehouses
  - Creating initial Cost and Balance objects for the Products
- **Generation of inventory reports.** This process generates reports on the state of the Inventory System. The reports may contain information on the following:
  - The balances of products in each warehouse
  - Cost information for each product
  - A history of stock transactions

Note that these processes, like the stock transaction process, are responsibilities of the Inventory System as a whole rather than of any single constituent object of the Inventory System.

Commands can also be used to selectively expose business operations from a subsystem to users of that subsystem. Under these circumstances, the set of commands defined for a subsystem makes up the user interface, or API (application program interface), of the subsystem, in effect creating a facade for the subsystem.

Applicability

Consider using the Business Process Command pattern when any of the following criteria apply:

- A logical business object or subsystem does not have a one-to-one mapping with a physical object within the application, but instead is represented by multiple cooperating objects.

- Some processes associated with the logical business object or subsystem are responsibilities not of any one of the constituent physical objects within the application, but rather of the logical object itself.

- Circumstances make it useful to restrict access to the full capabilities of a subsystem by selectively exposing a subset of its business methods.

The Business Process Command approach can also be used to provide the user of an application with coarse-grained functions that span multiple logical business objects or subsystems. For example, a command class could be provided to produce an all-inclusive report that spans the Warehouse and Financial subsystems.

Structure

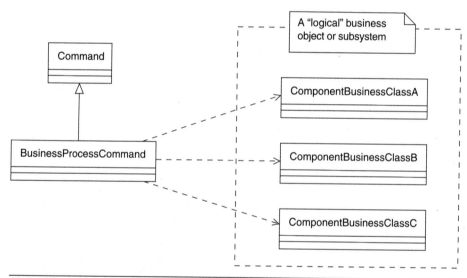

Figure 6.2. Command Structure

Participants

- **ComponentBusinessClasses** (Warehouse, Product, Balance, Cost). Sets of physical business objects that combine to represent a logical business object or subsystem.

- **BusinessProcessCommand** (StockTransactionCommand). A command class that encapsulates a process for which the logical business object or subsystem is responsible.

- **Command.** A common base class for command classes. The command class introduces a virtual do method that is implemented by command subclasses.

Collaborations

- Clients create and execute an instance of the BusinessProcessCommand class.
- When executed, the BusinessProcessCommand interacts with the constituent objects that make up the logical business object or subsystem as necessary to perform its encapsulated algorithm.

Consequences

The Business Process Command pattern has the following tradeoffs, benefits, and drawbacks:

Tradeoffs

- **Understandability versus performance overhead.** Using a command to encapsulate a business process as described in this chapter allows a more accurate and intuitive modeling of the business domain. This approach increases understandability of the application design and implementation. However, using a command rather than a method defined on one of the constituent business objects does come at some cost to performance. Entailed in the command approach is the overhead of creating the command object before executing the encapsulated process. It may be necessary in some performance-critical situations to resort to placing the business process in a method on one of the constituent business objects.

Benefits

- **Intuitive modeling of domain.** The Business Process Command pattern provides a more accurate and intuitive modeling of the target business domain.
- **Encapsulation.** The Business Process Command pattern encapsulates the business process.
- **Extending the application.** The Business Process Command pattern provides a natural extension point for the application.

Drawbacks

- **Cost of command creation.** Using a command to represent a business process introduces the performance overhead of command creation.

Implementation

Consider the following implementation issues for the Business Process Command pattern:

- **Creation interface for the command.** What information, object references, and so on will the command need when it is created in order to execute its encapsulated process later? Common requirements include inputs for the encapsulated process, as well as references to some (or all) of the constituent objects involved in the process. In the Inventory System example, the involved Warehouse and Product objects probably would be passed to the StockTransactionCommand object during its creation. The reference to the Product would allow the command to access Cost and Balance objects.

- **Use of a Template Method in the command.** Often the general steps in a business process are always executed in a certain order, whereas the specific implementation of those steps may be customized for different uses. If this is the case, the do method of the Business Process Command should be implemented as a Template Method, by the introduction of separate (typically protected) methods on the command class to represent the different steps in the business process. The do method of the command then calls these methods in the proper order. Subclasses of the Business Process Command may then selectively override the implementation of these auxiliary methods.

- **Abstract and concrete Business Process Command classes.** Should the Business Process Command class be abstract or concrete? Like a policy (see Chapter 7), the use of a command allows the application developer to provide a single concrete implementation of the Business Process Command class that may later be subclassed as needed, or to implement an abstract version of the Business Process Command class that requires subclasses to provide the implementation of some or all of the encapsulated process. The former approach is commonly used when there is a single prevailing implementation of the business process; the latter approach is useful when different implementations are known to exist.

Sample Code

Here's a simplified example of an abstract command base class for the stock transaction creation process described earlier:

```
public class StockTransactionCommand extends Object {
    // Subclasses will need to override the following abstract
    // methods:
    protected abstract StockTransaction createStockTransaction();
    protected abstract void updateBalances();
    protected abstract void updateCosts();
    protected abstract FinancialTransaction
        createFinancialTransaction();

    // The command's do method implemented as a Template Method:
    public void do() {
    ivStockTransaction = createStockTransaction();
    updateBalances();
    updateCosts();
    ivFinancialTransaction = createFinancialTransaction();
    }

    // Initialize the data in this class
    // The passed warehouse and product will serve as the target
    // for creation of the stock transaction
    public void initialize(Warehouse whs,
                           Product prd,
                           Quantity amt) {
                               ivProduct = prd;
                               ivWarehouse = whs;
                               ivAmount = amt;

    }

    // These attributes are set at creation
    public Warehouse ivWarehouse = null;
    public Product ivProduct = null;
    public int ivAmount = 0;

    // These attributes will be set when the command is run
    public StockTransaction ivStockTransaction = null;
    public FinancialTransaction ivFinancialTransaction = null;
}
```

Subclasses of StockTransactionCommand will override the createStock-Transaction, updateBalances, updateCosts, and createFinancialTransaction methods to provide implementations specific to the type of stock transaction represented by each subclass.

Known Uses

The Business Process Command pattern is used within the SanFrancisco framework in the Warehouse Management and General Ledger Core Business Processes.

The Warehouse Management package uses the pattern for stock transactions, as was described in a simplified form in our example. Warehouse Management provides the class StockTransactionCreateCmd, an abstract command class that represents the stock transaction process. The StockTransactionCreateCmd uses a Template Method approach to implementation of the do method. A concrete subclass, called ManualStockTransactionCreateCmd, is also provided. The ManualStockTransactionCreateCmd subclass represents a manual transaction of stock between warehouses and provides specific implementations of the auxiliary methods called through the do method.

In the General Ledger package, the General Ledger is a logical business subsystem that is implemented as numerous cooperating financial objects, such as Journals, Dissections, AnalysisCodes, Balances, and so on. The business process of year-end closing involves the creation of Journals and the updating of account Balances at the end of a fiscal year. Like the stock transaction example, year-end closing is not a natural responsibility of the collection of Journals, nor the account Balances, but of the General Ledger subsystem itself.

Related Patterns

- **Command.** Business Process Commands are a specific usage of the Command pattern defined in *Design Patterns*.

- **Template Method.** A Business Process Command base class may implement its do method as a Template Method (as described in *Design Patterns*).

- **Facade.** Business Process Commands may be used as a facade (as defined in *Design Patterns*) for a subsystem.

Part II

Behavioral Patterns

SanFrancisco's behavioral patterns describe various methods of incorporating flexible algorithms throughout a business application. Each of the behavioral object patterns described in this book defines a variation or extension of the Strategy pattern defined in *Design Patterns.*

The Simple Policy pattern (Chapter 7)—named as such because business experts typically describe variable algorithms within a domain as business policies—defines three distinct scoping variations of the Strategy pattern: object-specific scope, company-wide scope (i.e., scoped by the application's currently active business context), and application-wide scope. These variations give an application developer control over the range to which a particular algorithm applies: to a specific business object only, to all business objects of a particular type associated with a specific company, or to all business objects of a type regardless of where they reside within the company hierarchy.

The Chain of Responsibility–Driven Policy pattern (Chapter 8) combines the Chain of Responsibility pattern, also defined by *Design Patterns,* with the Simple Policy pattern to allow application developers to vary business algorithms according to the objects being processed, as well as the object doing the processing.

The Token-Driven Policy pattern (Chapter 9) allows specific policies for a business method to be selected on the basis of the business process using the method.

7

Simple Policy

Intent

Define a family of algorithms, encapsulate each one, and make them interchangeable. This pattern is similar to the Strategy Pattern in the book *Design Patterns*. It lets the algorithm vary independently from the business objects affected by it.

Motivation

Business application users often identify recurring activities in which the logic used to make certain decisions could vary depending on the specific situation or objectives of the company. Each company could use various criteria and related logic to determine how different events within the business are handled.

The company's approach could be driven by many factors, some external to its business (such as government regulation and competition) and some that result from internal factors (such as the company's style of doing business or the types of products sold). In addition, the business logic necessary for different core business processes may require different scope. For example, determining a discount may differ for different specific products, but calculating the tax is the same for all products offered by a company. Flexible applications should be designed to support a wide variety of business environments and minimize the impact on core business objects.

Consider the following example from our case study (see Chapter 2):

Food Warehouse has a subsidiary company in Belgium. Both the parent company and the subsidiary keep track of all their financial transactions in journals. These journals must be posted to the proper accounts, but first the journals must be validated. FW maintains a consistent set of validation rules for the entire company, and all journals must meet these requirements before they can be posted. However, since the Belgian subsidiary is located in the European Union, it must follow additional validation requirements imposed by the EU.

Figure 7.1 shows a simplified view of company, journal, and journal posting objects for our journal validation example. In this example, a business algorithm needs to vary on a company-by-company basis. Implementing journal validation rules directly into the Journal class would result in an inflexible design. First, this approach would increase the size and complexity of the Journal class, making it more cumbersome and harder to maintain. Because validation rules in Belgium differ from those in the United States, we would also need to provide multiple Journal subclasses, each with its own validation algorithm. Then, if company policies or government regulations changed in the future, we would need to modify some or all of these Journal subclasses, even though the general business behavior of the Journal class would not have changed.

One way we can effectively address this requirement is to isolate the volatile business behavior in a separate class: the journal validation policy class. We can then introduce a single journal validation policy per company that is used for all postings within a given company (see Figure 7.2).

By taking this approach, we can easily vary journal validation behavior between companies while allowing multiple companies to share common

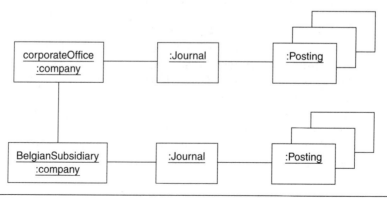

Figure 7.1. Simplified View of Company Hierarchy, Journals, and Postings

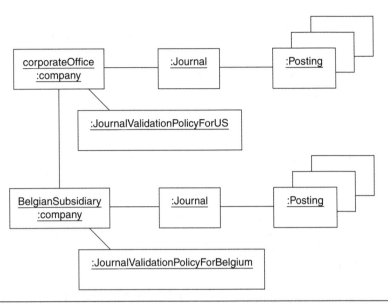

Figure 7.2. Journal Validation Policies

validation rules. Other companies in our company hierarchy can either choose to introduce their own specialized validation rules (just as the Belgian subsidiary in Figure 7.2 does) or share rules with the parent company. For example, if we were to introduce the West Region subsidiary as another Company object underneath the Corporate Office company in Figure 7.2, then when our application was operating in the West Region, any journal postings could automatically use the validation policy defined at the corporate level.

Figure 7.3 shows the classes in this example. We have introduced a small policy class hierarchy to represent the business rules used during posting validation. By defining this class hierarchy to encapsulate different business algorithms, we can isolate the variable portions of a business object from the portions that are unlikely to change over time. Business objects can then delegate their execution of business logic to these policies. The business objects to which a policy instance applies are collectively called the *scope* of applicability of that policy. In this example we have company-wide policy scope. SanFrancisco defines three distinct scopes:

- **Object-specific scope.** This scope most closely resembles the Strategy pattern of *Design Patterns*. The algorithm used for a business operation may vary among the different instances of a class. The product discount algorithms described in Chapter 2 have object-specific scope.

  A domain business object that implements a business algorithm with object-specific scope contains an instance of the policy base class for that algorithm

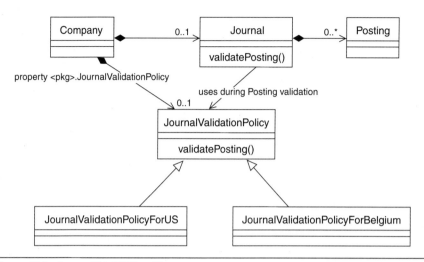

Figure 7.3. Journal Validation Classes

as one of its attributes. The policy object held is an instance of one of the concrete subclasses—the default or a subclass provided by the application. Typically this instance is passed as a parameter upon creation of the DomainBusinessObject. The policy instance may optionally contain state (see the "Implementation" section later in this chapter for a discussion of policy state).

- **Company-wide scope.** The same algorithm is used for all business objects of a particular type within a single company, as in our journal validation example. Objects in different companies may have different policies.

  In company-wide policy structure, the policy base class is contained as a property of the Company object.[1] The DomainBusinessObject instance retrieves the policy from the Company by requesting it via policy base class name (the property will be an instance of one of the concrete subclasses). The Company implements the Property Container pattern (see Chapter 5), which allows the policy to be attached to the current Company or anywhere within its hierarchy. Again the policy may optionally contain state.

- **Application-wide scope.** Every business object instance in the entire application uses the same algorithm (regardless of the particular Company

---

1. The Company object hierarchy serves as the business context for the application; however, this concept of *business context* can be extended to business object hierarchies other than Company.

with which the objects are associated). Business objects that have application-wide scope tend to be uncommon. One example of such an object
within SanFrancisco is the policy used for price calculation. This policy
allows special tax calculations, for example, to be easily incorporated into
the framework.

The structure for the policy with application-wide scope of applicability
appears very similar to the object-specific structure. The domain class contains a policy base class instance as an attribute. The policy attribute is
changed by class replacement. Unlike the situation with object-specific
policy scope, in this case the policy that is the attribute of the domain class
is set by replacement of the FixedPolicy class so that a specialized class is
instantiated by the FixedPolicy constructor each time it is called (see Chapter 3 for a discussion of class replacement).

Every business occasionally needs to override the algorithm that would
normally be used for a given business task. By specifying the policy base class
as an optional parameter on the business object method that is delegating to a
policy, we can easily accommodate these special cases.

Applicability

Consider using the Simple Policy pattern when any of the following criteria
apply:

- A business algorithm is volatile and likely to change.
- Different versions of the algorithm are required.
- The algorithm will introduce undue complexity to the business object.
- The implementation requires multiple conditional statements to determine
  the particular algorithm to be used.

Structure

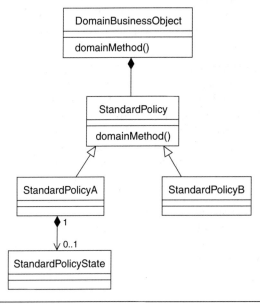

Figure 7.4. Object-Specific Policy Structure

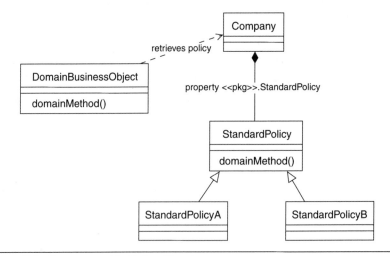

Figure 7.5. Company-wide Policy Structure

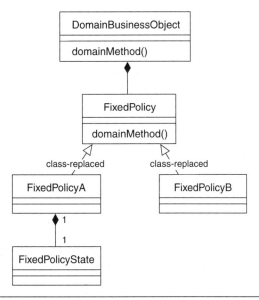

Figure 7.6. Application-wide Policy Structure

Participants

- **DomainBusinessObject** (Journal). The business object class (referred to as the context object in the Strategy pattern of *Design Patterns*) that contains the externally visible policy method and is the target of the request. For object-specific or application-wide policy scopes, the business object holds an instance of one of the concrete policy classes. When company-wide policy scope is appropriate, the business object delegates responsibility to its policy by first retrieving the policy instance from the active Company (as noted previously, other business context objects can also be used to hold policy instances). In either approach, the business object can use any of the different implementations of the algorithm.

- **StandardPolicy** (JournalValidationPolicy). An abstract class that declares an interface common to all the supported algorithms in the object-specific and Company-wide scope forms of the pattern. Optionally, it may define utility methods to be used by all the concrete policy classes.

- **StandardPolicyDefault** (JournalValidationPolicyForUS). A default concrete policy provided by the framework and intended as a sample implementation. Application developers typically provide other policies specific to their business needs. These default policies may be provided by the framework or by specific applications that use the framework.

- **FixedPolicy.** A concrete policy used by all instances of the domain class. The algorithm in this application-wide policy is changed only by class replacement.

- **StandardPolicyState, FixedPolicyState.** The encapsulated state (internal attributes) associated with a particular policy. Business policies that use encapsulated state are rare.

Collaborations

- The method supported by the policy on the business object contains only a call to the policy method of StandardPolicy or FixedPolicy. Typically, a default implementation is not placed in the business object class.

- StandardPolicy or FixedPolicy should typically take the business object instance as a parameter on the policy method, thereby allowing the two objects to interact to complete the algorithm.

- How the policy object is attached and when it is created depend on its scope of applicability:

  - In **object-specific scope,** the policy instance typically is passed in during business object creation, thus allowing the business object to establish a reference to that instance.

  - In **company-wide scope,** these policies are held as properties on one of the Company objects. They are usually set up at the time the Company object is defined within the application.

  - In **application-wide scope,** these policies are held as attributes of the business object, but they are usually identified through configuration and established at the time the application is installed. Such policies are created by the business object while it is itself being created.

Consequences

The Simple Policy pattern has the following tradeoffs, benefits, and drawbacks:

Tradeoffs

- **Enforcing versus relaxing policy contravariance.** Policy users can choose to enforce *contravariance*[2] (the preservation of a base class contract by its

---

2. Contravariance is colloquially known as the "require no more, promise no less" rule, which states that the preconditions specified by a base class are not made more stringent by subclasses, and the specified postconditions, consequences, and side effects are supported by subclasses at least as rigorously as by the base class.

subclasses) or to selectively violate contravariance on a policy subclass-by-subclass basis. Enforcing contravariance ensures that all application code using the business method supported by a particular policy class hierarchy will see consistent business method behavior regardless of which policy is used. In selected cases, however, particularly when the code using the business method needs a great deal of control over the behavior of that method, there may be reasons to violate contravariance. For instance, we can increase framework flexibility by violating policy class hierarchy contravariance as long as all users of the method supported by that policy class hierarchy are aware of the violation and take necessary precautions against any potential adverse effects. Needless to say, violating contravariance should be approached with caution.

Benefits

- **Alternative to business object subclassing.** Policies provide a means other than creating subclasses of a business object to support a variety of algorithms or behaviors. Subclassing the business object allows the addition of the logic needed to support the business process; however, such an implementation hardwires the algorithm into the business object. It also integrates the business object details with the algorithm implementation, making the business object much more volatile.

- **Elimination of conditional statements.** The Simple Policy pattern offers a means to minimize the use of conditional statements in order to direct the execution of specific business logic, thereby allowing separation of the business logic into meaningful units (e.g., by specific business use) rather than the alternative of merging all options into a single large and complex method implementation.

- **Choice of implementations.** Policies can provide different implementations of the same algorithm, thereby allowing clients to determine the algorithms appropriate for their needs.

- **Focusing of expertise.** An expert in a particular business area (e.g., tax codes) can work on these policies without interfering with the expert in another area (e.g., discounts). Experts work on algorithms and classes associated only with their specific areas.

- **Transparency to the client.** The client of the policy does not need to know which algorithm is being used. It simply calls the policy method on the business object, which triggers the correct algorithm.

Drawbacks

- **Additional overhead.** For each business method implemented using the Simple Policy pattern, the business object must obtain the policy object and then invoke the policy method.

- **Increased number of objects.** Having policies increases the number of objects within the application.

Implementation

Consider the following implementation issues for the Simple Policy pattern:

- **Policy objects and state.** A policy is an object that exists because of the algorithm it contains and does not usually contain state. However, it may contain state if necessary. If a policy needs to contain state, the state may be used by the algorithm but should not affect the algorithm (e.g., checking the value of the state and conditionally executing different algorithms should not be done within the policy method). It is more desirable to have the policy contain its state indirectly in one of several ways:

  - As an attribute of the associated business object. The business object is always passed as a parameter of the policy method. Therefore the policy will always have access to the business object and can access its attributes.

  - As a property of the associated business object. For more information on properties, see Chapter 5.

  - As an object with a user alias. User aliases for objects can be established in many ways; for example, through JNDI (Java Naming and Directory Interface) capabilities in Java. SanFrancisco provides a transactional naming mechanism to identify an object uniquely so that it can be retrieved by that name later.

- **Sets of policy objects.** In some cases it may be advantageous to allow the end user to choose which concrete policy will be used at runtime. Concrete policy objects may be kept in a collection as described by the Controller pattern (see Chapter 10). Following this approach, you can choose the specific policy at runtime and use it by overriding the business object's policy as already described.

- **Policy interfaces.** The interface for the policy method must be defined with great care. This method cannot change its interface without severely affecting the code that will use the policy. For example, if we design a credit check method with only customer and amount as parameters, and then discover later that a time stamp object is also required as a parameter, every user of this method will have to be changed to pass the new parameter. One way to reduce the risk of such a serious effect from a change is to pass the domain object as a parameter to the policy. Often the business object will have relationships to additional business information that can be used by the policy algorithm. In extreme cases, the additional parameters may be temporarily added as properties of the domain object before the call to the method, then removed after the method returns. Some policies can also benefit from the passing of another business object as a parameter that serves as a *smart parameter list*—i.e., an object with business meaning containing numerous attributes that may be useful to the business algorithm implemented by the policy. This business object can be extended (e.g., via class replacement) and the accompanying policy can take advantage of this expanded interface.

- **Grouping of cooperating algorithms.** Usually a policy base class should supply only a single business method. In some situations, however, a policy should support multiple methods. Consider this approach only when multiple business algorithm methods are likely to be changed in concert; otherwise this approach results in a poorly factored design with unnecessarily duplicated business logic from unchanged methods.

Sample Code

The Strategy pattern implementation outlined in *Design Patterns* provides examples of how object-specific and application-wide policy behavior can be implemented. The company-wide policy is different and warrants a separate explanation.

In our example, the business object that implements a company-wide policy, the Journal, will access its policy through the business context object, the Company, where the Company object holds the policy as a property:

```
public class Journal extends Object {

  public void validatePosting(Posting posting) {

    // Get the active Company
    Company activeCompany = CompanyContext.getActiveCompany();

// Retrieve the validation policy by property and delegate to it
    // Validation policy takes Journal as an additional
    // parameter to increase policy flexibility
    (JournalValidationPolicy)activeCompany.getPropertyBy(
      "gl.JournalValidationPolicy").validatePosting(posting, this);
  }
```

```
    ...

    Set ivPostings;
}
```

Defining the interface for the policy method is important. The policy method defines as a parameter not only the Posting, but also the Journal, to increase policy implementation flexibility. The policy base definition may be simply an interface (if no implementation is to be provided at the base level, as shown in the code that follows), or it may provide partial implementations via such approaches as the Template Method pattern (described in *Design Patterns*).

```
public interface JournalValidationPolicy {

    public void validatePosting(Posting posting, Journal journal);
}
```

The retrieved Posting validation policy contains the logic to use when validating postings to the Journal. A skeleton implementation of this policy looks like this:

```
public class JournalValidationPolicyForUS implements
JournalValidationPolicy extends Object {

    public void validatePosting(Posting posting, Journal journal) {

        boolean validated = true;
        int reasonCode;
        // Get the necessary information from the passed-in
        // Journal object to use during validation
        ...

        // Compare retrieved information to passed-in Posting info
        // Set validated to false and set reasonCode if validation fails
        ...

        // If validation fails, throw exception
        if (!validated) {
            throw new ValidationException(reasonCode);
        }
    }
}
```

Other examples of policy sample code can be found in the documentation provided for the Strategy pattern in *Design Patterns*.

Known Uses

Many SanFrancisco business objects use the Simple Policy pattern. NaturalCalendar is an example of a SanFrancisco business object that makes use of multiple policies. NaturalCalendar is a calendar composed of Day objects, which can be used to represent working days. Each Day object can have one or more work periods defined. All Day objects have a policy (WorkPeriodManagerPolicyDefault) to add work periods. This policy has an application-wide scope of applicability. NaturalCalendar also has a policy (NaturalCalendarWorkTimePolicyDefault) that can be used to check any given time to determine if it is within a work period and when the previous or next work period will begin. This policy is an example of an object-specific policy that is attached to the NaturalCalendar object.

The SanFrancisco General Ledger framework makes considerable use of the Simple Policy pattern. One example is the process that is followed when Journal objects are being deleted. When a Journal is deleted, its associated objects should also be cleaned up. If the deletion of the Journal is delegated to a deletion policy, that policy can perform the necessary additional cleanup. This policy is a company-wide policy: It will be used by all Journal objects for a company.

Related Patterns

- **Template Method.** The policy base class may implement the business algorithm in the form of a template method, relying on subclasses of the policy base class to implement various hook methods used by the template method implementation described in *Design Patterns.*

- **Property Container.** If the scope of applicability of the policy is company-wide, the Property Container pattern (see Chapter 5) will be used to locate the policy in the company hierarchy.

- **Controller.** Multiple policy objects can be managed through a controller (see Chapter 10).

- **Class Replacement.** If the policy's scope of applicability is application-wide, the Class Replacement pattern (see Chapter 3) is used to change the particular policy that is used for all business objects of the type using the policy within the application.

8

Chain of Responsibility-Driven Policy

Intent

Define a family of encapsulated domain algorithms and associated chains of responsibility to locate the correct algorithm to be used and make the family members interchangeable so that either a domain algorithm or a chain of responsibility can be configured into a business object. Encapsulated chains of responsibility search for the correct domain algorithm based on business objects involved in the processing being done by the domain algorithm.

Motivation

Typically there are many algorithms for any particular business object behavior, such as putting away stock in a warehouse (referred to as putaway). Often the end user of an application specifies the algorithm(s) to be used. The Simple Policy pattern is often used in such situations; however, this approach often does not meet the flexibility needs of an application for a particular domain behavior. Sometimes an application algorithm needs to vary according to not only the object doing the processing but also the objects being processed. Consider the following example from our case study (see Chapter 2):

Most warehouses owned by Food Warehouse have the same configuration and thus can use the same putaway policies when storing incoming goods.

However, FW also leases some warehouse space that is configured differently and requires different putaway policies. In addition, some products require special putaway policies to ensure proper inventory rotation.

In this example, Food Warehouse needs to be able to configure its application so that different putaway policies will come into effect under different circumstances. Moreover, sometimes the policy needs to vary according to the product being placed into stock, and at other times the warehouse controls the putaway algorithm.

Assume that the Product class has domain responsibility for the putaway method. One possible approach in this situation is to define a policy class hierarchy for the putaway method (as shown in Figure 8.1) and build various concrete policy classes, some of which take into account the warehouse where the goods are being stored and others of which implement special stock rotation algorithms. This approach meets our requirements but has two major drawbacks:

1. Some of our concrete policy implementations are more complex than necessary because they must not only implement multiple putaway policies but also make decisions based on the particular warehouse to select the correct policy.

2. If our business becomes more complex in the future, such that other business objects can affect the putaway algorithm, we will have to reimplement most if not all of the existing concrete policy classes to take into account these additional business objects.

You may have already noticed that a chain of responsibility is involved in this example: First the product is checked for special handling rules, then the warehouse is checked to see if it requires a special putaway algorithm, and finally the default putaway algorithm defined for the company is used.

We can apply the Chain of Responsibility pattern of *Design Patterns* in combination with the Simple Policy pattern to this problem to eliminate the first of

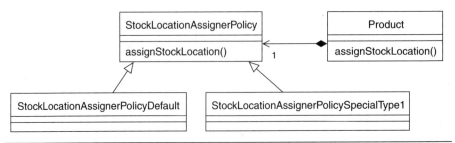

Figure 8.1. A Policy Class Hierarchy for the Putaway Method

the two drawbacks. Each business object can be defined to contain an optional policy object, and a chain of responsibility can be implemented in the involved business objects (Warehouse, Product, and Company in Figure 8.2) to check for the presence of a policy in the business object and use that policy if present, or otherwise pass responsibility on to the next business object in the chain.

However, this approach doesn't help us deal with the second drawback. What would happen if the end user of the application needed to introduce additional business objects into the decision process? We would then have to modify the hard-coded chain of responsibility to add other business objects—not a very flexible solution. How are we going to solve this problem? The Chain of Responsibility-Driven Policy pattern introduces a second policy class hierarchy called the *selection policy* to give us the needed flexibility.

A selection policy searches for the correct domain algorithm to use (i.e., the correct domain algorithm policy instance) during processing. Selection policy subclass implementations follow a unique chain of responsibility that searches through some or all of the objects being processed by the domain algorithm in a prescribed order. The selection policy checks each object in the search path to see if it contains an instance of the domain algorithm policy. The most flexible way

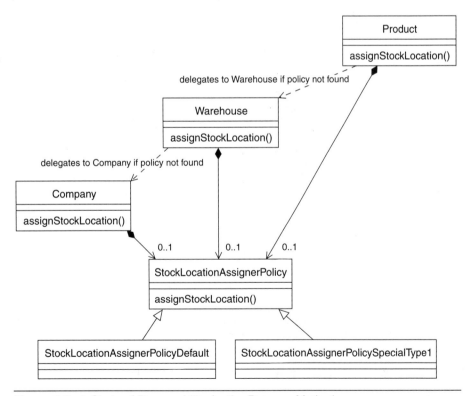

Figure 8.2. A Chain of Responsbility for the Putaway Method

to maintain these instances is by property (see Chapter 5). Within SanFrancisco, if a domain algorithm policy instance is present, it will have a property name of the following form: "<pkg>.<PolicyBaseClass>." In our location assignment example, the property name would be "whs.StockLocationAssignerPolicy."

The selection policy subclass continues to search until it finds a domain algorithm policy object instance or reaches the default policy object instance (typically held by the currently active Company object in the application). Thus, the policy used may be the default version defined for the application, or it may be an overriding version held by one of the objects being processed by the algorithm. For example, the default algorithm for our location assigner selection policy example is to search first the Product, then the Warehouse, and finally the Company for the domain algorithm policy instance. Figure 8.3 shows this extension for our example.

This approach eliminates the second drawback, but we can do better. We would like the flexibility to use a chain of responsibility, or not, without having to change our business object implementations. By combining the policy class hierarchy with the selection policy class hierarchy, we have a very flexible solution (shown in Figure 8.4) that allows us to make either a selection policy subclass or a policy subclass the policy attribute on Product. The domain algorithm policy and selection policy class hierarchies can be merged because each declares a common domain method.

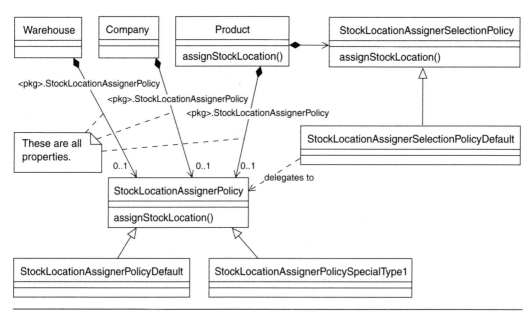

Figure 8.3. Encapsulating Where to Look for the Putaway Method

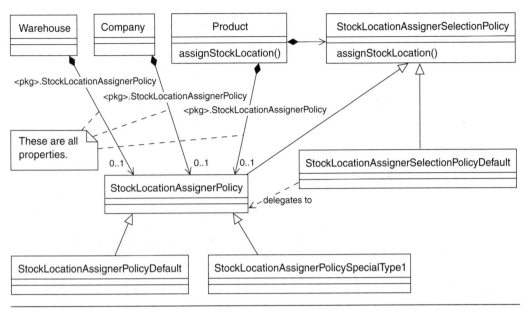

Figure 8.4. Combining the Class Hierarchies

You might think it odd that the domain algorithm policy class hierarchy inherits from the selection policy class hierarchy, but policy classes can also be thought of as selection policy classes, which implicitly select themselves rather than following a chain of responsibility (in other words, they implement a single-object chain of responsibility). Thus, if a policy subclass instance is in place on Product, the location assigner algorithm behaves identically to the standard object-specific Simple Policy pattern. If a selection policy subclass instance is in place, then the chain of responsibility implemented by that selection policy will be followed until a policy subclass instance is found.

Let's look at a specific example. Assume our products are stored in two warehouses. Warehouse A uses a special putaway policy. Warehouse B relies on the default policy established by the enterprise. Figure 8.5 shows how we would deploy the various policy instances in this case. If we invoke the assignStockLocation method on our product, passing warehouse A as one of the parameters, the collaboration diagram appears as in Figure 8.6. And if if we pass warehouse B as one of the parameters, the collaboration diagram looks like Figure 8.7.

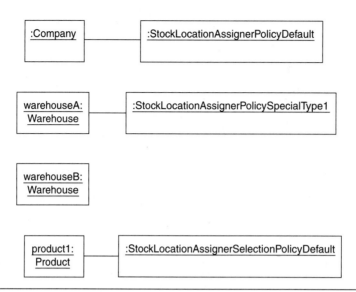

Figure 8.5. Sample Putaway Policy Setup

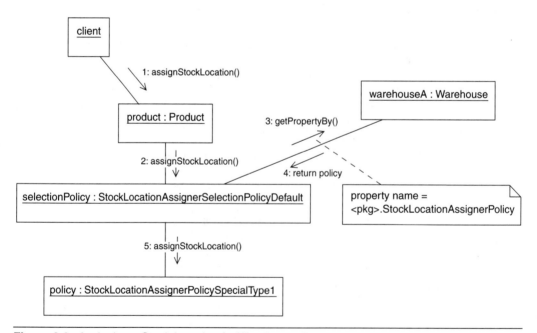

Figure 8.6. Assigning a Stock Location for Warehouse A

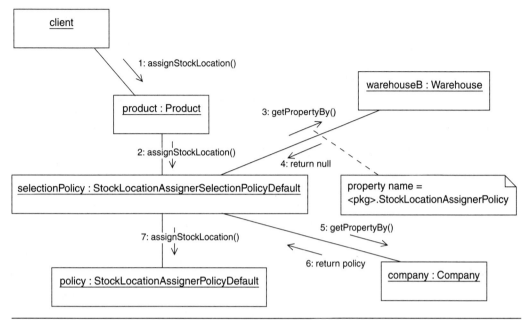

Figure 8.7. Assigning a Stock Location for Warehouse B

Applicability

Consider using the Chain of Responsibility-Driven Policy pattern when any of the following criteria apply:

- Multiple domain algorithms are typically used in conjunction with a business object behavior.
- Configuring a default behavior for a domain algorithm (typically on a company-by-company basis) is useful.
- Overriding that default behavior is desirable on an object-by-object basis for any objects involved in the domain algorithm.
- Making performance-versus-flexibility tradeoff decisions on an object-by-object basis is advantageous for the business object.

Structure

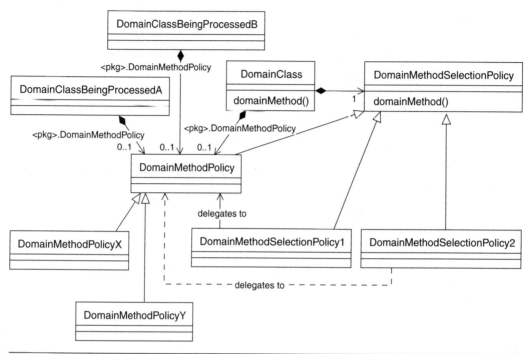

Figure 8.8. Chain of Responsibility-Driven Policy Structure

Participants

- **DomainClass** (Product). The class that plays the role of the context class in the Simple Policy (Strategy, in *Design Patterns* terms) design pattern.

- **DomainMethodSelectionPolicy** (StockLocationAssignerSelectionPolicy). An abstract class that plays the role of the Strategy class in the Simple Policy (Strategy) design pattern.

- **DomainMethodPolicy** (StockLocationAssignerPolicy). An abstract class that often implements protected helper methods that can be used by subclass implementations of domainMethod. It may also provide a template method implementation (as described by the Template Method pattern of *Design Patterns*) for the domainMethod that uses the protected helper methods.

- **DomainMethodSelectionPolicy1, DomainMethodSelectionPolicy2** (StockLocationAssignerSelectionPolicyDefault). Two of potentially many SelectionPolicy subclasses that implement various chains of responsibility on the basis of the objects being processed by domainMethod.

- **DomainMethodPolicyX, DomainMethodPolicyY** (StockLocation-AssignerPolicyDefault). Subclasses of DomainMethodPolicy that implement various domain algorithms.

- **DomainClassBeingProcessedA, DomainClassBeingProcessedB** (Warehouse, Company). Two of potentially many domain classes that are used during business algorithm processing. Instances of these classes may be passed in by parameter or retrieved as attributes from other business objects passed into the policy. Multiple domain classes may be involved in chain of responsibility. Often the DomainClass (Product in our example) is also one of the domain classes being processed.

Collaborations

- DomainClass delegates its responsibility for domainMethod to DomainMethodSelectionPolicy, just as in the Simple Policy pattern.

- DomainMethodSelectionPolicyA searches through DomainClassBeingProcessedA and other domain class instances that are part of its implemented chain of responsibility until it finds a DomainMethodPolicy instance.

- DomainMethodSelectionPolicy instances delegate responsibility for implementation of the domain algorithm to DomainMethodPolicy instances.

- Typical object interactions under the Chain of Responsibility-Driven Policy pattern are as follows (referenced steps refer to Figure 8.9):

  1. Client code invokes the domain method on the target domain object (step 1).

  2. The domain object delegates responsibility to its associated domain method selection policy (step 2).

  3. The selection policy attempts to retrieve the domain policy from the first domain object in the chain—in this case, the domain object responsible for the domain method (step 3).

  4. If a policy instance is found, the selection policy delegates responsibility for the domain method to the retrieved policy; otherwise it continues the search (step 4).

  5. The selection policy attempts to retrieve the domain policy from the second domain object in the chain (step 5).

  6. If a policy instance is found, the selection policy delegates responsibility for the domain method to the retrieved policy; otherwise it continues the search (step 6).

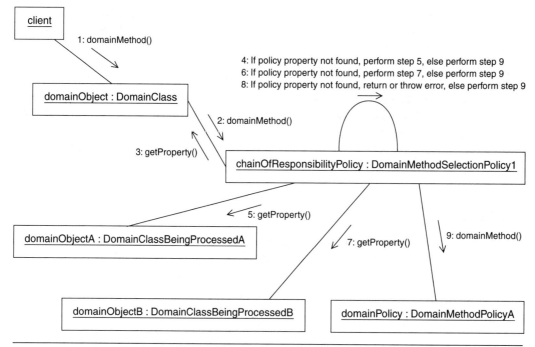

Figure 8.9. Typical Object Interactions

7. The selection policy attempts to retrieve the domain policy from the final domain object in the chain (step 7).

8. If a policy instance is found, the selection policy delegates responsibility for the domain method to the retrieved policy; otherwise it throws or returns an error (step 8).

9. The selection policy invokes the domain method on the retrieved policy instance, which completes the domain method using its implemented algorithm (step 9).

Consequences

The Chain of Responsibility-Driven Policy pattern has the following tradeoffs, benefits, and drawbacks:

Tradeoffs

- **Performance versus flexibility.** When configuring a business object that has implemented the Chain of Responsibility-Driven Policy pattern, the end user or application must decide whether the additional flexibility provided by the selection policy is worth the overhead involved in processing the chain of responsibility. If a chain of responsibility is deep (i.e., includes a large number of business objects) and overrides are not common, the search path for retrieving the policy to use will be more expensive than for a shallower chain or a chain in which overrides are typical.

- **Complexity versus flexibility of selection policy hierarchy.** Introducing a selection policy hierarchy increases a design's complexity, during both the design process and the debugging of the design's implementation. In particular, determining which policy instance is used during a specific invocation can be challenging.

- **Exposing versus hiding flexibility.** Application developers must decide whether to expose the flexibility of selection policies to clients during object configuration. In some cases exposing the full set of selection policies and policies to the end user is warranted; in other cases the application may decide to automatically configure the proper selection policy into the business object responsible for the behavior and define the default policy behavior at the Company level, while leaving the choice of overriding policy behavior to the end user. Still other applications may abstract this configuration choice at a higher level, allowing end users to select from conceptual options, which then result in specific selection policy and policy configurations within the affected business objects.

Benefits

- **Policy-related benefits.** Both selection policies and domain algorithm policies have the same benefits as other policies. These benefits include eliminating conditional statements, providing an alternative to subclassing, and defining a family of useful algorithms.

- **Additional flexibility.** The Chain of Responsibility-Driven Policy pattern allows the application developer or end user to attach different domain algorithms to business objects of different classes.

- **Reduced configuration complexity.** If most of the time the algorithm attached to the context object is the correct algorithm, most business objects of a particular class do not need to be configured to hold an overriding policy.

Drawbacks

- **Increased design complexity.** The combined hierarchy of selection policies and policies increases the number of classes involved in the design.

Implementation

Consider the following implementation issues for the Chain of Responsibility-Driven Policy pattern:

- **Defining the DomainClass and SelectionPolicy interfaces.** Great care should be taken when defining the DomainClass interface for the behavior in question to ensure that sufficient information can be provided to the policy that is implementing the behavior. SanFrancisco implementations of this pattern always pass the DomainClass along with any other client-provided parameters to the SelectionPolicy, in order to give the policy class the most flexibility in accessing information during the processing of its algorithm.

- **Terminating chains of responsibility.** When configuring a set of domain objects that implement the Chain of Responsibility-Driven Policy pattern, you should always ensure that a default domain policy algorithm has been placed at the end of the chain of responsibility. Otherwise, runtime errors will result that may be very difficult to debug.

- **Supporting policy overrides by the client.** When defining the DomainClass interface for the behavior, the designer needs to choose whether to allow an instance of the domain algorithm policy or selection policy base class to be passed in as an additional parameter to be used as an overriding policy. In particular, passing an instance of the selection policy base class gives the client complete flexibility with minimal additional overhead, and as such it is a standard approach throughout SanFrancisco.

- **Converting a Simple Policy-based design into a Chain of Responsibility-Driven Policy.** If a designer comes across a class in which a simple policy design has been implemented but a chain of responsibility would also be useful, alternate policy subclasses that implement chains of responsibility can be defined. Although the result is a cluttered and somewhat confusing class hierarchy, as long as concrete class names clearly delineate policy behavior (either domain algorithm or chain of responsibility), this approach allows the designer to retrofit an existing class with a more flexible design.

- **Associating policy instances with domain objects being processed.** The Property Container pattern (see Chapter 5) provides a very flexible and easy-to-use approach for associating policy instances with domain objects. Another alternative approach is to define a side dictionary that is keyed by domain object ID and whose values are policy instances.

- **Recursively delegating to selection policy instances.** For very sophisticated algorithms, the selection policy class hierarchy could be made to delegate back to itself, thus allowing for unlimited chaining of selection policies before a domain policy is reached. In general, this level of flexibility is not required.

- **Eliminating the DomainMethodPolicy base class.** The DomainMethodPolicy base class may not be needed in all situations. This class is most useful when many of the potential policy algorithms can be implemented in a uniform manner through a template method. Even if the Template Method pattern (described in *Design Patterns*) is not used to implement a predominant policy algorithm, you may wish to introduce a DomainMethodPolicy base class to aid in organizing the domain algorithm subclasses separate from your selection policy implementations.

Sample Code

In our example, the Product class provides the method assignStockLocation, which delegates responsibility to its contained StockLocationAssignerPolicy instance unless the calling client passes in an overriding policy instance. The method is defined to return one or more stock locations in a set to the client.

```
public class Product {

    // ...

    public Set assignStockLocation(Warehouse warehouse,
                StockZone stockZone,
                Lot lot,
                Measurement measurement,
                ProductTransactionQuantity quantity,
                StockLocationAssignerSelectionPolicy overridingPolicy) {

        if (policy == null) {
        // Client has not overridden object's policy behavior,
        // so delegate to contained policy instance
            return ivSelectionPolicy.assignStockLocation(this,
                                            warehouse,
                                            stockZone,
                                            lot,
                                            measurement,
                                            quantity);

        } else {
        // Client has overridden object's policy behavior,
        // so delegate to passed-in policy instance
            return overridingPolicy.assignStockLocation(this,
                                            warehouse,
                                            stockZone,
                                            lot,
                                            measurement,
                                            quantity);

        }
    }
```

```
// ...

protected StockLocationAssignerSelectionPolicy ivSelectionPolicy;

// ...
}
```

Each selection policy concrete class searches through the business objects involved in the chain of responsibility to find the correct policy instance to use. Note that the Product (the domain class responsible for the behavior) is also involved in the chain of responsibility. In addition, the default policy behavior is attached to the context Company object, which is always accessible in a SanFrancisco-based application.

```
public class StockLocationAssignerSelectionPolicyDefault {

    // ...

    public Set assignStockLocation(Product product,
                            Warehouse warehouse,
                            StockZone stockZone,
                            Lot lot,
                            Measurement measurement,
                            ProductTransactionQuantity quantity) {


        StockLocationAssignerPolicy assignerPolicy = null;

        // Try the Product first
        assignerPolicy = (StockLocationAssignerPolicy)
            product.getPropertyBy("whs.StockLocationAssignerPolicy");

        // If not on the Product, try the Warehouse
        if (assignerPolicy == null) {
            assignerPolicy = (StockLocationAssignerPolicy)
                warehouse.getPropertyBy("whs.StockLocationAssignerPolicy");
        }


        // If not on the Product, get the default from the active Company
        if (assignerPolicy == null) {
            assignerPolicy = (StockLocationAssignerPolicy)
                CompanyContext.getActiveCompany().getPropertyBy(
                    "whs.StockLocationAssignerPolicy");
        }

        // Delegate the assignStockLocation request
        return assignerPolicy.assignStockLocation(product,
                            warehouse,
                            stockZone,
                            lot,
```

```
                                         measurement,
                                         quantity);
    }

    // ...

}
```

Finally, each location assigner policy concrete class implements its algorithm according to the needs of the application, just as in the Simple Policy pattern.

Known Uses

SanFrancisco Core Business Processes rely heavily on the Chain of Responsibility-Driven Policy pattern. Some sample uses in the Warehouse Management package are as follows:

- Assigning locations into a particular warehouse for incoming product stock (the primary example in this chapter)
- Selecting lots for an outgoing product quantity from a particular warehouse
- Selecting locations for an outgoing product quantity from a particular warehouse
- Determining how to deal with a shortage of goods when picking stock out of a particular warehouse

Related Patterns

- **Simple Policy.** Both selection policy and domain algorithm policy class hierarchies follow the Simple Policy pattern (see Chapter 7).
- **Chain of Responsibility.** Selection policy subclasses implement encapsulated chain of responsibility algorithms, as described in *Design Patterns*.
- **Template Method.** The domain algorithm policy base class may implement the algorithm as a template method (defined in *Design Patterns*).
- **Property Container.** Business objects that implement the Property Container pattern (see Chapter 5) can easily be included in a selection policy's chain of responsibility.

9

Token-Driven Policy

Intent

Define a family of encapsulated domain algorithms for a behavior and make them interchangeable, establish groupings of these algorithms and configure these groupings into business objects responsible for the behavior, and control which algorithm is used, on the basis of the client (represented by token) using the behavior.

Motivation

Warehouse applications need to be able to check the availability of stock to be taken out of a warehouse at a specified time. Typically, an application needs numerous product availability algorithms, and the end user of an application often specifies the algorithm(s) to be used. The Simple Policy pattern is usually used in such situations; however, in some cases using a standard policy does not meet the flexibility needs of an application. Availability-checking algorithms often need to vary on the basis of not only the object responsible for the processing but also the business process using the behavior. Consider the following example from our case study (see Chapter 2):

Case Study   Food Warehouse prides itself on effective inventory management and its ability to consistently meet delivery date commitments it makes to its customers. Accordingly, FW defines very sophisticated availability-checking algorithms to be used during sales order entry. These algorithms take into account, among other factors, existing sales orders and expected goods receipts, along with the amount of goods currently in stock. In addition, FW uses different order entry availability-checking algorithms for high-volume products than for low-volume products. FW also checks product availability when preparing pick lists to ensure that goods will be available in the selected warehouse stock locations when warehouse personnel go to retrieve those goods for shipment. The availability-checking algorithm that FW uses in this case takes into account only goods in stock.

In this example, Food Warehouse needs to be able to configure its application so that different product availability-checking policies will be used depending on the business process doing the availability checking. In other words, information describing the current business process needs to be given to the business object responsible for the behavior.

Assume that the Product class has domain responsibility for checking product availability. One possible approach in this situation is to define a policy class hierarchy for availability checking and build multiple concrete policy classes that take various types of information into account in their algorithms. However, the Simple Policy pattern by itself does not allow the client (i.e., the code calling the method) to affect which checking algorithm is used. How can we ensure that this client information is taken into consideration? Somehow the client process needs to be represented on the call to the business object method so that it can be used during selection of the availability-checking algorithm.

As Figure 9.1 shows, the Token-Driven Policy pattern builds on the Simple Policy pattern by doing the following:

- Defining a class (ProductPolicyOrganizer in our example) whose purpose is to organize multiple policy instances and provide access to those instances by key.

- Defining a parameter (ProcessTokenValue in our example) to be passed on the method call. This parameter represents the business process using the method and is used as the key when a policy is being retrieved from the policy organizer.

In our example, the getProductAvailabilityCheckerPolicyBy method on the ProductPolicyOrganizer class uses the input key parameter, a ProcessTokenValue, to determine which policy instance to return. The ProcessTokenValue object represents a particular domain process (order entry or picking in our example).

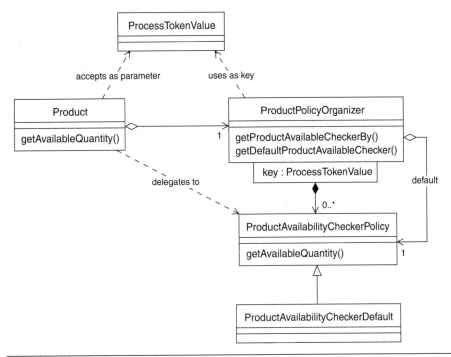

Figure 9.1. Product Availability Checking Using Process Tokens

Product holds onto an instance of the ProductPolicyOrganizer class and uses that object to select the correct policy instance to use when the getAvailableQuantity method is invoked by a client. Different Product objects can be configured with different organizer objects so that, for example, high-volume products and low-volume products can use different concrete policies. The getAvailableQuantity interface on Product includes a ProcessTokenValue as a parameter, and Product uses this parameter to retrieve the correct policy instance. If Product is unable to find a policy instance for the passed-in ProcessTokenValue, it retrieves the default policy instance held by the Product-PolicyOrganizer.

The getAvailableQuantity interface declared by the ProductAvailability-CheckerPolicy also takes a ProcessTokenValue as one of its input parameters. Passing a ProcessTokenValue to the policy implementation is useful for the following reasons:

- The concrete policy implementation might want to call other domain methods that are implemented by the Token-Driven Policy pattern.

- If ProcessTokenValue implements the Property Container pattern (see Chapter 5), the application may add properties to the passed-in ProcessTokenValue to provide pertinent domain information.

Applicability

Consider implementing the Token-Driven Policy pattern when any of the following criteria apply:

- Multiple domain algorithms are typically used in conjunction with a business object behavior.
- The process using the business object behavior needs to affect which domain algorithm to use.
- A default behavior for a domain algorithm can be defined.
- Different business objects need to use different sets of algorithms, depending on their characteristics.

Structure

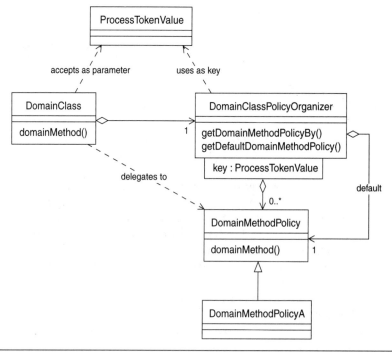

Figure 9.2. Token-Driven Policy Structure

Participants

- **DomainClass** (Product). The class that plays the role of the context class in the Simple Policy (Strategy, in *Design Patterns* terms) design pattern.
- **DomainMethodPolicy** (ProductAvailabilityCheckerPolicy). An abstract class that plays the role of the Strategy class in the Simple Policy (Strategy) design pattern.
- **DomainMethodPolicyA** (ProductAvailabilityCheckerPolicyDefault). One of potentially many subclasses of DomainMethodPolicy that implement the domain algorithm.
- **DomainClassPolicyOrganizer** (ProductPolicyOrganizer). A class that holds various combinations of DomainMethodPolicy subclass instances associated with various client processes, along with a default policy instance that is used when a client process using the domain method has not been configured into the organizer.
- **ProcessTokenValue.** The object representing the client process that is using the domain method. This object is used as a key to retrieve the correct DomainMethodPolicy instance and optionally to carry additional information that can be used by the algorithm implemented by the selected policy.

Collaborations

- DomainClass delegates its responsibility for domainMethod to DomainMethodPolicy, just as in the standard Simple Policy pattern.
- DomainClass uses the passed-in ProcessTokenValue instance to retrieve the correct policy instance from DomainClassPolicyOrganizer.
- DomainClassPolicyOrganizer serves as an intermediary between DomainClass and its maintained collection of DomainMethodPolicy instances.

Consequences

The Token-Driven Policy pattern has the following tradeoffs, benefits, and drawbacks:

Tradeoffs

- **Policy-related tradeoffs.** The tradeoffs of the Simple Policy pattern also apply to the Token-Driven Policy pattern.

Benefits

- **Policy-related benefits.** Domain algorithm policies provide the same benefits as other policies. These policy-related benefits include eliminating conditional statements, providing an alternative to subclassing, and defining a family of useful algorithms.

- **Families of policies.** Application developers can define families of policies by configuring different DomainClassPolicyOrganizer instances. These families of policies can then be associated with specific business object characteristics, such as product sales volume in our example.

- **Selective overriding of default behavior.** Because DomainClassPolicy-Organizer holds a default policy instance, application developers and end users can decide which client processes, if any, should use specialized policies; that is, they can selectively override the default behavior. If no specialized policies are defined, the behavior of this pattern becomes semantically identical to that of the object-specific Simple Policy pattern.

Drawbacks

- **Increased design complexity.** The DomainClassPolicyOrganizer, ProcessTokenValue, and policy class hierarchy increase the number of classes involved in the design.

Implementation

Consider the following implementation issues for the Token-Driven Policy pattern:

- **Defining the DomainClass and policy interfaces.** As in any other policy-based pattern, great care should be taken in defining the DomainClass interface for the behavior in question to ensure that sufficient information can be provided to the policy that is implementing the behavior. In SanFrancisco, the most effective approach is to pass DomainClass along with any other client-provided parameters to the policy because this approach gives the policy class the most flexibility in accessing information during the processing of its algorithm.

- **Supporting policy overrides by the client.** When defining the DomainClass interface for the behavior, the designer needs to choose whether to allow an instance of the domain algorithm policy base class to be passed in as an additional parameter to be used as an overriding policy. Contrary to the Chain of Responsibility-Driven Policy pattern (see Chapter 8), the standard SanFrancisco implementation of the Token-Driven Policy pattern does not allow the client to override the policy directly.

SanFrancisco assumes that the client in this case should affect the algorithm used only via the token passed to DomainClass.

- **Primitive type versus object as process token value.** Passing a full-fledged object as the process token value adds weight to the method call as compared to passing a primitive type such as int to represent the client process. If an object is passed, however, particularly an object that implements the Property Container pattern (see Chapter 5), additional information can be passed to the policy algorithm. Even if the token class is not implemented as a property container, an application developer can choose to subclass the token class, adding domain-specific attributes that can be used during policy processing. In SanFrancisco, instances of ProcessTokenValue are always passed to give users of the framework maximum flexibility.

- **ProcessTokenValue as controlled class.** SanFrancisco defines the ProcessTokenValue class as a controlled class (see Chapter 10) so that domain processes can register their presence by creating a new ProcessTokenValue instance in the ProcessTokenValue controller.

- **DomainClassPolicyOrganizer as controlled class.** SanFrancisco treats the DomainClassPolicyOrganizer class as a controlled class (see Chapter 10) so that preconfigured policy families can be defined and associated with DomainClass instances.

- **Delegating responsibility for policy selection to organizer.** DomainClass may delegate to its contained organizer full responsibility for selecting the policy to be used. In this case, the organizer takes on the responsibility of finding an appropriate policy to return or use when it does not find an existing policy associated with the passed-in token. This approach simplifies the DomainClass code but also limits what DomainClass can do in this case. For example, an application could define a set of related tokens that DomainClass could use for additional searches if the token initially passed in were not associated with a policy. When implementing the Token-Driven Policy pattern, SanFrancisco places responsibility for alternate policy retrieval on DomainClass.

Sample Code

The Product class provides the method getProductAvailability. This method retrieves the correct policy to use from its contained ProductPolicyOrganizer object using the passed-in ProcessTokenValue as key, then delegates responsibility to the retrieved policy. If no policy is associated with the passed-in key, the Product uses the default policy held by the organizer. The getProductAvailability method is defined to return a ProductTransactionQuantity that represents the quantity of goods available to the client.

```
public class Product {

    // ...

    public ProductTransactionQuantity getAvailableQuantity(
                            ProductTransactionQuantity quantity,
                            ProcessTokenValue processToken,
                            Warehouse warehouse,
                            Lot lot,
                            StockLocation location,
                            Time requestedTime,
                            MannerOfTransport mannerOfTransport) {

        ProductAvailabilityCheckerPolicy myCheckerPolicy = null;

        // Attempt to retrieve correct policy on basis of
        // client process
        myCheckerPolicy =
            ivOrganizer.getProductAvailabilityCheckerPolicyBy(processToken);

        if (myCheckerPolicy == null) {
            // Client process doesn't have a specialized policy
            // defined, so use default policy
                myCheckerPolicy =
                    ivOrganizer.getDefaultProductAvailabilityCheckerPolicy();
        }

        // Delegate responsibility for behavior to retrieved policy
        return myCheckerPolicy.getAvailableQuantity(this,
                                        quantity,
                                        processToken,
                                        requestedTime,
                                        warehouse,
                                        lot,
                                        location,
                                        mannerOfTransport);
    }

    // ...

    protected ProductPolicyOrganizer ivOrganizer;

    // ...
}
```

The ProductPolicyOrganizer class is implemented simply to contain a keyed collection (i.e., a map) and a default policy instance. The organizer wires through its keyed retrieval method to its contained collection and downcasts the result to the ProductAvailabilityCheckerPolicy base class so that the returned object is ready for use by the Product.

Finally, each product availability checker policy concrete class implements its algorithm according to the needs of the application, just as in the Simple Policy pattern. Note that the ProcessTokenValue object is passed to the policy to allow the policy to extract pertinent information stored by the client process on the object as properties or attributes.

Known Uses

SanFrancisco uses the Token-Driven Policy pattern when determining product availability (the primary example in this chapter) or when verifying the credit-worthiness of a customer.

Related Patterns

- **Simple Policy.** The domain policy class hierarchy follows the Simple Policy pattern (see Chapter 7).
- **Template Method.** The domain policy base class may implement the algorithm as a template method (described in *Design Patterns*).
- **Property Container.** SanFrancisco implements ProcessTokenValue as a property container (see Chapter 5) so that additional information can be attached to tokens for use by concrete policy implementations.
- **Controller.** Both the DomainClassPolicyOrganizer and ProcessTokenValue classes are controlled classes (see Chapter 10) so that they can be easily maintained and retrieved during application processing.

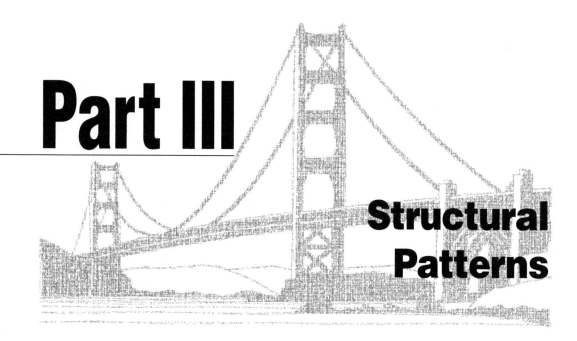

Part III

Structural Patterns

anFrancisco's structural patterns are concerned with how business information is organized and accessed. Structural object patterns define how business information (in the form of business objects) is organized within a complex business environment. The Controller pattern (Chapter 10) in its various manifestations provides a way to selectively expose, hide, or override specific business object instances throughout the business hierarchy represented by the application.

The Key/Keyable pattern (Chapter 11) defines ways to build composite views of otherwise unrelated business information for a particular purpose, representing both the business information that is of interest (SpecificationKeys) and specific combinations of business information within a particular definition (AccessKeys).

The Generic Interface pattern (Chapter 12) is an extension of the Facade pattern of *Design Patterns,* which provides a form of cross-application loose coupling by defining a focused interface that all instantiations of a particular application must support. Applications of other types can then interact with the target application through its set of generic interfaces without being concerned about how that application is implemented.

Part III

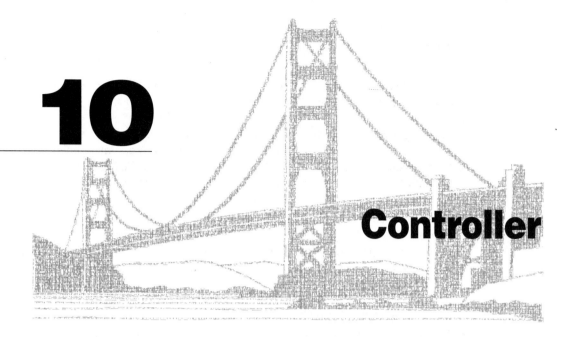

10

Controller

Intent

Provide a composite view of objects of a specific type across a hierarchical context. Users of this view are not aware of which context provides a particular object. Objects within the view may be aggregated (retrieved) from a higher-level context or provided locally at the current context. Locally defined objects either are newly introduced or override an aggregated object. The pattern also provides a way to hide objects that would otherwise be aggregated.

Motivation

Business enterprises are typically organized into multiple operating units. Divisions, areas, departments, operating companies, and subsidiaries are just some of the possible units a business might choose for organizing itself. Each of these units needs access to different business information within the enterprise. Some of this information is unique to a specific operating unit; other information must be shared across multiple units, or perhaps even across the entire enterprise. Consider the following example from our case study (see Chapter 2):

Case Study Food Warehouse is composed of five distribution groups, three trucking units, a sales force within each of its five regions, and a corporate office. It also maintains a wholly owned subsidiary in Belgium for importing European goods into the United States. This business structure affects the information each unit can use in its operations. For example:

1. The corporate office defines a chart of accounts for the enterprise's general ledger. This chart of accounts applies to all of FW's operating units. Certain accounts, however, such as those used to record CEO expenses, should be used only by the corporate office when posting to the general ledger.

2. Food Warehouse sells goods in the United States and Canada. Its corporate office can define currencies and exchange rates that apply throughout the enterprise. However, the Belgian subsidiary needs to deal not only with U.S. dollars but also with the currencies of the European countries from which it purchases goods for export to the United States. Because the Belgian subsidiary is not set up to export goods to Canada, it should be prevented from working with Canadian dollars.

3. Each of the warehouses used by FW for its U.S. and Canadian operations is owned and managed at the corporate level. Some of these warehouses are dedicated to a particular distribution group; others are shared by more than one group, with dedicated zones within those warehouses for each group. The warehouses used by the Belgian subsidiary are managed directly by that subsidiary.

Each operating unit in the Food Warehouse example has a different view over the general ledger accounts, currencies and exchange rates, and warehouses. This view affects FW's operations; in effect, every business unit provides a unique context within the overall enterprise for the operations and information of that unit.

Figure 10.1 is a partial representation of FW's organizational structure. Each object shown, with the exception of the object labeled "Corporate Office," is a separate instance of type Company. The object labeled "Corporate Office," being the root of the object hierarchy, is an instance of type Enterprise. According to the convention established by SanFrancisco, only one Enterprise instance can be present in any configured installation. On the other hand, as many Company instances as are needed to represent the remaining components of the organizational structure can be created while the application is being configured.

Now that we have an organizational structure in place, how can we configure that structure to provide the various views of business information (based on organizational unit) that we need?

The Controller pattern allows us to configure each company within this organizational structure. This configuration consists of a mix of business objects and supporting data, in which some of these objects and data are shared

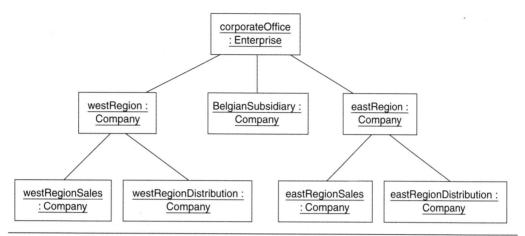

Figure 10.1. Simplified Food Warehouse Organizational Structure

with a parent organization and some are specific to a company. In particular, if a parent company introduces a set of instances of a given type of business objects, a child company has the option to do any of the following:

- Introduce its own set of business objects, isolating itself from the parent's set (the warehouses owned and managed by the Belgian subsidiary)

- Share the parent's set entirely, with no set being defined at the child's level (the warehouses shared by West Region Sales and West Region Distribution within the West Region operating unit)

- Add additional business objects to the parent's set (the European currencies introduced by the Belgian subsidiary)

- Share the parent's set but hide certain business objects in the set (preventing Canadian dollars from being used as a currency by the Belgian subsidiary)

- Share the parent's set but override certain business objects with those contained by a set at their own level (e.g., inhibit postings to the CEO expenses account by establishing the setting "post inhibit" on the CEO expenses account for all companies within the hierarchy; note that overriding is different from hiding because overriding keeps the account valid and visible but prevents someone from creating a new account with the same settings as the existing CEO expenses account, either accidentally or maliciously)

- Partially share the business objects themselves in the parent's set, where a subset of the business object's data is public (the warehouse information managed by the parent company) and the remaining data is private (the warehouse zones assigned to each operating unit sharing a specific warehouse)

Controllers own instances of a particular type after those instances are created and provide application users with a central point from which to manage them. As you distribute controller instances throughout a company hierarchy, they interact with each other through the hierarchy, relying on the chained property container behavior supported by the companies.

When your application is running in a particular Company context, it works directly with that Company to retrieve controller instances. The application code then retrieves object instances from the retrieved controllers and works with those instances. Controllers hide the complexities of the company hierarchy from most of the application code.

Controlled Classes

Not all object types need to be controlled, but which types of objects do need to be controlled in a particular application? First, types that are not meaningful outside of the context of another object type do not need to be controlled. For example, consider a Decimal type. Would it be meaningful to provide a controller for all Decimal instances used by a particular business unit? No, because a decimal value gains meaning only if it is placed in a broader application context—for example, as an exchange rate factor.

Object types whose instances have an independent lifecycle are candidates to be controlled objects. However, there is no need to control an object type that has a natural owner (e.g., lots of a product are naturally owned by that product). In effect, the owner of the object type serves many of the same functions that a controller would, such as providing a "home"[1] for those objects and giving users a way to access object instances.

What are we left with? Object types that do not have a natural business object owner are good candidates to be controlled classes. Typically, these types are meaningful at the context level of the application. For example, many operational units within an enterprise maintain their own set of financial journals. Certain products might be sold by one unit and not by another. Both Journals and Products are good candidates for controlled classes.

Root, Aggregating, and Hiding Controllers

Before we examine the Food Warehouse examples in more detail, let's take a look at the types of controllers defined by SanFrancisco. SanFrancisco controllers are composed of a class hierarchy that includes an abstract base controller

---

1. EJB (Enterprise JavaBean) specification-defined ejbHomes serve some of the same functions as controllers, such as providing a point of access for accessing object instances. In that sense, controllers can be thought of as homes for object instances of a particular type.

class and some concrete controller classes. The abstract base controller class presents the common methods defined for accessing the controlled business objects. Clients use the interface presented by this abstract class to retrieve business objects from a controller.

The first concrete controller class is the *root controller*. As you might remember from Chapter 5, the company hierarchy provided by SanFrancisco implements a chained property container. A root controller is the end station for a particular company's chain of responsibility: Only those business objects in a particular root controller's collection can be accessed through that controller. Thus, when a company keeps a set of business objects in a root controller, it is isolating itself from its parent's set (if one exists).

The second concrete subclass is an *aggregating controller*. Like the root controller, an aggregating controller holds a collection of business objects that it directly controls. Unlike the root controller, it has access to a parent controller, which may be either a root controller or another aggregating controller. To find its parent controller, the aggregating controller first goes to its associated Company (to which it maintains a reference). Then it finds its immediate parent company through the organizational tree structure of companies and uses the PropertyContainer interface (see Chapter 5) of the parent company to request the parent controller.

This modeling of the relationship between parent and child controllers allows controllers to be added, removed, or changed at any level of the organizational structure without adverse effects on controllers at other levels. Aggregating controllers at lower levels are not required to rebuild parent controller links when a new controller is added to a company between it and its current parent controller.

When a client retrieves a business object through an aggregating controller, the controller first checks its own collection for the requested business object. If the aggregating controller finds the requested business object, it returns this object. This could be the first instance of this business object that occurs in the company hierarchy, or the aggregating controller could be overriding a parent's business object with its own (i.e., the unique domain identifier of the locally contained object is identical to that of another object defined in a parent controller).

If the aggregating controller does not find the requested business object, it retrieves its parent controller (through the company hierarchy) and attempts to retrieve the requested business object from that controller. This behavior continues until one of the aggregating controllers in the chain finds the requested business object or until a root controller is encountered. Thus, an aggregating controller appears to a client to have a logical scope that includes the business objects it controls directly, as well as the objects in its chain of parent controllers.

A specialization of the aggregating controller is a subclass known as a *hiding controller*. A hiding controller does everything an aggregating controller does, and it also maintains a collection of unique domain IDs for business objects held by parent controllers that it wishes to hide. When a business object with a given ID is requested from a hiding controller, the controller first checks its collection of hidden IDs. If the controller finds the ID among them, it immediately returns a null value to the client indicating that the requested business object is not found. If the hiding controller does not find the ID in its hidden key collection, it uses normal aggregating controller behavior to try to find the requested object. Hiding controllers allow a child company to hide specific business objects in the parent company's set while sharing others.

Food Warehouse Examples Revisited

Now that we have discussed the various controller types, let's apply them to each of the Food Warehouse examples we introduced at the beginning of the chapter, starting with the corporate chart of accounts.

Example 1: Chart of Accounts (Aggregating Behavior)

Simply put, a *chart of accounts* is a list of the financial accounts (the asset, liability, equity, income, and expense accounts) of an enterprise. In SanFrancisco, the chart of accounts is represented by a controller that maintains these accounts for use by the general ledger. Because FW's chart of accounts is defined at the corporate level, we need to place this controller on the Enterprise object.

Let's look at the characteristics we described for the chart of accounts. First, it is shared by every operating unit of Food Warehouse. This arrangement fits our definition of a root controller: a controller that exists at any level within the company hierarchy and exists on its own (i.e., it is not dependent on a parent controller in the hierarchy). Once this controller is in place, every company in FW's hierarchy can access the accounts defined at the corporate office level.

Although this is the behavior we want for most accounts, remember that some accounts (such as the CEO's expense account) should not be used except by the corporate office. How can we enforce this restriction? Aggregating controllers can help us out here. An aggregating controller depends on a parent controller for its basic contents but can add additional contents or override its parent's contents. For our chart of accounts, we don't want to add any new accounts, but we do want to override the CEO's expense account to prohibit any of our operating units from using this account (in accounting terms, we want to make the setting on the account "post inhibit").

Figure 10.2 shows a subset of the original FW company hierarchy with the chart of account controllers and specific account objects that we just discussed introduced into the hierarchy. As you can see, the corporate office chart of accounts has all the accounts defined for the enterprise (only three of those accounts are shown).

In the West Region operating unit, we have added an aggregating chart of accounts that holds only one account, the CEO expenses account. This new

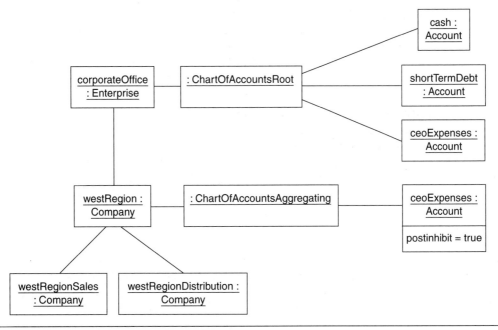

Figure 10.2. Chart of Accounts Example

account overrides the CEO expenses account at the corporate level, with "post inhibit" set to prevent this account from being used by the West Region operating unit or any of its subunits. Because we have not introduced any other accounts at this level, the remaining accounts defined by the corporate office are available for use throughout the West Region. The aggregating chart of accounts makes these other accounts visible.

Note that we have not defined charts of accounts for West Region Sales or West Region Distribution. If your application is running with one of these companies as its current context and the application attempts to retrieve an account, the application will automatically fall back to the chart of accounts defined at the West Region level (because of the chained property behavior implemented by the company hierarchy). You can think of this behavior as introducing a "phantom" controller. Child companies in the company hierarchy automatically gain access to all controllers defined above them in the hierarchy, and if they have not introduced dedicated controllers at their level, they will get exactly the behavior defined above them in the hierarchy.

Now suppose we introduce an additional level within FW's corporate structure: the U.S. subsidiary, which resides between the corporate office and the West Region. If we were to do this without introducing a new chart of accounts at this level, nothing would change in the way our example behaves. The West Region and its subdivisions would still get all their accounts from the chart of accounts defined at the corporate office level, with the exception of the CEO expenses account. In effect, the U.S. subsidiary company is transparent to Food Warehouse and will remain so until one or more controllers are introduced directly on the U.S. subsidiary. Only at that time will the introduction of this new level affect the application's behavior.

Example 2: Currencies (Hiding Behavior)

Next, let's take a look at the currency structure within Food Warehouse. With the exception of its Belgian subsidiary, all of FW's operating units deal strictly with U.S. or Canadian customers and suppliers. Thus, FW can define the valid currencies (U.S. and Canadian dollars) once at the corporate office. (Although FW will also need to define the valid exchange rates to use when converting between currencies, we will ignore that aspect of currency definition in this example.) To define valid currencies, we will use another root controller, one that meets the needs of every subunit of FW except the Belgian subsidiary.

Because the Belgian subsidiary buys goods from countries throughout Europe, it has to deal with many more currencies than do FW's other operating units. It is best for the Belgian subsidiary to manage these currencies directly rather than relying on the corporate office to do so because it has employees with the right expertise to ensure that all the necessary rules are being followed in each European country, such as dealing with the transition to the new European Economic and Monetary Union (EMU) currency, the euro. The Belgian subsidiary resells the goods it purchases to operating units in the U.S., so it needs to work not only with various European currencies and exchange rates, but also with U.S. dollars. We have already defined the currency "U.S. dollar" at the corporate office, so it makes sense for the Belgian subsidiary to use an aggregating currency controller to add the new currencies it must handle. By doing so, it automatically gains access to the U.S. currency through the chaining mechanism implemented by aggregating controllers.

If we simply use an aggregating controller, however, the subsidiary will have access to too much information because both U.S. and Canadian currencies will be visible to it. Since the Belgian subsidiary does business with only the FW operating units that are located in the United States, we should use a hiding currency controller on the Company object that represents the subsidiary. We can then configure this controller to hide Canadian dollars from the subsidiary so that only the U.S. currency will be retrieved from the corporate office.

The resulting company and controller structure for currencies looks much like the previous chart of accounts example (see Figure 10.2), except this time the hiding controller defined for the Belgian subsidiary doesn't override any currencies; it only adds numerous new currencies to the list of valid currencies for the subsidiary (see Figure 10.3). It also contains an entry to hide "Canadian dollar" so that business processes working with currencies in the Belgian subsidiary won't be able to see or work with Canadian dollars.

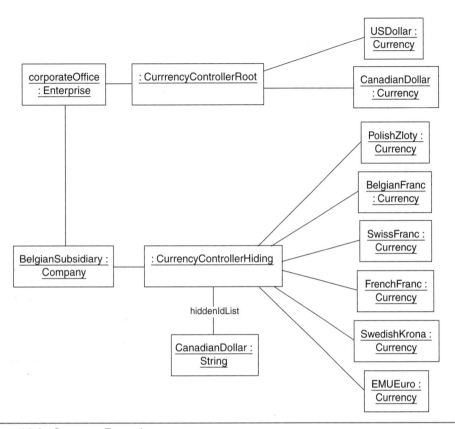

Figure 10.3. Currency Example

Example 3: Warehouses (Shared and Private Information)

Finally, let's examine the third and most complex example: the warehouses of Food Warehouse, of which there are three categories:

1. Warehouses that are owned and managed by the corporate office and whose zones are allocated for use by different operating units

2. Warehouses that are owned and managed by the corporate office and fully allocated to a particular operating unit

3. Warehouses that are owned and managed by a particular operating unit (e.g., the Belgian subsidiary)

Let's break down these categories into their specific requirements and look at how those requirements are handled by the Controller pattern. A common thread running through each category is the concept of ownership: FW's warehouses are owned by a specific operating unit or by the corporate office. Each controller inherently establishes an ownership relationship between the controlled item (in this case, warehouses) and the company where the controller resides, so controllers easily handle this requirement.

The first category of warehouses (those with zones allocated across multiple operating units) introduces a unique twist to ownership. Each warehouse in this category is owned by the corporate office, but individual stock zones within the warehouse are conceptually owned by the operating unit to which they have been allocated. In other words, the physical building is owned by the corporate office, but this building is logically subdivided among the operating units that use it, as Figure 10.4 shows. The physical building and its attributes (such as address) are shared information, but the specific stock zones allocated to each company are private to those companies.

The Controller pattern deals with such situations by treating some aspects of a business object as private and others as shared. Shared aspects of each warehouse are attributes like the postal address of the warehouse and its legal description. Private aspects of each warehouse are attributes like the stock zones (and associated locations) allocated to each operating unit, and algorithms like stock putaway, which might vary among operating units. The private and shared aspects combine to make up a view of a particular business object from the perspective of a specific company context.

In SanFrancisco, analysis-level business objects that have both private and shared aspects are factored at design time into two distinct objects: the domain object itself, which maintains all private aspects itself and presents the complete analysis-level business interface; and a shared attributes object, which maintains the attributes and behavior of the analysis-level object that should be shared across all company-specific views of the domain object. (Note that the shared attributes object could also contain business algorithms, as well as attributes meant to be shared by all "views" of the business object.) This separation provides a simple usage view via the domain object while still providing

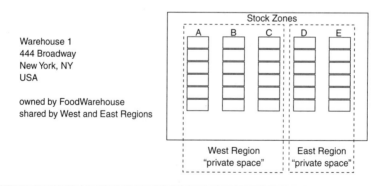

Figure 10.4. Shared Warehouse Example

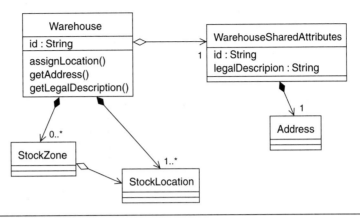

Figure 10.5. Warehouse Class Structure

the flexibility of the factoring. Figure 10.5 shows the the Warehouse business object factored into its private and shared parts.

Note that even though the WarehouseSharedAttributes class defines the attributes legalDescription and address, get methods are defined for those attributes on the Warehouse class. An instance of the Warehouse class is not complete unless it is associated with an instance of the WarehouseSharedAttributes class, and Warehouse delegates some of its behavior to its contained Warehouse-SharedAttributes class. Furthermore, the ID attributes of related Warehouse and WarehouseSharedAttributes objects must be identical because only the composite of both objects makes up the full domain definition of a warehouse. SanFrancisco generates special object construction code for classes like Warehouse that are composed of both private and shared aspects. This special code ensures that an instance of the shared attributes class (WarehouseSharedAttributes in our example) exists and has the same ID as the instance of the domain class (Warehouse in our example) being created.

Because Warehouse and WarehouseSharedAttributes are controlled objects, and each object is separately controlled, we can distribute controllers of the correct type throughout the company hierarchy to reflect the structure that Food Warehouse has set up for its warehouses. Figure 10.6 shows how we'll distribute the Warehouse controllers for the first category (warehouses with zones assigned to specific operating units).

Each Warehouse object in Figure 10.6 shares the same ID but contains different zones. Each operating unit in effect has its own view of warehouse 1. The East Region can use only zones D and E for storage of goods, the West Region only zones A, B, and C. If asked, however, both views of warehouse 1 will return "New York, NY" as the address because this information is part of the WarehouseSharedAttributes object with which each Warehouse object is associated.

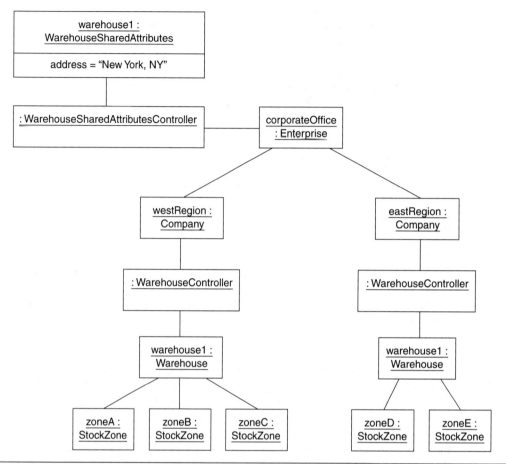

Figure 10.6. Shared Warehouse Example: Object Structure

The other two categories of warehouses are simplifications of the first. In the second category, only one Warehouse object with a particular ID will be present across all operating units. In Figure 10.7, the corporate office holds the shared attributes objects for both warehouse 2 and warehouse 3 (because in our example these warehouses are owned and managed by the corporate office). The private-aspect object for warehouse 2 exists only in the West Region because this warehouse has been allocated solely to the West Region operating unit. Likewise, warehouse 3 exists only in the East Region. Although Figures 10.6 and 10.7 do not show the sales and distribution subunits of the East and West Regions, remember that these subunits will be able to work with the warehouses defined for their parent units through the chained property container capabilities implemented by the company hierarchy (see Chapter 5).

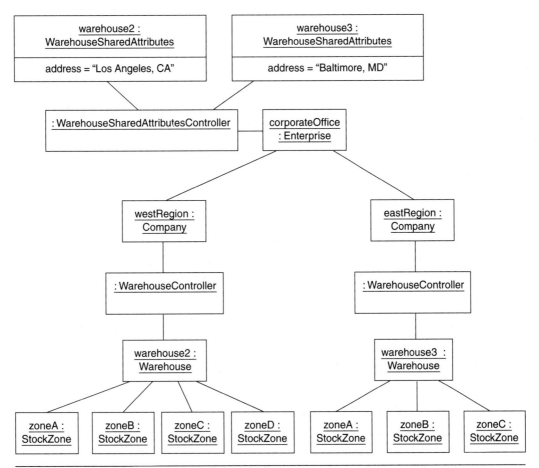

Figure 10.7. Dedicated Warehouse Example (Owned by Corporate Office): Object Structure

The third category is simpler still. Warehouses in this category are both owned by and allocated entirely to the same operating unit (see Figure 10.8). Note that in this case, both the Warehouse and the SharedWarehouseAttributes controllers are attached to the Belgian subsidiary. The reason is that the Belgian subsidiary both owns warehouse 4 and has allocated all zones of that warehouse for its dedicated use. Another point worth mentioning is that if we knew beforehand that every warehouse had this characteristic, there would be no need for the additional complexity of shared and private objects and their separate controllers; the shared and private objects could collapse into a single controlled object.

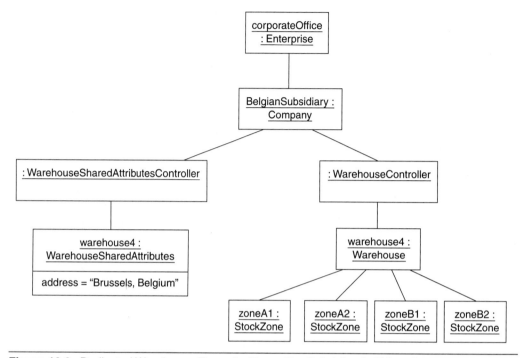

Figure 10.8. Dedicated Warehouse Example (Owned by Subsidiary): Object Structure

Dictionaries and Default Objects

Often the business objects used during a particular business process are chosen by the person using the application. Sometimes, however, application code (including code that is part of another business object) needs to directly retrieve one or more business objects during processing. If the user is responsible for defining and creating these business objects, how can the code be written to retrieve the correct object? To quote Marshall Cline, "All object-oriented design problems can be solved with another level of indirection."[2] Controller dictionaries introduce this additional level of indirection.

A *controller dictionary* maps object tokens to specific business objects visible to the controller.[3] These tokens are defined by the application, but it is up to the

2. In *C++ FAQs*, 2nd ed. (1999), by Marshall Cline, Greg Lomow, and Mike Girou (Addison-Wesley, Reading, MA).

3. In reality, dictionary tokens are mapped to the unique domain IDs of their associated objects rather than directly to their associated objects. By taking this approach, we can take advantage of aggregating-controller behavior to automatically retrieve the current business object mapped to the token regardless of when new business objects with the same domain IDs are introduced into the controller hierarchy.

application user to configure the mappings between each token and its associated object. Once these mappings have been made, the application will operate as expected. If a mapping is missed, however, a business process dependent on that mapping will fail because it will not be able to determine which business object to use to complete the process.

Let's take a look at a specific business example from Food Warehouse (shown in Figure 10.9). Choosing the correct exchange rate for converting from one currency to another can be very complex. Often multiple exchange rates are defined between two currencies. Some of these exchange rates (like rates used during value-added tax calculations in Europe) might be mandated by legal authorities, and others (like rates for intercompany transfers or purchase orders) might be under the discretion of the financial officers of the business. Still others (like the "EuroFood purchase order" example in Figure 10.9) might result because of special negotiations or contracts between a company and one of its business partners.

Because of this complexity, an exchange rate controller should have a dictionary that can be used by application code to retrieve the correct exchange

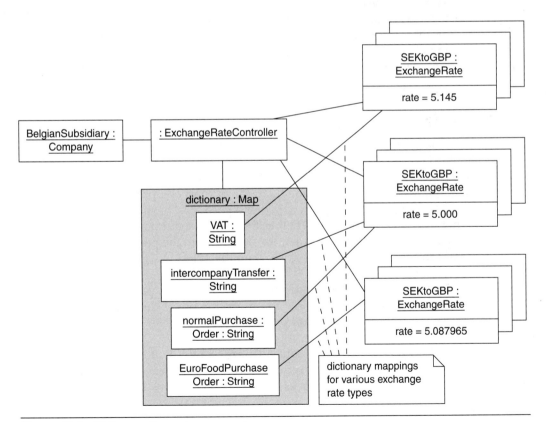

Figure 10.9. Dictionary Example

rate between two currencies when converting currencies for value-added tax, intercompany transfer, external sales, or other defined conversions. All application code dealing with exchange rates should use the dictionary entries (in other words, the tokens defined by the application) to retrieve exchange rates. It is up to the end users to map these tokens to the underlying exchange rates they have defined. A simple installation of the business application in our example might map all tokens to a single set of exchange rates; a complex installation would set up one-to-one mappings from each token to a unique set or a combination of shared and dedicated mappings (as in Figure 10.9).

We can handle default objects to be used by an application similarly because we can think about "default value" as a particular role a business object can play. In SanFrancisco, controllers maintain their default objects with designated attributes, but default objects could be just as easily maintained with "default" tokens in a controller's dictionary.

Contexts Other than Company Hierarchy

Depending on the objectives of the application, it might be appropriate to consider a context hierarchy other than the company hierarchy. A couple of possibilities to consider include a hierarchy based on location or on business partner (customer or supplier). As long as the context structure is well defined, the Controller pattern works with any hierarchical context.

Applicability

Consider using the Controller pattern for object types that do not have a natural business object owner. Typically, these types are meaningful at the context level of the application. Good examples of such objects (mentioned in the "Motivation" section earlier) include financial journals and product instances.

Another way to determine whether a particular business object should be controlled is to think about whether the object would normally be associated with a particular Company when considered from the perspective of a typical expert in the object's domain. If so, then the object is a good candidate to be controlled.

Once you've selected the Controller pattern for a particular object type, you also need to think about how controllers should be distributed throughout the company hierarchy in your application. Here are some options to consider:

- All instances held by a controller are shared by all subcompanies, and subcompanies cannot introduce additional instances, nor can they remove or replace existing instances in the parent company. These controller-held object instances are monolithic (i.e., their attributes cannot be split into private or shared sets). A single root controller instance placed on the parent company is sufficient in this case.

- All instances held by a controller are shared by all subcompanies, but subcompanies are allowed to introduce additional instances and remove, replace, or hide existing instances in the parent company. These controller-held object instances are monolithic (i.e., their attributes cannot be split into private or shared sets). A root controller placed on the parent company in combination with aggregating and hiding controllers distributed throughout the subcompany hierarchy wherever additional instances can be added or existing instances can be overridden will meet these requirements. If desired, you can repeat this structure throughout the company hierarchy by distributing root controller instances as needed in the hierarchy and introducing aggregating or hiding controller instances in subcompanies underneath these instances. Each root controller terminates the chain of responsibility and isolates its company subhierarchy (i.e., the company on which it resides and all children of that company) from the remainder of the company hierarchy.

- All instances held by a controller can be split into private and shared aspects, each of which is represented by a separate controlled class. In this case, objects representing the shared attributes of the domain class are held in a controller that is installed on a parent company (typically the Enterprise object). Each company in the company hierarchy may then introduce a controller for objects representing the private aspects of the domain class. Object instances in those controllers are linked by ID to the appropriate shared attribute object. Aggregating behavior is usually not appropriate for these types of business objects, because the objects themselves are being split into multiple views, each of which is visible to a particular company in the company hierarchy.

Structure

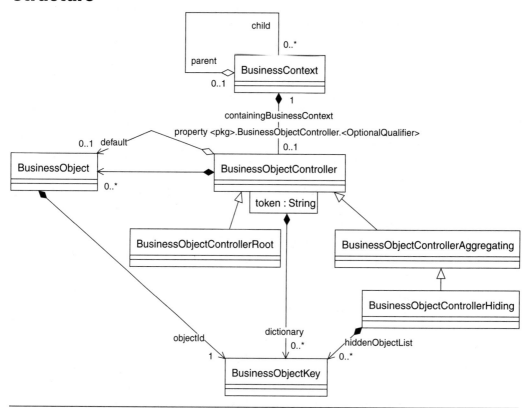

Figure 10.10. Aggregating and Hiding Controller Structure

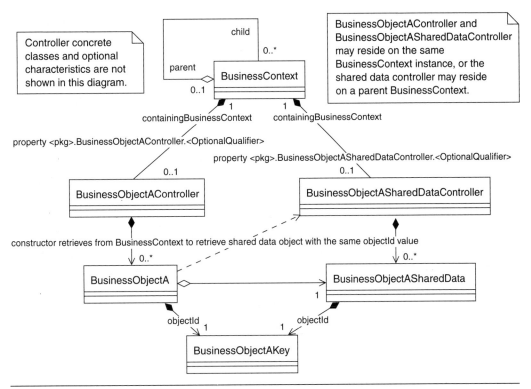

Figure 10.11. Shared and Sharing Controller Structure

Participants

- **BusinessContext** (Company). An object that represents the active view within the business application. The BusinessContext serves as a collection point for all business information and processes that are valid for and available to a particular operating unit within an enterprise. BusinessContext objects exist within a hierarchy: A child BusinessContext can delegate some or all of its capabilities to its parent BusinessContext. SanFrancisco provides an implicit business context in the form of its company hierarchy. Another potential context could be based on hierarchies such as the internal representation of a business partner's (e.g., customer's or supplier's) organization. In general, any hierarchical structure that affects a broad range of business information and processes is a BusinessContext candidate.

- **BusinessObject** (Currency, Account, Warehouse, ExchangeRate). The domain object being controlled. This is a top-level object—in other words, an object whose natural domain owner is the BusinessContext with which it is associated.

- **BusinessObjectController** (CurrencyController). The object responsible for managing the valid set of business objects available to a particular business context (typically a Company object within the enterprise's company hierarchy). This base class is not instantiable, but its interface provides the capabilities that clients acting within a particular BusinessContext can use when working with BusinessObjects.[4] BusinessObjectController instances are loosely coupled to their BusinessContext objects via property.

- **BusinessObjectControllerRoot.** A controller whose instances exist at any level within the BusinessContext hierarchy and are capable of existing on their own (i.e., are not dependent on a parent controller in the hierarchy). Only those BusinessObjects directly held by a BusinessObjectControllerRoot are available for use by the BusinessContext that holds the controller; any BusinessObjects defined above the level of this BusinessContext are not visible to the context.

- **BusinessObjectControllerAggregating.** A controller whose instances are dependent on a parent controller for their basic contents but can add additional contents or override their parents' contents. BusinessObjectController-Aggregating instances cannot be held by the root BusinessContext object of a particular context hierarchy. A BusinessObjectControllerRoot object must always be present in the context hierarchy at a level above a BusinessObjectControllerAggregating instance.

- **BusinessObjectControllerHiding.** A subtype of BusinessObjectController-Aggregating whose instances can also selectively hide their parents' contents.

- **BusinessObjectAController** (WarehouseController). A controller whose instances make up the private data of a business object following the shared and private information structure described in example 3 of the "Motivation" section.

- **BusinessObjectA** (Warehouse). The private portion of a business object following the shared and private information structure described in example 3 of the "Motivation" section.

- **BusinessObjectASharedDataController** (WarehouseSharedAttributes-Controller). A controller whose instances make up the shared data of a business object following the shared and private information structure described in example 3 of the "Motivation" section.

- **BusinessObjectASharedData** (WarehouseSharedAttributes). The shared portion of a business object following the shared and private information structure described in example 3 of the "Motivation" section.

---

4. One exception to this rule occurs when working with the methods introduced specifically on the hiding controller interface (see the "Sample Code" section later in this chapter for details).

- **BusinessObjectKey, BusinessObjectAKey.** Two of potentially many objects that uniquely identify a particular BusinessObject. These objects are used in the following situations:
  - By BusinessObjectControllerHiding instances to represent the set of BusinessObjects that are not to be visible to the BusinessContext where the controller resides.
  - For the retrieval of shared data instances in the construction of the private portion of a business object following the shared and private information structure described in example 3 of the "Motivation" section.
  - By clients to retrieve BusinessObjects from controllers and as the values in controller dictionary key/value pairs. Typically the BusinessObjectKey is a String, although in some cases a more complex object type may represent the unique identifier of a BusinessObject.

Collaborations

- BusinessObjectController provides the valid set of BusinessObjects to the BusinessContext with which it is associated.

- BusinessObjectControllerAggregating relies on other BusinessObjectControllers distributed above it in the BusinessContext hierarchy to provide some or all of the BusinessObjects that are valid in its BusinessContext.

- BusinessObjectControllerHiding uses BusinessObjectKeys to list the BusinessObjects that are available above it in the BusinessContext hierarchy but that are not to be made available to its BusinessContext.

- BusinessObjectController optionally maintains a default BusinessObject.

- BusinessObjectController optionally maintains a map of tokens representing specific business object roles to their associated business objects (represented by BusinessObjectKeys).

- BusinessObjectA (the private portion of a business object following the shared and private information structure described in example 3 of the "Motivation" section) retrieves its associated shared data controller during construction to locate its associated shared data object.

Consequences

The Controller pattern has the following tradeoffs, benefits, and drawbacks:

Tradeoffs

- **Full versus partial controller distribution.** When configuring an application during its installation, you must consider where to place controller instances throughout the business context hierarchy. An application could (1) choose to populate the hierarchy fully with controller instances, thus simplifying the creation of new controlled object instances regardless of the current business context; (2) choose to create controllers only where specifically directed to by the application installer; or (3) attempt to distribute controllers intelligently throughout the hierarchy on the basis of an algorithm derived from information provided by the end user during product installation. In general, the application will perform better if controllers are introduced only in contexts in which the set of valid controlled objects has been altered (e.g., new objects have been introduced, existing objects have been overridden or hidden).

- **Allowing versus preventing dynamic controller maintenance.** If an application chooses to allow dynamic addition and/or removal of controllers once it is in production mode, it must also maintain proper references to the controlled business objects affected by the addition or removal of a controller. For example, consider a three-level hierarchy in which a PaymentTerms object for "three easy payments"[5] exists at the top level of the hierarchy (see Figure 10.12). If the application user introduces a new PaymentTerms controller in the middle level of the hierarchy and defines a PaymentTerms object for "three easy payments" at that level, any references to that object at either the middle or bottom level of the hierarchy (such as the reference established by Customer, as shown in Figures 10.12 and 10.13) will become invalid unless the application dynamically updates those relationships to refer to the newly defined object at the middle level. Likewise, if the user later deletes that object, the application needs to update any references to it so that they refer to the object defined at the top level of the hierarchy. See the discussion on controller maintenance in the "Implementation" section later in this chapter for more details.

  If this approach is prevalent throughout an application, the application can choose to dynamically retrieve controlled objects (i.e., retrieve objects as needed by their unique IDs) rather than maintaining direct references

---

5. Each PaymentTerms object describes a predefined payment schedule, potentially including multiple installments, discount agreements for early payments, and other information describing the schedule.

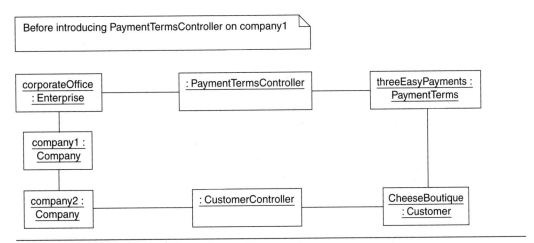

Figure 10.12. Before Adding Controller on Company 1

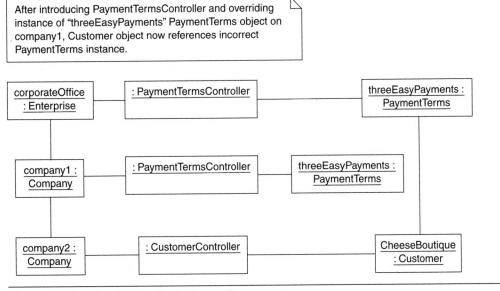

Figure 10.13. After Adding Controller on Company 1

to controlled objects. Such an approach may result in slightly slower object retrieval times, depending on how controlled objects are persisted and indexed. For some applications, the dynamic lookup approach may result in incorrect behavior, so alternative approaches should be carefully analyzed early during application design.

Benefits

- **Partitioning business information across a business context.** The Controller pattern provides an effective way to partition business information across the complex underlying structure of a hierarchically organized business enterprise. Application code does not need to be aware of the specific context in which it is operating; instead, it can use the controllers available in its context to retrieve business objects of interest and then execute its business processes via methods provided by those objects. Controllers ensure that only business objects applicable to a particular context can be used when operating in that context.

- **Controller as metaclass.** A controller can serve as a type of metaclass for its contained business objects, helping to manage some of the object lifecycle issues associated with a class. For example, controllers can be used to ensure uniqueness during object creation. They can also provide a default object instance to client code where appropriate.

- **Consolidation of shared and private aspects of a business object.** When business objects have both shared and private aspects from the business context perspective, controllers for those separate aspects can collaborate to provide a view of the business object that is tailored to a particular context. They can also ensure that only valid business objects are created and maintained within a context. The business object client deals only with a simple usage view provided by the business object that contains the private aspects of the view. This approach simplifies how clients interact with what could be a complex set of domain object information while still providing the flexibility of the factoring.

- **Configuration flexibility resulting from indirect object references.** Dictionaries and default values incorporated into controllers introduce a level of indirection during client retrieval of business objects, thereby freeing clients from having to be aware of specific object identity. Instead, clients rely on the object roles defined by dictionary entries (or the default business object) to retrieve business objects for later use.

Drawbacks

- **Additional overhead for simple business structures.** Controllers introduce additional overhead during business operations. For very simple business structures (i.e., a business with no or very few internal hierarchies), a more direct and explicit approach to managing business objects can be considered as an alternative to the Controller pattern.

- **Alternative or multiple context structures.** Businesses that are not hierarchically organized (e.g., a matrix-managed organization) are not inherently supported by the Controller pattern relying on a company context.

For such structures, it may be possible to align the controllers used by the business with a context other than company structure. In other cases, it may be necessary to provide multiple context structures for differing business information and connect controller instances directly to those structures to achieve the correct delegation behavior.

Implementation

Consider the following implementation issues for the Controller pattern:

- **Creation of controlled objects.** When we create a controlled object, we must guarantee its uniqueness compared to other objects that exist in the context of the newly created object. Because aggregating and hiding controllers are designed to allow business objects defined at a higher level in the application context to be overridden, this statement is less restrictive than "the object must have a unique domain ID." In SanFrancisco, factory create methods provided for business object types are responsible for checking uniqueness. Alternatively, this responsibility could be delegated to the controller itself, or to the persistent store of the application if that store is capable of ensuring object uniqueness (e.g., objects are persisted into a relational database table in which a primary key composed of one or more columns has been established).

- **Controlled item key types.**
  - **Dynamic ID.** Dynamic ID classes are used in a way similar to that in which an enumerated type would be used. Dynamic ID classes and their controllers should be used when an application user is allowed to define the set of values for the enumerated type. Often dynamic ID values are used to classify other business objects, allowing business objects that reference a certain type's value to be identified and grouped through queries according to the referenced value.

    Dynamic IDs are conceptually similar to enumerated types. Enumerated types or their equivalents should be used when the set of values for the type is fixed (e.g., days of the week, months of the year); otherwise, dynamic IDs should be used.

    A dynamic ID class may have additional behavior beyond its enumerated type characteristics. For example, it may have control attributes or algorithmic methods attached. Because the primary purpose of most dynamic ID values is classification of other objects, however, these classes tend to be data-centric, with little behavior.

    The key of a dynamic ID class is always an ID (String) and will never be more than that. In SanFrancisco, dynamic ID classes always inherit from the Distinguishable interface, which declares the getId method, returning a String. Such inheritance has two benefits: It standardizes the public interface defined for dynamic ID controllers, and it allows various support classes to work with dynamic ID classes polymorphically. Dynamic ID controllers have a more restrictive interface than other controllers: The key used for controlled item retrieval is always a String.

Currency is an example of a dynamic ID. Each currency used by an application (U.S. dollar, French franc, and so on) needs to be represented uniquely, and it is up to the user of the application to decide which currencies are valid for its particular installation. Other examples of dynamic IDs are Color (e.g., the application could initially define Red, Green, and Blue as valid colors, but the application user could choose to remove Red and add Purple) and Region (the Food Warehouse example has two regions defined: West Region and East Region).

– **Distinguishable controlled items.** Some controlled classes that inherit from Distinguishable are not dynamic IDs. Such classes are not dynamic IDs because their primary purpose is not to serve as an enumerated type. Business object classes in this category still have a key that is a String ID. However, because you may want to be able to retrieve instances of these classes using attributes other than the String ID, the controller interface for these classes should be more flexible than one for a dynamic ID. SanFrancisco provides the MethodAccessKey interface for these controllers to use when managing their controlled instances. This interface is used wherever a key parameter or return value is required in a controller method. SanFrancisco also provides a concrete implementation class—SimpleMethodKey—that implements the MethodAccessKey interface. SimpleMethodKey is used to retrieve items from such controllers. This concrete key class encapsulates a String ID for use by the controller. The controller code works with the abstract interface defined on MethodAccessKey, thus allowing you to define alternative retrieval key subclasses. Some examples of distinguishable controlled item classes in SanFrancisco include BusinessPartner, Product, and Journal.

– **Nondistinguishable controlled items.** These classes have a complex key structure, typically composed of multiple attributes that must be supported by a specialized MethodAccessKey subclass. An example of such a class in SanFrancisco is Bank. Its key is composed of the combination of country ID and bank code.

• **Dynamic ID metatypes.** Dynamic IDs can be implemented in two different ways. The standard approach is to create a separate dynamic ID controller for every unique dynamic ID type. Another approach is to define a generic dynamic ID controller whose instances can be initialized to represent specific dynamic ID types. SanFrancisco provides a Classification controller that supports this second approach.

In both cases controllers are involved. When creating a controller for a particular type, however, we make the controller (type) and its controlled type instances (values) specific. For example, you might define an AreaController with Areas, rather than a generic ClassificationTypeController that represents the Area type, containing generic ClassificationTypeValues that represent specific Areas. Using specific controllers encourages type safety because attributes, return types, and parameters can be typed to their specific domain classes, such as Area. Applications that take the second approach for some or all of their dynamic IDs use a generic class, such as ClassificationType, to represent their identifiers. These applications then must do additional runtime checking to ensure that particular objects are of the intended type. On the other hand, the generic support such as that provided by SanFrancisco's Classification controller, combined with the Property Container pattern (see Chapter 5), means that the end user could easily define a new type (and its associated values) and use it to classify domain objects.

In general, an application should use a type-specific dynamic ID controller when it knows beforehand that a particular classification type will be needed. The mechanism provided by a generic dynamic ID controller, such as SanFrancisco's Classification controller, should normally be used when the classifications cannot be determined until runtime.

• **Controller dictionaries and default values.** When defining a controller with a dictionary, make sure that only the application can define dictionary tokens. If the application code doesn't know about a token, it will never use it, so a user-defined token entry will be useless.

Sometimes an application provides one or more business objects preconfigured into a controller. For example, if a financial application is sold primarily in the United States and Canada, the Currency controller might be preconfigured with business objects representing U.S. and Canadian dollars. If that application defines a default currency, it might choose to preconfigure the default value of each currency controller as the U.S. dollar object for applications sold in the United States and as the Canadian dollar object for applications sold in Canada. The same consideration should be given to any dictionary entries defined for a controller. By establishing these mappings at installation time, you can ensure that your application will run with minimal user configuration required. Eventually users will remap some or all of the preconfigured token entries and default values to adapt the application to their specific needs.

When implementing a dictionary or default value, consider implementing aggregating behavior for it, thus allowing a token to be overridden on a subcompany basis. SanFrancisco automatically provides aggregating behavior for all dictionaries and default values.

- **Fixed content controllers.** Some controllers in your application may have fixed content. Such controllers will not have an associated end user maintenance interface, and their contents will be established when the application is installed (possibly modified as additional application modules are installed or the application is upgraded). All the IDs of controlled items maintained by these controllers will be well known to the application code; thus, the code can retrieve these items directly from the controller. Typically, such controlled items are managed by a single root controller installed on the Enterprise object that can be accessed regardless of which Company is set as the active Company. One possible use for a fixed content controller is as a registry of an application's installed business processes.

- **ID generation.** Some controlled item classes have IDs that should be generated automatically rather than being assigned by the creator of the item. For example, the IDs for journal entries in a general ledger are typically generated; in fact, some countries have specific legal requirements for how these IDs are generated. You can incorporate ID generation into a controller by assigning responsibility for ID generation to a contained ID generation policy (see Chapter 7). This policy comes into play when the created instance is registered with the controller. If you take this approach, consider designing the generation policy to handle both the case in which an initial ID is specified by the creator of the item and the case in which the ID is not specified. In the first case, the ID generation policy can be designed to modify the initial ID (perhaps by appending or prepending additional information to the ID). In the second case, the ID generation policy will generate a new ID and assign it to the newly created instance.

Automatic ID generation can become a point of high contention in a multiuser application, so in some cases preallocating IDs will result in better application throughput. This approach is consistent with the first case mentioned here, in which the ID generation policy merely modifies the passed-in ID according to a standard pattern.

Some object IDs may have specifically defined legal or corporate restrictions. For example, a business may want to enforce a sequential numbering scheme with no gaps for its sales orders. Preallocating order IDs could result in an aborted order, in which a customer begins the order process but terminates it before the order is completed. Domain requirements must be considered early in design to ensure that the application is flexible enough to support various ID handling policies.

- **Typed controllers.** Typically, for a particular controller type, only a single controller instance exists on a particular Company. In some situations, however, multiple controller instances of a particular type are required on a single Company. For example, SanFrancisco defines the OrderPartner class to represent customers, suppliers, and internal suppliers such as warehouses. It's necessary to keep the sets of different order partners separate from each other, because a particular order partner could be both a customer and a supplier. If customers and suppliers were not kept separate, the IDs of the two instances could collide.

  SanFrancisco achieves this separation by defining a dynamic ID that represents order partner controller types, and instances of that ID for customer, supplier, and internal supplier. This ID is then held as an attribute of both the OrderPartner and the OrderPartnerController classes. Three instances of OrderPartnerController are created and attached to a Company, of which one represents customers, one represents suppliers, and one represents internal suppliers. The property names of these controllers are scoped by usage on the basis of the ID of their contained order controller types (e.g., "om.OrderPartnerController.OM_CUSTOMER"). As instances of OrderPartner are created, they are associated with one of the three controllers on the basis of their type.

- **Controller maintenance.** Over time, controllers distributed throughout a company hierarchy will be modified by end users of that application. In many cases, such modification can be done safely at any time (e.g., financial journal objects can be created and accumulated in a journal controller without affecting other aspects of the financial application). However, when application code retrieves controlled items by ID, by dictionary token, or as a default value, care should be taken to avoid corrupting existing objects when doing the following:

  - **Modifying the controller hierarchy.** Sophisticated applications may want to support dynamic setup of controllers—that is, allow the end user to create and add controllers to various companies throughout the company hierarchy (as mentioned in the "Tradeoffs" section). As long as the application has not entered into production mode, such support can be accomplished easily and safely. Extreme care should be taken in modification of the controller hierarchy after an application has entered into production mode. It is possible to corrupt existing objects by making their object references to controlled objects invalid. For example, if a controller on the Enterprise object contains controlled item A, then a process running in the context of a subcompany will retrieve item A from the Enterprise when passing ID "A" as the lookup key. If later a controller that contains an overridden version of controlled item A is added to the subcompany, a different object will be returned when item

A is retrieved. This situation could cause persistent objects created by the process to become inconsistent (e.g., two objects created at different times in the same company context could hold references to different objects even though those objects have the same ID).

– **Overriding and hiding controlled items.** If controlled items with the same ID are introduced or hidden at different times in the various controllers in the company hierarchy, the same situation as that just described can occur, even if the controllers in the company hierarchy were defined at application installation time.

– **Removing controlled items.** If controllers implement aggregating behavior for default values or dictionary entries, additional steps must be taken in the removal of a controlled item to ensure that dictionary entries or default value settings do not become invalid. For example, a controller asked to remove a controlled item may not check for default or dictionary usage of that item in itself or any of its child controllers. In this case, a client that is removing a controlled item from its controller (i.e., deleting that item) should ensure that no dictionary or default entries refer to the object to be removed. The client should also remove any hidden ID entries in child hiding controllers that refer to the object to be removed. When making this check, remember that overriding instances of this object in child controllers terminate the search tree.

– **Changing attributes of a controlled item that affect its key.** For the following reasons, care must be taken in the modification of object attributes that either partially or entirely make up the unique key of the object:

• A duplicate key could be created in the controller that directly owns the instance being modified or its children.

• Child controllers of the controller that directly owns the instance being modified could be affected.

• Dictionary entries for the controller that directly owns the instance or that controller's children could be affected.

The client code that makes such an attribute change should ensure the following:

• That the changed attribute does not result in a duplicate key for the controller that directly owns the modified object or that controller's children (we can accomplish this objective by creating a key that represents the changed object and checking all affected controllers to see if they already contain this key)

• That dictionary entries for the controller that directly owns the modified object and that controller's children are updated to refer to the new key

- That objects owned by child aggregating or hiding controllers that override the modified object are updated to refer to the new key

- That hidden ID entries in child hiding controllers that refer to the modified object are updated to refer to the new key

  To assist client code in making these checks, you might consider providing a method on your controllers that returns a collection of the controller's children (i.e., all aggregating and hiding controllers located below this controller in the company hierarchy). The sample code later in this chapter shows how this method can be implemented.

- **Controlled classes that extend other controlled classes by aggregation.** Aggregation is a well-known technique for extending business objects. For example, SanFrancisco provides a Product class, which contains attributes and behavior related to warehouse management information and processes. SanFrancisco also extends the Product class by introducing an OrderProduct class that contains additional attributes and behavior related to order management information and processes. An instance of this OrderProduct class contains an instance of the Product class. This type of structure is common when a higher-level package needs to extend the behavior of a class provided by a lower-level package. If the extending domain class (e.g., OrderProduct) is a controlled class, special rules should be followed in the implementation and use of its controller:

  - The extending class controller (e.g., OrderProductController) should contain a reference to the extended class controller (e.g., ProductController).

  - When creating an instance of the extending class, you should take care to ensure that an instance of the extended class controller exists on the Company that owns the controller of the extending class instance being created, thereby helping to ensure that instances of the extending class are paired with extended class instances from the same Company, because from the application user's perspective, these two objects are parts of a whole and must be treated as such (see Figure 10.14). Once this check is made, the object being created should also attempt to retrieve the extended object whose domain ID is identical to its own.[6] If an extended object with this ID doesn't exist, the create should fail.

  - When working with instances of the extending class, you should retrieve the extending class controller only as a directly contained property (see Chapter 5). Otherwise it would be possible to retrieve a

---

6. It's safer to let the object being created (the extending object) retrieve its contained object (the extended object) automatically as part of the creation process rather than allowing the contained object to be passed in as a parameter on the create method.

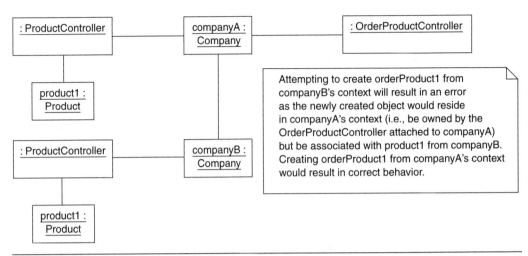

Figure 10.14. Ensuring You Get the Right Instance

controller instance from a Company higher in the hierarchy, even though an instance of the extended class controller exists on the active Company. In the example shown in Figure 10.14, if we were operating in Company B's context and attempted to create a new OrderProduct instance with domain ID "1," we would completely bypass the associated Product instance at Company A's level. The result would be an inconsistent view of the extending class instance (OrderProduct 1) from the perspective of Company B because the extending class instance holds on to an extended class instance (Product 1 in this case) defined at a company lower in the hierarchy (Company B) even though an instance of the extending class is defined on the parent company.

– If the extending class will support chained property behavior, you should take care in how you do the chaining. If the extended class is within a hierarchy, simply chaining the extending class to the extended class may not provide the expected chaining. The extended class may immediately traverse up its hierarchy, not taking the extending classes of other extended classes into account. Typically, the correct behavior in this situation is to alternate between extending and extended classes, zigzagging up the hierarchy until the property is found. An example of such behavior in SanFrancisco is the alternation between BusinessPartner (the extending class) and BusinessPartnerSharedData (the extended class). SanFrancisco BusinessPartner objects can represent a customer or supplier's hierarchy, just as SanFrancisco Company objects represent the internal hierarchy of the enterprise using the application. In this case, property delegation should pass from BusinessPartner to

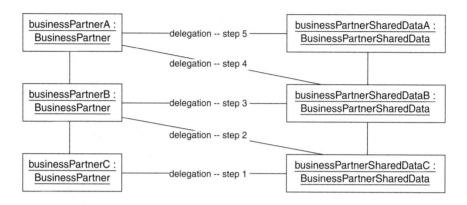

Chained property delegation within a business partner hierarchy must alternate between the BusinessPartner and BusinessPartnerSharedData objects as it zigzags up the hierarchy.

Figure 10.15. Extending Chained Property Behavior When Shared Data Is Involved

BusinessPartnerSharedData for a single level in the customer or supplier's hierarchy, then step up to the parent instance in the hierarchy, repeating the pattern as shown in Figure 10.15.

Sample Code

Using Currency as an example, let's start with a view of the common controller interface:

```
public interface CurrencyController {

// In general, two types of object access methods are provided: one that
// presents the caller with the complete collection of objects visible to
// the caller, and one that presents only those objects present at the
// controller's level in the contextual hierarchy. Typically, the first
// form of method is used during operational activity, and the second
// is used during maintenance activity (i.e., object lifecycle activity)
// within the application.


// The primary interfaces for dealing with a controller are through the
// controlled item's key. Methods to set new elements into a controller
// are not present on SanFrancisco controllers because the create method
// for a controlled object directly inserts the created object into the
// controller, thereby ensuring that no instances of the controlled object
// type exist outside of a controller.
```

```
// Type 1 (operational) methods:

    public abstract Currency getCurrencyBy(String key);

    public abstract boolean containsCurrencyKey(String key);

// Type 2 (maintenance) methods:

    public abstract Currency getDirectlyOwnedCurrencyBy(String key);

    public abstract boolean directlyContainsCurrencyKey(String key);


// Because the controller acts as an intelligent collection, a typical
// controller interface also provides collection-like methods for working
// with its contained objects

// Type 1 (operational) methods:

    public abstract QueryCollection queryOwnedCurrencies(String select,
                                                        ...);

    public abstract QueryCollection getOwnedCurrencies();

// Type 2 (maintenance) methods:

    public abstract QueryCollection queryDirectlyOwnedCurrencies(String select,
                                                        ...);

    public abstract QueryCollection getDirectlyOwnedCurrencies();

    public abstract void removeDirectlyOwnedCurrencyBy(String key);

    public abstract void removeAllDirectlyOwnedCurrencies();

    public abstract boolean isCurrenciesDirectlyEmpty();


// Dictionary and default object behavior is optional. Again, both
// operational and maintenance methods will be present in each case.

// Type 1 (operational) methods:

    public abstract boolean containsCurrencyDictionaryEntryKey(String
        dictionaryKey);

    public abstract Currency getCurrencyDictionaryEntryBy(String dictionaryKey);

    public abstract Currency getDefaultCurrency();
```

```
// Type 2 (maintenance) methods:

    public abstract boolean directlyContainsCurrencyDictionaryEntryKey(String
        dictionaryKey);

    public abstract Currency
        getDirectlyContainedCurrencyDictionaryEntryBy(String dictionaryKey);

    public abstract void setDirectlyContainedCurrencyDictionaryEntry(String id,
                                                String dictionaryKey);

    public abstract Currency getDirectlyContainedDefaultCurrency();

    public abstract void setDirectlyContainedDefaultCurrency(Currency
        baseCurrency);


// A typical controller provides methods to retrieve its associated
// parent controller (the controller directly above it in the context
// hierarchy) and its child controllers (all controllers existing below
// it in the context hierarchy), as well as a method
// to retrieve the context object with which it is associated, in this
// case a Company object

    public abstract CurrencyController getParentController();

    public abstract Set getChildControllers();

    public abstract Company getContainingCompany();

} // End of interface CurrencyController
```

Now let's take a look at some sample implementation classes for controllers. First we'll look at a sampling of methods that can be implemented on the controller base class:

```
public abstract class CurrencyControllerImpl implements CurrencyController {

// All ". . . DirectlyContained . . ." methods can be implemented by the
// controller base class. These methods are rather straightforward,
// accessing the controller's contained collection or attribute in a
// wire-through manner.


// Here are some sample methods that deal with managing the Currency
// objects directly owned by this controller. Remember that because of
// the tightly coupled creation rules for controlled objects followed
// by SanFrancisco, there is no setDirectlyOwnedCurrencyBy method.
```

```
public Currency getDirectlyOwnedCurrencyBy(String key) {

    return (Currency)ivCurrencies.getElementBy(key);
}

public void removeDirectlyOwnedCurrencyBy(String key) {

    // Remove the owned object, thereby causing
    // the object to be deleted
    ivCurrencies.removeOwnedElementBy(key);
}


// The following methods show how dictionary entries are managed

public Currency getDirectlyContainedCurrencyDictionaryEntryBy(
                                        String dictionaryKey) {

    Currency element = null;

    String id = (String) ivCurrencyDictionary.getElementBy(dictionaryKey);
    if (id != null) {
        element = getCurrencyBy(id);
    }

    return (element);
}

public void setDirectlyContainedCurrencyDictionaryEntry(String id,
                                        String dictionaryKey) {

    // If the specified element ID is null, remove dictionary entry
    if (id == null) {
        ivCurrencyDictionary.removeElementBy(dictionaryKey);
    }
    // Otherwise, modify dictionary to reflect new relationship
    // between dictionaryKey and element
    else {
        // Ensure that element to be associated exists
        if (containsCurrencyKey(id)) {
            // Element exists; update dictionary
            if (ivCurrencyDictionary.containsKey(dictionaryKey)) {
                // Modify existing dictionary entry
                ivCurrencyDictionary.replaceElementBy(id, dictionaryKey);
            }
            else {
                // Add new dictionary entry
                ivCurrencyDictionary.addElementBy(id, dictionaryKey);
            }
        }
        else {
```

```
                    // Element does not exist, throw exception
                    MyException exception = new MyException("element doesn't exist");
                    throw (exception);
                }
            }
        }

        public boolean directlyContainsCurrencyDictionaryEntryKey(
                                                    String dictionaryKey) {

            return ivCurrencyDictionary.containsKey(dictionaryKey);
        }


// Finally, here are some additional methods for managing default values

        public Currency getDirectlyContainedDefaultCurrency() {

            return ivDefaultCurrency;
        }

        public void setDirectlyContainedDefaultCurrency(Currency defaultCurrency){

            if (defaultCurrency != null) {
                // Retrieve ID of passed-in object and ensure that
                // it is logically contained in this controller
                String key = defaultCurrency.getId();
                if (!containsCurrencyKey(key)) {
                    // Passed-in parameter is not logically contained;
                    // throw exception
                    MyException exception =
                    new MyException("object not logically contained");
                    throw (exception);
                }
            }
            ivDefaultCurrency = defaultCurrency;
        }


// Two of the three utility methods can be implemented by the base class.
// Only getParentController must be implemented by either the Root or
// the Aggregating subclass.

        public Handle getContainingCompany() {

            return ivContainingCompany;
        }

        public Set getChildControllers() {
            // Create a Set to hold all found children
            Set childControllers = new Set();
```

```
            // Use recursive protected method to find child controllers
            return (getChildControllers(getContainingCompany(), childControllers));
    }

    protected Set getChildControllers(Company startingCompany,
                                      Set childControllers) {

        Iterator iter = startingCompany.createSubcompanyIterator();
        Company childCompany = null;
        while ((childCompany = startingCompany.getNextSubcompany(iter)) != null) {

            // For each child Company, check if it directly contains
            // a CurrencyController (relying on the Property Container pattern;
            // see Chapter 5)
            if (childCompany.directlyContainsPropertyKey("CurrencyController")) {
                CurrencyController currencyController =
                 (CurrencyController)childCompany.
                 getDirectlyContainedPropertyBy("CurrencyController");
                // If the CurrencyController is not a root,
                // include it in our collection
                if (!(currencyController instanceof CurrencyControllerRoot)) {
                    childControllers.addElement(currencyController);
                    // Recursively process the child Company, looking for more
                    // aggregating controllers and place those in our collection
                    getChildControllers(childCompany, childControllers);
                }

                // Root controllers are not added to the collection and
                // cause the recursive search to be terminated for that branch
                // of the company hierarchy
            }
            else {
                // Even if the child Company does not have a controller
                // itself, we want to continue to recursively process
                // its children, looking for more aggregating controllers
                getChildControllers(childCompany, childControllers);
            }
        }
        return (childControllers);
    }

    // The base controller class also contains the attributes necessary to
    // manage the objects being controlled and to access the context object

    protected QueryCollection ivCurrencies;
    protected Map ivCurrencyDictionary;
    protected Currency ivDefaultCurrency;
    protected Company ivContainingCompany;

}
```

Root, aggregating, and hiding controllers are responsible for implementing the operational methods of the controller. As root controllers terminate the composite views of their controlled objects within the context hierarchy, they can simply delegate their behavior to the ". . . DirectlyControlled . . ." methods implemented by the base class.

```
public class CurrencyControllerRootImpl extends CurrencyControllerImpl {

    public Currency getDefaultCurrency() {
        return getDirectlyContainedDefaultCurrency();
    }

    // Other operational methods are similarly implemented

    // Because the root controller terminates the chain, it has
    // no parent controller

    public CurrencyController getParentController() {
        // By definition, root controllers have no parents
        return null;
    }
}
```

Aggregating controllers, on the other hand, must implement these operational methods by first checking for a local object instance. If a local instance is not found, the aggregating controller delegates responsibility for the method to its parent controller:

```
public class CurrencyControllerAggregatingImpl extends CurrencyControllerImpl {

    public Currency getDefaultCurrency() {

        Currency defaultCurrency = getDirectlyContainedDefaultCurrency();
        if (defaultCurrency == null) {
            defaultCurrency = getParentController().getDefaultCurrency();
        }
        return (defaultCurrency);
    }

    // Other operational methods are similarly implemented

    // We locate an aggregating controller's parent controller by first
    // retrieving the controller's parent context object, then getting the
    // correct controller from that context object

    public CurrencyController getParentController() {

        // Get the parent Company of our containing Company
        Company containingCompany = getContainingCompany();
        Company parentCompany = containingCompany.getParentCompany();
```

```
        // Return the parent controller
        return
            (CurrencyController)parentCompany.getPropertyBy("CurrencyController");
    }
}
```

Finally, a hiding controller must first check to determine if the requested object has been hidden before passing control to its aggregating controller base class:

```
public class CurrencyControllerHidingImpl extends
        CurrencyControllerAggregatingImpl {

    public Currency getCurrencyBy(String key) {

        Currency returnedCurrency = null;

        // First check if passed-in key is associated with a hidden object
        if (!ivHiddenObjectKeys.containsElement(key)) {
            // If object has not been hidden, attempt to retrieve object
            returnedCurrency = super.getCurrencyBy(key);
        }
        return returnedCurrency;
    }

    // Other operational methods are similarly implemented

    // A hiding controller must maintain a list of hidden objects. Hiding
    // controllers typically implement a set of wire-through methods that provide
    // users of the controller with maintenance capabilities for the hidden
    // object list (not shown in this sample code). Note that because these
    // methods are introduced only at the hiding controller level, application
    // code for maintaining objects in a hiding controller must be aware of the
    // fact that it is working with a hiding controller. This is the one
    // exception to the rule that client code always uses the abstract
    // controller interface when working with a controller.

    List ivHiddenObjectKeys;
}
```

Known Uses

The Controller pattern is used pervasively in SanFrancisco. The business objects used as examples in the "Motivation" section earlier in this chapter, along with other business objects, such as Product, Journal, and BusinessPartner, are all implemented as controlled objects in SanFrancisco.

Related Patterns

- **Property Container.** BusinessObjectController instances are loosely coupled to their BusinessContexts via property. Business objects that implement the Property Container pattern (see Chapter 5) also allow users of an application to introduce new classifications of those business objects at runtime.

- **Iterator.** Controllers can be thought of as "smart collections" of business objects; that is, they allow their users to iterate over their contents, as described for the Iterator pattern in *Design Patterns.*

- **Simple Policy.** Policies (see Chapter 7) can be used to automatically generate unique IDs for newly created controlled objects.

11

Key/Keyable

Intent

Encapsulate a set of diverse business information in such a way that the set can be used as an independent whole for processing information. These uses include mapping, combining, filtering, and caching information.

Motivation

Often a business process has to work with a set of diverse business information. In many such cases the business information (or criteria) will change depending on the needs of the business; however, what is done with that business information (in other words, the business process) remains essentially the same. These situations are very diverse, often involving one or more of the following information-handling processes:

- **Mapping** from one set of business information to other information, such as having a map from the day of the week and zone to the picker assigned for that zone on that day of the week

- **Combining** information on the basis of its associated business information, such as combining a group of product requests into a consolidated pick list based on the product and location

- **Filtering** information on the basis of its associated business information, such as filtering all orders to be able to look at the sales of lettuce for a particular period
- **Caching** the results for a query over particular business information, such as the results of determining the availability of lettuce in a particular warehouse

In the following sections we will look at the motivation for each of these processes, using examples from the Food Warehouse requirements (the case study introduced in Chapter 2), and we will explore how each situation is addressed by the Key/Keyable pattern.

Mapping

The most straightforward way to use a set of business information is as an identifier of another piece of information. In other words, the set is used as the key in a mapping to an associated piece of information, thereby allowing that associated information to be retrieved quickly from the map.

For example, Food Warehouse needs to manage which picker (the person who goes to the warehouse and gets a product) is assigned to each zone in the warehouse. Figure 11.1 shows an example of using a map for this assignment. In this example, the key consists of the day of the week and the zone. A map with multiple entries, each with a unique key, is created. When we need to know which picker picks from the freezer on Thursday, we use this business information to create a key, and the key retrieves Alf, the picker defined in the map for this key.

If later we needed to add more criteria to the key—for example, if assignments changed according to the month—we could simply add the new criterion (the month) to the key and still retrieve the picker by building and using a key. The only change to the code would be how the key was constructed.

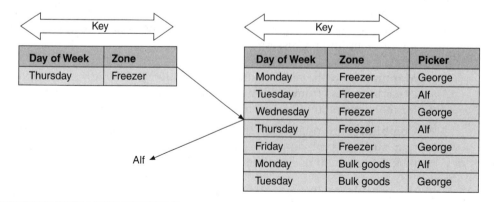

Figure 11.1. Mapping Using Business Information

As Figure 11.2 shows, we can update the key in the previous example to include the month. We can then repopulate the map. Then when we need to know which picker is picking in the freezer on Thursdays in January, we can simply use this business information to create a key and retrieve the associated picker, Fred, from the map.

This simple lookup is sufficient when we are using only specific values for each of the criteria. However, it is inefficient when there are a lot of similar entries. For example, consider what the map looks like if George and Alf pick during the summer months and two other employees pick during the remainder of the year. Instead of having to add entries to the map for each month, we would like to indicate a set of months and a set of days of the week when the picker should be assigned the particular zone. We want a key that can represent a set of the keys described here so that we can add a smaller number of entries to the map while still defining the full set of necessary mappings; that is, we want to be able to encapsulate groups of criteria, as well as specific values.

Figure 11.2 shows an entry with the business information for month omitted. We could interpret this entry to indicate that Alf should always pick bulk goods on Monday, no matter what month it is. We would reach this conclusion by changing the algorithm to build the key from the business information—such as "Monday, March, bulk goods"—and trying to find a match and after not finding one, removing some of the business information from the key—leaving, for example, "Monday, *omitted*, bulk goods"—and trying again to find a match, in this case retrieving Alf. This approach allows us to create a default for all months and then override it with only those months that are different. In our example, we could add an overriding entry using the key "Monday, April, bulk goods," which assigns Mary as the picker.

Let's take a look at another Food Warehouse requirement, the retrieval of discounts. FW wants to be able to do things like define default discounts—for all customers, for a particular customer, or for a particular product. In addition,

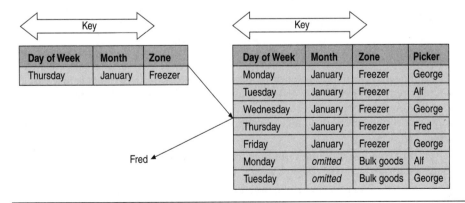

Figure 11.2. Adding More Business Information to the Mapping

FW wants to define discounts for combinations of criteria, such as for a particular customer buying a particular product. To support this requirement we need to be able to define the mapping from groups of criteria to various discounts.[1]

The Key/Keyable pattern can be used for these types of mapping. We refer to a key containing specific values for each piece of business information as an *access key*.[2] As you may have already surmised, keys can also represent groups of business information. We call such keys *specification keys*.[3] In both cases, the key is made up of key elements, called *keyables*. The access key is made up of access keyables, the specification key of specification keyables. These keyables encapsulate the business information or group of business information, respectively, in such a way that the business information can be used abstractly by the containing key.

The abstract keyable class is subclassed to support different kinds of business information. For example, an application could provide specific keyable classes for the day of the week or the zone. The existence of the keyable will be assumed in the remaining discussion of keys. Thus, as Figure 11.3 shows, when we say that the access key contains a zone, we mean that the access key contains an access keyable subclass that identifies a specific zone.

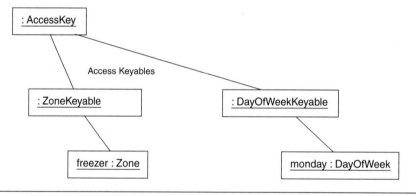

Figure 11.3. An Access Key Consisting of Access Keyables

---

1. Defining complex mappings of discount criteria to various discounts is just part of FW's requirements. FW also wants to be able to use these criteria in different ways, depending on priority ordering, to find the discount (or discounts) that apply. This use of keys is described in more detail as part of the Keyed Attribute Retrieval pattern (see Chapter 14).

2. The term "access key" came from the fact that these keys typically are used for accessing a map.

3. The term "specification key" came from the fact that these keys specify a set of access keys.

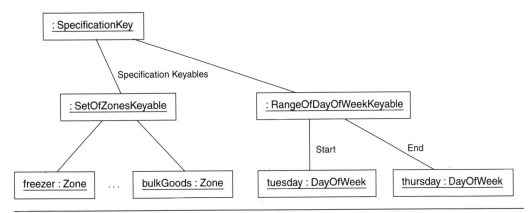

Figure 11.4. A Specification Key Consisting of Specification Keyables

Similarly, as Figure 11.4 shows, when we say that a specification key has a set of zones, we mean that the specification key contains a subclass of the specification keyable that identifies a set of zones. And when we say that a specification key has a range of days of the week (e.g., Tuesday through Thursday), we mean that the specification key contains a subclass of the specification keyable that identifies a start and end day of the week.

When access keys are used, a map simply uses the equals operation implemented by the key to find the correct match. So in the example shown in Figure 11.1, in which the day of the week and the zone define the picker to use, an access key containing (via keyables) the day of the week and the zone would be used. Building the key for a particular day of the week and zone and then adding the picker to the map using that key would populate the map. Then when the picker is needed, we can build a retrieval key for the business information of interest and use that key to retrieve the person from the map. We perform this retrieval simply by finding a key that equals the requested key. The AccessKey class implements the equals operation by comparing each of its contained keyables against the keyables of the passed-in AccessKey instance. Keys whose keyables all match are equal.

With specification keys, the equals operation is needed, but it is not sufficient. Equals is needed for maintaining the map—that is, building the groups of business information and using them as the key for an entry. For example, if we want to define a discount for customer George for products lettuce and celery, we want to build the specification key that contains this set of products and then use that key to enter the discount (e.g., 10 percent) into the map (see Figure 11.5).

When we want to work with that definition—that is, remove it or update it—we need to use the equals operation to find the particular entry. When we look up the discount, however, we will be looking for the discount for a particular customer (e.g., George) and a particular product (e.g., lettuce). We do

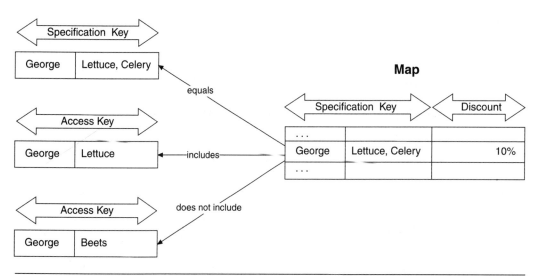

Figure 11.5. Specification Key Operations

this by creating an access key containing the particular values and then looking for the specification key that includes that business information. That is, when looking at each entry in the map, we retrieve its key, which is a specification key, and ask it if it includes the requested access key.

An access key is included whenever for each of its individual pieces of business information (represented by access keyables), the associated group of business information (represented by specification keyables) in the specification key includes the individual criteria. In our example (see Figure 11.5), the specification key containing George and lettuce and celery includes an access key containing George and lettuce (or celery), but not one containing George and beets.

The need to map from a specification key to associated information is common enough that a special map is defined. Called a *specification key map*, this map (see Figure 11.5) supports additional retrieval methods that take advantage of the fact that the key is known to be a specification key. In addition to the standard retrieval using a key (via equals), the specification key map supports the retrieval of information by use of an access key to get all entries associated with specification keys that include the access key. And it supports the retrieval of information by use of a specification key to get all entries associated with specification keys that are a subset (or superset) of the passed-in specification key. The specification key map can be used to implement the Keyed Attribute Retrieval pattern (see Chapter 14) and the Cached Aggregate pattern (see Chapter 13).

Combining

In order fulfillment, the products specified must be retrieved from the warehouse. We specify the products by creating pick lists that list the items to be picked and the locations from which they are to be picked. These lists are assigned to a person (picker) who goes to the warehouse and retrieves the requested items. Food Warehouse naturally wants to make this picking process as efficient as possible. For example, one of FW's objectives is to combine different order requests so that only one picker picks from a particular bin and so that the picker visits that bin only once on the pick list. However, many different criteria can be used for combining the items into individual pick lists. For example, products may be controlled by location, meaning that a product must be picked from a particular location in the warehouse. Let's take a look at FW's requirements in a bit more detail:

Case Study

Food Warehouse needs to be able to generate pick lists for each of its warehouses. The criteria for building those pick lists varies from warehouse to warehouse, but the basic algorithm is the same.

- Warehouse A is a simple warehouse in which all requests for the same product should be picked at the same time. The requests are equally divided among the pickers.

- Warehouse B is controlled by location, so all requests for the same product in the same zone can be combined. The zones are assigned to particular pickers and are used to divide the requests into pick lists.

To support these requirements, we need to define two pick list generation policies. These two policies are very similar. For warehouse A, each pick request can be used to build an access key containing simply the product. This key is then used to access a map of pick list details. If a map entry for the key does not yet exist, the policy will create a pick list detail associated with the request and add that detail (with its associated access key) to the map. If an entry is already in the map, the request is associated with the pick list detail already in the map. When all requests have been processed, the map contains the set of pick list details, which can then be divided into pick lists. Figure 11.6 shows how pick lists for three orders are generated for warehouse A.

Remember that in this case the access key contains only the product because that is the only sorting aspect applicable in warehouse A. Focusing on just the lettuce portion of the orders, the first item of order 1, lettuce, causes a key containing just lettuce to be created. Because we don't have an entry for lettuce already in the map, we will add this key and set its associated quantity

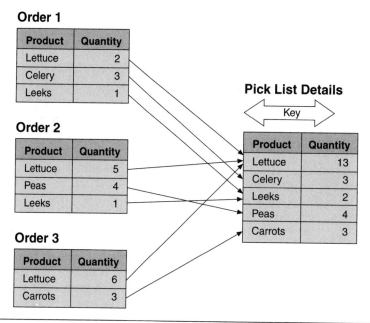

Figure 11.6. Generating the Pick List Details for Warehouse A

to 2. When order 2 is processed, its first item, lettuce, causes the same key to be created. Since we will find a duplicate key in the map, we can update its associated quantity to 7 (2 + 5). When the first item of order 3, also lettuce, is processed, it matches this entry's key, so the quantity is set to 13 (7 + 6).

For warehouse B, the pick list details can be created in the same manner. However, in this case the key created contains not just the product, but also the location. Figure 11.7 shows how the pick list details can be created for the data of the warehouse A example with location added. Again focusing on just the lettuce portion of the orders, the first item of order 1, lettuce, causes us to create a key containing lettuce and location A. Because this is the first entry, we will add it to the map and set its associated quantity to 2. When order 2 is processed, its first item, lettuce, causes a key containing lettuce and location B to be created. This key does not match the key previously created, so it is not in the map and thus has to be added with a quantity of 5. When the first item of order 3, also lettuce, is processed, its key is lettuce and location A, which matches the key for order 1. Thus, the quantity associated with this key in the map is updated to 8 (2 + 6).

Once the set of pick list details is generated, it has to be divided into pick lists. For warehouse A, our policy will generate pick lists simply by dividing the pick list details evenly among the pickers. For warehouse B, the location's associated zone defines the picker, and thus the pick list, with which each pick

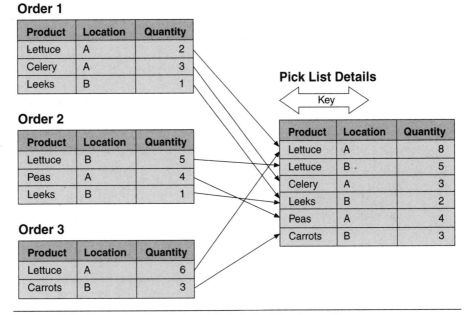

Figure 11.7. Generating the Pick List Details for Warehouse B

list detail should be associated. We can accomplish this association by creating a pick list for each picker, going through each pick list detail, and adding the details to the appropriate picker's pick list.

If these criteria were also likely to change, however, we could implement the pick list generation policy of warehouse B to use keys. For each picker the policy creates a specification key containing all the locations assigned to the picker. These keys are used as the key in a map (possibly a specification key map) to each picker's pick list. Then each pick list detail is used to create an access key containing the location. The specification key that includes this access key is then found in the pick list map, and the pick list detail is added to the associated pick list. If later Food Warehouse decides to add criteria when determining the picker to whom the pick list detail is to be assigned, only the access key and the specification key need be modified.

Filtering

Often the different aspects of a particular piece of information are used to filter it in a meaningful way. For example, Food Warehouse wants to be able to look at all sales of lettuce for all periods, for each customer. The company also wants to be able to look at sales of lettuce for all periods, regardless of customer. Eventually the decision makers in Food Warehouse may need to consider every permutation of these aspects. To accomplish this task, we can run queries for each possibility (probably with inadequate performance), or we can run an initial query and then filter the results in different ways to combine or separate different aspects for analysis.

Usually a particular set of aspects (criteria) defines a particular piece of information, much as running a query specifies the specific set of criteria for which information is desired. Thus, we can think of an access key as identifying a specific set of query criteria. Likewise, a group of criteria defines a particular group of information. A specification key, then, can be thought of as identifying a group of query criteria. In other words, it is as if each specific piece of information had an associated access key created for it, and then the specification key was used as a filter to determine if that access key was included in its group of criteria and thus if the information was part of the requested result.

This thinking allows us to write a generic algorithm for filtering information that uses keys to encapsulate the filter criteria. For each piece of information, we create the associated access key. If the access key is included in the specification key that identifies the request, we include it in the results; otherwise we exclude it. By associating a specification key with a map that maps from access keys to the information, we can have the specification key define which access keys can be in the map. In other words, the specification key filters the access keys applied against it.

Filters of the simplest form indicate that all values are acceptable or that certain criteria should be completely ignored. This concept is supported by specification keyable subclasses that specify all values are to be accepted (AllValuesKeyable) or all values are to be ignored (IgnoredKeyable). When AllValuesKeyable is specified, any specific criterion is acceptable. When IgnoredKeyable is specified, the particular criterion is not used in the filtering process.

Figure 11.8 shows an example of information filtering. The table on the left shows the raw sales records for produce from 1 January to 30 June. If we want to analyze lettuce sales, we can build a specification key that contains lettuce, AllValuesKeyable for period, and AllValuesKeyable for customer. In other words, we can look at who was buying lettuce when (summarized on the right-hand side of Figure 11.8). Note that as part of the filtering process the date has been transformed to the period (quarter in this case) because it is typical to look at sales on the basis of period.

Because our key contains the period, the information will be consolidated to some extent; that is, information for dates in the same period will be consolidated. Had we used the date in our example instead, the information would only have been filtered. The table on the right in Figure 11.8 shows the result of the filtering (and consolidation). The second-quarter (2Q) entry for Marinda, for example, consolidates the 10 May, 12 May, and 23 June records for lettuce.

Produce Sales Records

Date	Product	Customer	#
3 Jan	Beets	Alfred	3
12 Jan	Lettuce	Marinda	2
17 Jan	Lettuce	Lee	1
19 Jan	Lettuce	Sally	4
10 May	Lettuce	Marinda	10
11 May	Celery	Sally	2
12 May	Lettuce	Marinda	20
2 Jun	Lettuce	Sally	1
4 Jun	Lettuce	Sally	1
23 Jun	Lettuce	Marinda	2
23 Jun	Corn	Marinda	6
29 Jun	Lettuce	Sally	1
29 Jun	Lettuce	Lee	1

Specification Key: lettuce, *all, *all

Access Key

Product	Period	Customer	Amount
Lettuce	1Q	Marinda	2
Lettuce	2Q	Marinda	32
Lettuce	1Q	Sally	4
Lettuce	2Q	Sally	3
Lettuce	1Q	Lee	1
Lettuce	2Q	Lee	1

Figure 11.8. Filtering

However, the 23 June record for corn is omitted because it is not specified by our filter.

Once the information is filtered, we can use the resulting map to create similar maps for related specification keys by using the generic filtering algorithm we have described here, in which the input comes from the existing map. In particular, SpecificationKey has a method called isSubsetOf that determines if it is a subset of another specification key. Specification key A is a subset of specification key B if specification key A's groups of criteria are a subset of those in specification key B. For example, if specification key B has lettuce, celery, and leeks, then specification key A is a subset if it contains only lettuce and celery; however, it is not a subset if it contains lettuce and beets.

Any criterion is a subset of AllValuesKeyable because AllValuesKeyable includes everything. On the other hand, when IgnoredKeyable is specified, the particular criterion is not of interest. It is as if the criterion were not included in the associated query. Thus, no criterion is a subset of IgnoredKeyable. In other words, if we didn't take a particular criterion into account at some point earlier, we cannot take it into account now. For example, if we had said we didn't care about the customer and filtered the data such that we had the sales based on just lettuce and period, we would no longer have enough information to retrieve the data for a particular customer.

The process by which a new map is generated from an existing map for a new specification key is called *consolidation*. The algorithm for consolidation can be written to work just with keys, so it is independent of the particular criteria in the map. This independence is achieved by the introduction of a convert method on the specification key. The convert method takes an access key and transforms it for use with the specification key; that is, it modifies the access key so that it is compatible with the new map being built. If the convert method cannot convert the access key, the information is excluded. For example, if the new specification key contains only lettuce, any access keys that contain beets will be excluded.

The algorithm converts each access key by using the convert method on the specification key. The convert method returns a new access key, which is then used to do a lookup in the map associated with the specification key. If there isn't already an entry, the access key (along with its information) is entered in the map. If an entry is found, then the information is combined with (usually added to) the information already in the map.

Figure 11.9 shows an example of consolidation. In this example the map generated in Figure 11.8 is used as a starting point. This map shows the sales of lettuce for each customer for each period. Now we want to look at the overall sales of lettuce by customer, but disregarding period. To do so we create a specification key that contains lettuce, IgnoredKeyable for period, and AllValuesKeyable for customer. This is a subset of the existing map's specification key, since we want fewer criteria. All keyables are equal except the one for period, which changed from AllValuesKeyable to IgnoredKeyable.

The new specification key is then used to consolidate the information. For Marinda, the first entry's access key—"lettuce, 1Q, Marinda"—is passed to the

Specification Key: lettuce, *all, *all

Product	Period	Customer	Amount
Lettuce	1Q	Marinda	2
Lettuce	2Q	Marinda	32
Lettuce	1Q	Sally	4
Lettuce	2Q	Sally	3
Lettuce	1Q	Lee	1
Lettuce	2Q	Lee	1

Specification Key: lettuce, *ignore, *all

Product	Period	Customer	Amount
Lettuce	---	Marinda	34
Lettuce	---	Sally	7
Lettuce	---	Lee	2

Figure 11.9. Consolidation

convert method on the new specification key, which returns "lettuce, ---, Marinda" (where "---" indicates a criterion we wish to ignore). The converted key is not in the new map, so it is added with the value of 2. For the second entry, the access key "lettuce, 2Q, Marinda" is converted to "lettuce, ---, Marinda." This key matches the key of the previous entry added to the new map, so we add this entry's value (32) to the value of the entry already in the new map (2), thereby setting the entry's amount to 34.

Caching

Queries over large amounts of data can take a long time. When information is needed often and needed quickly, it makes sense to cache the information, rather than having to do a query to retrieve it each time. Each time lettuce is sold, for example, the cache of how much lettuce has been sold per customer is updated. Thus, we can immediately retrieve the current amount of lettuce sold per customer, rather than having to do a query over all sales orders. For more details on caching, see Chapter 13.

Applicability

Consider using the Key/Keyable pattern when any of the following criteria apply:

- The criteria used in an algorithm may change. The Key/Keyable pattern allows the criteria to change without affecting the algorithm. Such changes include the following:

  - Providing reusable algorithms, such as those provided by SanFrancisco for the Cached Aggregate pattern (see Chapter 13)

  - Mapping from a set of criteria to particular information

  - Consolidating information on the basis of a set of criteria

  - Filtering information on the basis of a set of criteria

- A set of criteria (access keys) must be managed. In the Key/Keyable pattern we can do this by using a specification key.

Structure

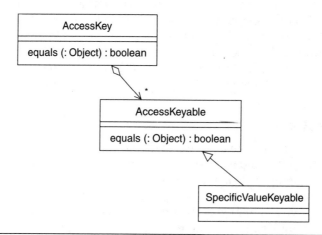

Figure 11.10. AccessKey Structure

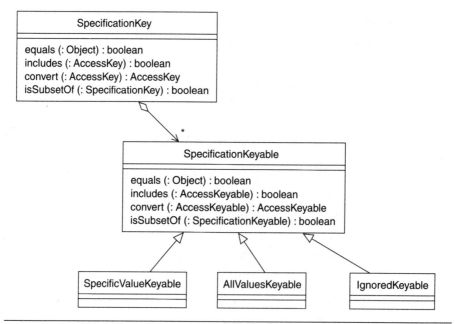

Figure 11.11. SpecificationKey Structure

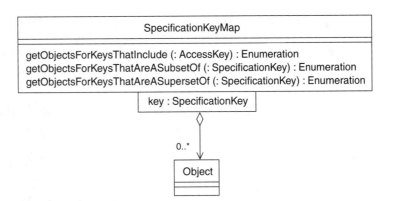

Figure 11.12. SpecificationKeyMap Structure

Participants

- **AccessKey.** A class that encapsulates a set of specific criteria by working with AccessKeyables, which encapsulate the criteria.

- **AccessKeyable.** A key element that encapsulates a specific criterion so that the containing AccessKey can work with it abstractly.

- **SpecificationKey.** A class that encapsulates a set of groups of criteria by working with SpecificationKeyables, which encapsulate the groups of criteria.

- **SpecificationKeyable.** A key element that encapsulates an individual group of criteria so that the containing SpecificationKey can work with it abstractly.

- **SpecificValueKeyable.** A key element that has a specific value of a particular criterion. SpecificValueKeyable is a subclass of both AccessKeyable and SpecificationKeyable. It is subclassed to provide support for particular criteria, such as lettuce (a particular product). Note that when it is used as an AccessKeyable, SpecificValueKeyable represents a particular value. When used as a SpecificationKeyable, it represents the specification of a particular value.

- **AllValuesKeyable.** A special SpecificationKeyable indicating that all criteria are acceptable.

- **IgnoredKeyable.** A special SpecificationKeyable indicating that the criterion in question should be ignored.

- **SpecificationKeyMap.** A special map ensuring that the key in the map is always a SpecificationKey. This class supports special operations related to methods supplied by the SpecificationKey, such as the following:

  - Finding all objects associated with SpecificationKeys that include a specified AccessKey

  - Finding all objects associated with SpecificationKeys that are a subset (or superset) of a specified SpecificationKey

Collaborations

- When comparing AccessKeys, the equals method delegates to each pair of AccessKeyables (the AccessKeyables that occupy the identical position in each AccessKey). These AccessKeyables (usually SpecificValueKeyables) know what they encapsulate and how to do the comparison. If any pair of AccessKeyables is not equal, then the AccessKeys are not equal. Thus, an AccessKey that contains the product lettuce (in a SpecificValueKeyable) will not equal an AccessKey that contains the product beets (in a SpecificValueKeyable) in the same position.

- In a fashion similar to that used to compare AccessKeys, when comparing SpecificationKeys the equals method delegates to each pair of SpecificationKeyables (the SpecificationKeyables that occupy the identical position in each SpecificationKey). These SpecificationKeyables know what they encapsulate and how to do the comparison. If any pair of SpecificationKeyables is not equal, then the SpecificationKeys are not equal. Thus, a SpecificationKey that contains the products lettuce and celery (in a SpecificationKeyable subclass) will not equal a SpecificationKey that contains the products lettuce, celery, and beets (in the same SpecificationKeyable subclass) in the same position.

- When determining if an AccessKey is included in a SpecificationKey, the method delegates to each SpecificationKeyable-AccessKeyable pair. The SpecificationKeyable knows how to work with its specification in such a manner that it can reduce the comparisons to comparisons between SpecificValueKeyables, which know what they encapsulate and how to do the comparison. If any AccessKeyable is not included in its corresponding SpecificationKeyable, the SpecificationKey does not include the entire AccessKey. Thus, the SpecificationKey with a SpecificationKeyable subclass that contains lettuce and celery will include the AccessKey that contains celery in an AccessKeyable.

- When comparing two SpecificationKeys, the isSubsetOf method delegates to each pair of SpecificationKeyables. The SpecificationKeyables understand how to compare the specification they represent, breaking it down to comparisons of SpecificValueKeyables as needed. For example, if the source SpecificationKey contains lettuce, celery, and leeks in one Specification-Keyable, the target SpecificationKey that contains a SpecificationKeyable with lettuce and leeks will be a subset of the source. In other words, the operation target.isSubsetof(source) will return true. If every element of each of the target's SpecificationKeyables is included in the source's corresponding SpecificationKeyables, the target SpecificationKey is a subset of the source SpecificationKey.

- The unique methods on the SpecificationKeyMap are applied to each SpecificationKey in the map and then use the result of that operation to determine if the associated Object should be included in the result. For example, when the getObjectsForSpecificationKeysThatInclude method is called, it iterates over the map, calling the includes method on the SpecificationKey that is the key for each element. When the includes method indicates that the passed-in AccessKey is included in the SpecificationKey, the Object associated with the SpecificationKey is added to the result.

Consequences

The Key/Keyable pattern has the following tradeoffs, benefits, and drawbacks:

Tradeoffs

- **Flexibility versus complexity.** Although use of the Key/Keyable pattern provides greater flexibility, the additional classes increase complexity.

Benefits

- **Isolation of the algorithm from the criteria.** Isolating the algorithm from the criteria not only allows the two to vary independently, but also helps clearly separate them.

Drawbacks

- **Decreased performance.** The Key/Keyable pattern is very powerful and can be used in many places. However, because a direct implementation of such criteria matching invariably performs better than the abstract key implementation, this pattern should be used only when there are clear requirements for the level of flexibility it provides.

Implementation

Consider the following implementation issues for the Key/Keyable pattern:

- **Keyable ordering.** AccessKeys and SpecificationKeys must act like an ordered collection of keyables. In most cases an actual collection, such as an array, will be used. When higher performance or less flexiblity is needed, specific implementations can be provided. For example, if a specification key is used only to indicate all values or is ignored and will always have five keyables, we could implement it by using five boolean attributes.

- **Coordination of interacting keys.** AccessKeys and SpecificationKeys that will be used together must be coordinated to ensure that the same family of criteria is in the same position. For example, an AccessKey with zone in the fourth position will be used with a SpecificationKey with a set of zones in the fourth position. We can encapsulate this coordination by providing classes specific for each usage. These classes provide methods related to use of the key; one such method is setProduct, which maps to the appropriate keyable position.

- **Providing reusable implementations.** The basic implementation for much of this pattern can be provided as reusable classes:

  - **AccessKey and SpecificationKey classes.** These classes can provide implementations of all the methods. The classes are subclassed for each specific use. This subclassing allows the exposure of usage-specific methods (e.g., setProduct) rather than the methods that directly manipulate the keyables, such as setKeyableAt. These subclasses provide type safety and a more domain-friendly interface.

  - **AccessKeyable and SpecificationKeyable abstract classes.** These classes can provide the basis for the ability of the keyables to work with each other at an abstract level. Without these abstractions, each keyable subclass would need to know how to work with every other keyable subclass.

  - **A SpecificValueKeyable class.** This class can provide implementations for all the methods except equals, which must be implemented by the specific subclasses.

  - **Various keyable subclasses.** SpecificValueKeyable subclasses can be provided for cases in which a certain type will be held. For example, since Object supports the equals method, an AnyObjectKeyable subclass could be provided. SpecificationKeyable subclasses for different kinds of specifications can be provided. For example, in addition to an AllValuesKeyable subclass and an IgnoredKeyable subclass, subclasses that support sets or ranges can be provided.

SanFrancisco, for instance, provides a DynamicSetKeyable that contains a set of SpecificValueKeyables. When the includes method is implemented, a SpecificValueKeyable is included in the set if one of the elements in the DynamicSetKeyable matches the passed-in SpecificValueKeyable.

SanFrancisco also provides a RangeKeyable that contains a pair of OrderableKeyables. An OrderableKeyable adds the lessThan method to a SpecificValueKeyable—for example, the DateKeyable. Thus, when the includes method is implemented, an OrderableKeyable is included in a RangeKeyable if it is equal to the start or end or falls between the start and end.

– **A SpecificationKeyMap class.** As shown in the "Motivation" section of this chapter, complete implementations can be provided for methods to get the set of objects associated with the specification keys that include an access key or are a subset (or superset) of a specification key. In addition, methods that find the best match can be provided. The "best key" is defined as the key that contains the minimum possible criteria but still has all the criteria of the specified key. An example is a method that finds the object associated with the specification key that best includes a specified access key or one that finds the best subset (or superset).

These "best" methods are used to minimize the amount of data being consolidated—an important function in determining which cached data to use to fulfill a request. For example, given a specification key with lettuce, beets, and celery and another with lettuce and carrots, a request with a key containing just lettuce would best match the specification key that contains lettuce and carrots. A request with beets, however, would best match the key that contains lettuce, beets, and celery.

• **Handling filtered-out data.** If needed, the concept of completeness can be added to SpecificationKeys. This concept determines what happens to filtered information that is outside of the filter criteria. If a SpecificationKey is complete, all AccessKeys can be converted. Any AccessKeyable that is not within the associated SpecificationKeyable criteria is replaced with a NotInSpecificationKeyable. If a SpecificationKey is incomplete, some AccessKeys may not be converted and will be excluded from the map.

• **Defining keyables.** The choice of which and how many keyables to include in the key can be crucial. If you add a new keyable to a key or you change the type of one of the keyables, you will have to recreate all the keys. This is not a big deal when the keys are generated each time, as in a process such as consolidation; when the keys are persisted as part of the cached product balances, however, this kind of change requires the deletion and recalculation of all the balances so that they are associated with the new key.

The ability to use a specification key to indicate that a keyable is ignored allows us to include criteria and then ignore them. That is, we can add the criteria we think we will need and then ignore or include them as needed. When the keys are persisted, it is easier to have the criteria and ignore them than to recreate all of the keys to add the criteria later.

Sample Code

In this section we show three specific code samples for managing information: mapping, combining, and filtering. The caching sample is shown as part of the Cached Aggregate pattern in Chapter 13. Before beginning the specific samples, let's look at a few general implementation samples.

General Implementation

Each key (AccessKey and SpecificationKey) delegates its operations to its keyables (AccessKeyables and SpecificationKeyables, respectively). The following code shows a sample implementation of the equals method on AccessKey.

```
public boolean equals(AccessKey otherKey){

    // Ensure that keys have same number of keyables
    if (ivNumKeyables != otherKey.ivNumKeyables) return false;

    // Check each keyable against the corresponding keyable
    // in the other key
    for (int i=0; i<ivNumKeyables; i++) {

        // If a keyable and its corresponding keyable are not equal,
        // then the keys are not equal
        if (!getKeyableAt(i).equals(otherKey.getKeyableAt(i)))
            return false;
    }

    // If all keyables are equal, then the two keys are equal
    return true;
}
```

The code for the other methods on the keys would be similar. For example, the equals method on the SpecificationKey would be identical, except that a SpecificationKey would be passed and the keyables would be SpecificationKeyables.

The AccessKey and SpecificationKey base classes can provide a default implementation that uses an array to hold on to the keyables. Each base class can provide a constructor that takes the number of keyables and creates the array. For example, the AccessKey constructor could be as follows:

```
public AccessKey(int numKeyables){

  ivNumKeyables = numKeyables;
  ivKeyables = new AccessKeyable[numKeyables];
  // Do not populate the array, since we don't know
  // what is needed. The subclass knows.

}
```

Subclasses of AccessKeyable must implement an equals method that takes a keyable (as an Object) and checks for equality between the keyables. The following sample is the ZoneKeyable subclass of AccessKeyable. Note that this example does not include considerations for interoperability with other keyables. Trying to compare two different AccessKeyable subclasses will result in a class cast exception. Throwing the exception may or may not be acceptable, depending on the particular use of the pattern.

```
class ZoneKeyable extends SpecificValueKeyable {

  private Zone ivValue;

  public void setZone(Zone newZone){
    ivValue = newZone;
  }

  public Zone getZone(){
    return ivValue;
  }

  public boolean equals(Object otherKeyable){
    // Get the Zone from the passed-in keyable and check equality
    if (((ZoneKeyable)otherKeyable).getZone().equals(ivValue))
        return true;
    else return false;
  }

  public ZoneKeyable(Zone initZone){
    ivValue = initZone;
  }
}
```

Other subclasses of AccessKeyable would look similar. If certain types of objects are used heavily, a generic AccessKeyable subclass can be created. For example, SanFrancisco has an abstract base class called Entity that provides persistence capabilities. It provides an equals method, so an AnyEntityKeyable can be provided that can be used to hold any Entity.

Mapping

The example in Figure 11.1 showed mapping from an AccessKey containing the day of the week and the zone to a particular picker. This mapping requires the creation of a subclass of AccessKey and two subclasses of AccessKeyable. Figure 11.13 shows these subclasses.

PickThePickerKey is the subclass of AccessKey. It adds usage-specific methods for working with the information it contains—in this case zone and day of the week. This information is held as AccessKeyables via the contained collection in the AccessKey. The particular AccessKeyables are the subclasses ZoneKeyable and DayOfTheWeekKeyable.

When an instance of PickThePickerKey is created, it will contain a ZoneKeyable and a DayOfTheWeekKeyable, which reference the appropriate Zone and DayOfTheWeek, respectively (see Figure 11.14). The methods on PickThePickerKey for working with Zone and DayOfTheWeek work with their respective keyables. For example, the setZone and getZone methods work with a ZoneKeyable:

```
public Zone getZone(){

  // The ZoneKeyable is in position 2
  return ((ZoneKeyable)getKeyableAt(2)).getZone();
}

public void setZone(Zone newZone){

  // The ZoneKeyable is in position 2
  ZoneKeyable keyableToUpdate = (ZoneKeyable)getKeyableAt(2);
  keyableToUpdate.setZone(newZone);
}
```

The PickThePickerKey create method will use the current date to set the DayOfTheWeek, so only the Zone is passed on creation:

```
public PickThePickerKey(Zone initZone){

  // Call parent to create the array, passing the number of keyables
  super(2);

  // Create the keyables
  setKeyableAt(1, new DayOfTheWeekKeyable());
  setKeyableAt(2, new ZoneKeyable(initZone));
}
```

Now we can use this key to work with a Hashtable. We can create instances of the key and use it to add items to the Hashtable or to look them up. If we assume that the variable pickerTable is the Hashtable we have been using, then

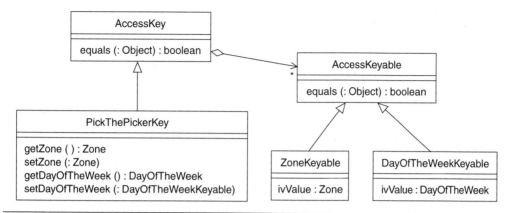

Figure 11.13. Picking the Picker

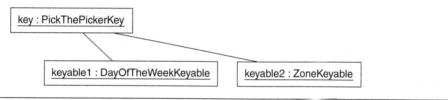

Figure 11.14. Picking the Picker Key

the following code can be used to look up which picker should be used for today's day of the week for zone A.

```
// Create a key to get today's picker for zone A
Zone theZone = new Zone('A');

AccessKey keyToUse = new PickThePickerKey(theZone);
// Day of the week defaulted to today's day of the week

Person thePicker = (Person)pickerTable.get(keyToUse);
```

In the example given in this chapter, we then wanted to add another piece of business information to the key, the month (see Figure 11.2). We can subclass PickThePickerKey to add the new information. A new subclass of AccessKeyable is needed to handle the month. Figure 11.15 shows the new class diagram.

The new subclass of PickThePickerKey, PickThePickerKey2, adds methods for working with the month. These methods work with the AccessKeyable subclass MonthKeyable. Thus, as Figure 11.16 shows, when a PickThePickerKey2 is created it will contain an instance each of DayOfTheWeekKeyable, ZoneKeyable, and MonthKeyable.

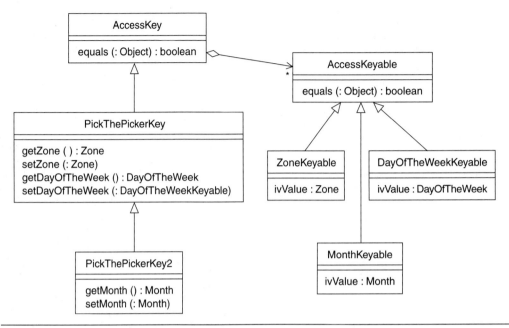

Figure 11.15. Extending Picking the Picker

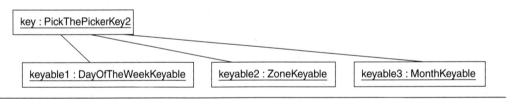

Figure 11.16. Extending Picking the Picker Key

The create method on PickThePickerKey2, just as on PickThePickerKey, takes the zone; the day of the week and month are retrieved from today's date:

```
public PickThePickerKey2( Zone initZone ){

    // Call parent to create the array, passing the number of keyables
    super(3);
    // Create the keyables
    setKeyableAt(1, new DayOfTheWeekKeyable());
    setKeyableAt(2, new ZoneKeyable(initZone));
    setKeyableAt(3, new MonthKeyable());
}
```

Now the key can be used to work with the Hashtable. If we want to look up the picker to use for zone A for today's day of the week and month, we use the following code:

```
// Create a key to get today's picker for zone A
Zone theZone = new Zone('A');

AccessKey keyToUse = new PickThePickerKey2(theZone);
// Day of the week defaulted to today's day of the week,
// and month defaulted to today's month

Person thePicker = (Person)pickerTable.get(keyToUse);
```

Except for the key that is created, this code is identical to the retrieval code from the first example. Manipulation of the map did not change. Creation of the key did change, although the change is not visible here because defaults could be used. However, the code that is used to populate the map (e.g., the screens that interact with the users) needs to change to allow working with this new item. This code would have changed anyway when the new item was added. What is gained is that the code working abstractly with the key does not have to change.

Combining

The examples in Figures 11.6 and 11.7 show the generation of pick list details from similar data for two warehouses, A and B, with differing requirements. These different requirements boil down to different criteria to be used when the order details of an order are combined into the pick list details. For warehouse A, all order details for the same product can be combined. This means that we need an AccessKey subclass that contains one keyable for the product. Figure

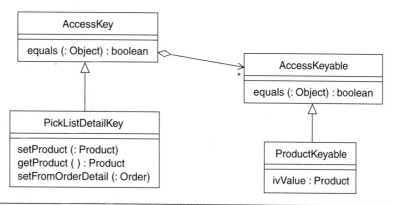

Figure 11.17. Combining Pick List Details

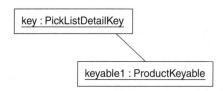

Figure 11.18. Key for Combining Pick List Details

11.17 shows these new classes. PickListDetailKey is the new AccessKey subclass, which uses the new ProductKeyable subclass of AccessKeyable.

Figure 11.18 shows a PickListDetailKey instance. It consists of a single Product-Keyable.

The one unique method is the setFromOrderDetail method on the PickListDetailKey. This method allows a PickListDetailKey to be reused for each OrderDetail by allowing the keyables in the key to be set by the information in the OrderDetail.

```
public void setFromOrderDetail( OrderDetail newOrderDetail ){

  setProduct( newOrderDetail.getProduct() );
}
```

The following algorithm uses the passed-in PickListKey to generate the pick list details for the passed array of orders. If we populate the order array as shown in Figure 11.6 and create a PickListDetailKey as already defined, the returned Hashtable will contain the pick list details shown in Figure 11.6:

```
public static Hashtable buildPickListDetailTable(
                        Order[] orders,
                        int numOrders,
                        PickListDetailKey pickListKey) {

// Create the Hashtable to populate
Hashtable pickListDetails = new Hashtable();

// Go through each order
for (int i = 0; i < numOrders; i++) {

  int numDetails = orders[ i ].getNumberOfOrderDetails();

  // Go through each order detail
  for (int j = 0; j < numDetails; j++) {

    // Set the values in the key for this order detail
    OrderDetail theOrderDetail = orders[i].getOrderDetail(j);
    pickListKey.setFromOrderDetail(theOrderDetail);
```

```
      // Use key to retrieve from Hashtable
      PickListDetail thePickListDetail =
                (PickListDetail)pickListDetails.get(pickListKey);

      // If found, then combine order detail into existing detail
      if (thePickListDetail != null)
                thePickListDetail.addOrderDetail(theOrderDetail);
      else {
        // If not found, then create a new detail and add to Hashtable
        thePickListDetail = new PickListDetail(theOrderDetail);
        pickListDetails.put(pickListKey, thePickListDetail);
      }
    }
  }
  return pickListDetails;
}
```

To support the needs of warehouse B, we must create a subclass of the
PickListDetailKey that adds the location and we must add a new AccessKeyable
subclass for location. Figure 11.19 shows the new PickListDetailKey2 using the
new LocationKeyable.

An instance of PickListDetailKey2 (see Figure 11.20) will consist of an instance each of ProductKeyable and LocationKeyable.

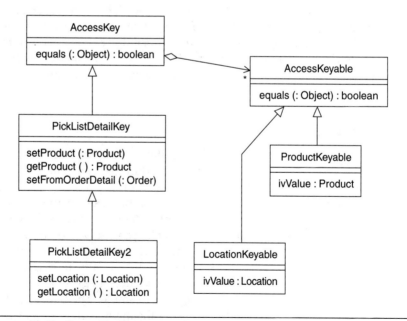

Figure 11.19. Extending Combining Pick List Details

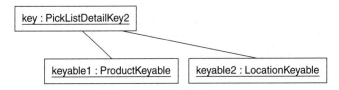

Figure 11.20. Extending the Key for Combining Pick List Details

To generate the pick list as shown in Figure 11.7, we simply have to create an instance of the new PickListDetailKey2 and pass it into the buildPickListDetailTable method shown in the preceding sample of code. How were we able to reuse the complete algorithm? The answer is the setFromOrderDetail method on the PickListDetailKey. This method is overridden by PickListDetailKey2 to set the additional keyable from the order detail:

```
public void setFromOrderDetail(OrderDetail newOrderDetail) {

    setProduct(newOrderDetail.getProduct());
    setLocation(newOrderDetail.getLocation());
}
```

At first this example may seem contrived; however, normally you are consolidating items on the basis of their attributes (or attributes of attributes—such as attributes on the order in the order detail case). Thus, by either providing a method to reset the key with the item or constructing the key from the item, a subclass that uses more (or different) criteria can be substituted without the algorithm being affected.

Filtering

The example in Figure 11.9 involves filtering (and combining) information from one map into another map. The key used in the map contains the product, period, and customer. Figure 11.21 shows the class diagram for this class, ProductFilterAccessKey, as well as the keyables used by the key. Note that these keyables subclass SpecificValueKeyable rather than AccessKeyable, as in earlier examples. The reason is that these keyables can also be used in a SpecificationKey as SpecificationKeyables; that is, they can be used to specify a particular product, period, or customer, such as lettuce, 1Q, or Sally, respectively.

This does not mean that the subclasses need to provide any more code than was shown in the earlier ZoneKeyable example. The SpecificValueKeyable is able to use the equals method to fulfill the methods required by implementing SpecificationKeyable. Figure 11.22 shows the SpecificValueKeyable relationship to AccessKeyable and SpecificationKeyable.

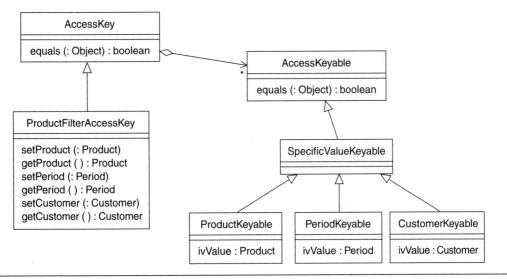

Figure 11.21. ProductFilterAccessKey and Its Keyables

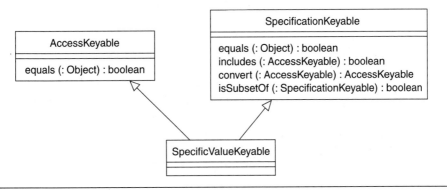

Figure 11.22. SpecificValueKeyable

The code provided by SpecificValueKeyable is as follows:

```
public class SpecificValueKeyable
                    implements SpecificationKeyable, AccessKeyable {

    public boolean includes(AccessKeyable theAccessKeyable) {
        return equals((SpecificValueKeyable)theAccessKeyable);
    }

    public AccessKeyable convert(AccessKeyable keyableToConvert) {
        if (equals((SpecificValueKeyable)keyableToConvert))
                                        return keyableToConvert;
```

```
      return null;
    }

  public boolean isSubsetOf(SpecificationKeyable otherKeyable){
    return equals((SpecificValueKeyable)otherKeyable);
  }
}
```

The equals signature from both the AccessKeyable and the SpecificationKeyable is the standard equals signature. The SpecificValueKeyable cannot provide a generic implementation of equals, so it is not provided here; instead it must be supplied by the SpecificValueKeyable subclasses. Support for the includes method maps to equals because a specific value, such as lettuce, can include only the same specific value. For example, lettuce includes lettuce but does not include beets.

Support for the convert method also uses equals. If the keyables are equal, then the conversion returns the specific value; if they are not equal, null is returned to indicate that the keyable cannot be converted. For example, a lettuce keyable can convert only lettuce and not beets. Finally, isSubsetOf is also supported by equals. Since these values are specific, the only subset that makes sense is the degenerative case of equals. (Note that the empty set cannot be represented as a specific value.)

To do the filtering, a SpecificationKey is needed. This new key is a subset of SpecificationKey and adds methods for working with the criteria. Figure 11.23 shows the new class, ProductFilterSpecificationKey.

Note that a different family of methods is provided for each item in the key. These methods depend on the specifications that are allowed. In this case, the ProductFilterSpecificationKey supports setting a specific product, ignoring the products, or including all products. If a set of products was supported, methods for working with the set (such as adding and removing) would need to be provided. The methods supporting Product could be implemented in the following way:

```
public void ignoreProducts() {
  setKeyableAt(1, new IgnoredKeyable());
}

public void allProducts() {
    setKeyableAt(1, new AllValuesKeyable());
}

public void setProduct(Product newProduct) {
  // Don't know what kind of keyable may already be present
  // in keyable position 1, so have to replace it instead of trying
  // to reuse it
  setKeyableAt(1, new ProductKeyable( newProduct));
}
```

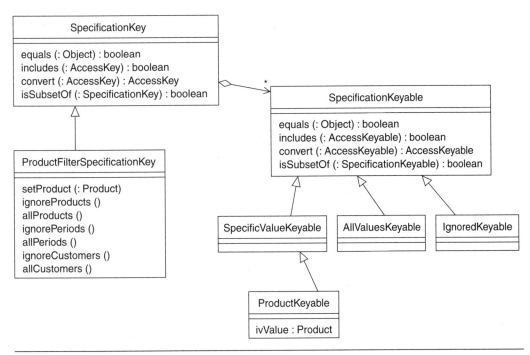

Figure 11.23. ProductFilterSpecificationKey

Note that the setProduct method could not simply get the keyable and set the product as was done in the AccessKeys. The reason is that the keyable in that position may be IgnoredKeyable, AllValuesKeyable, or ProductKeyable. (The method could check for the ProductKeyable case and simply set it in that case, but this capability depends on how the pattern is applied.)

It is crucial that the specification key and access key are coordinated so that they can work together. The keyables for the same criterion must be in the same position. That is, the keyable for product in the SpecificationKey must be in the same position as the keyable for product in the AccessKey. This is one reason that the subclasses of the keys for specific uses are recommended. As the code samples in this section show, this recommendation puts the burden of ensuring that the correct item goes in the correct position on the developer of the keys, rather than on the user of the keys.

In the example in Figure 11.9, the existing map is associated with a ProductFilterSpecificationKey that contains a ProductKeyable in position 1 that contains lettuce, an AllValuesKeyable in position 2, and an AllValuesKeyable in position 3. We create the new ProductFilterSpecificationKey by simply copying this key and calling the ignorePeriods method, which replaces the AllValuesKeyable in position 2 with an IgnoredKeyable.

With the new specification key in a variable called specificationKey2, we can then filter the Hashtable summaryInformation to generate the new Hashtable, result.

```
// Create the result Hashtable
Hashtable result = new Hashtable();

// Loop through the existing Hashtable
for (Enumeration keyEnum = summaryInformation.keys();
                                    keyEnum.hasMoreElements();) {

    // Get the original AccessKey
    AccessKey originalKey = (AccessKey)keyEnum.nextElement();

    // Convert the AccessKey for use with the new SpecificationKey
    AccessKey newKey = specificationKey2.convert(originalKey);

    if (newKey != null) {
      // If it could be converted, retrieve the existing information
      SalesSummary existingSummary =
         (SalesSummary)summaryInformation.get(originalKey);

      // Get information for key from current results
      SalesSummary summary = (SalesSummary)result.get(newKey);

      // If not already in result, then add it to the results
      if (summary == null)
         result.put(newKey, new SalesSummary(existingSummary));
      // Otherwise add to the entry already there
      else summary.addSalesSummary(existingSummary);
   }
}
```

Note that this code never needs to know the actual type of AccessKey or SpecificationKey being used. It is able to work with them completely abstractly; thus, this algorithm can be used for any AccessKey and SpecificationKey that work together.

Known Uses

SanFrancisco uses the Key/Keyable pattern extensively:

- In implementation of the Cached Aggregate pattern (see Chapter 13) in business partner balances (as part of the Common Business Objects), product balances (as part of the Warehouse Management Core Business Process), and account balances (as part of the General Ledger Core Business Process).

- In implementation of the Keyed Attribute Retrieval pattern (see Chapter 14) in prices and discounts (as part of the Order Management Core Business

Process) and lead times and transport times (as part of the Warehouse Management Core Business Process).

- For consolidation of journal entries (i.e., dissections) in the general ledger (as part of the General Ledger Core Business Process).

Related Patterns

- **Cached Aggregate.** The Key/Keyable pattern is used to implement the Cached Aggregate pattern (see Chapter 13).
- **Keyed Attribute Retrieval.** The Key/Keyable pattern is used to implement the Keyed Attribute Retrieval pattern (see Chapter 14).

12

Generic Interface

Intent

Provide an enforceable object-oriented way of working with another subsystem without coupling this use with the particular implementation of that subsystem.

Motivation

Most businesses (with the possible exception of Internet companies) plan to make a profit. The ability to make money requires knowing where your money is going. Thus, anything you do that affects the financial status of your company must be reflected in the general ledger. The general ledger provides the central point for combining all of the company's financial information and doing high-level analysis.

Most subsystems of a business application, such as the warehouse management subsystem, must be able to update the financial status in the general ledger. For example, when goods are sold, the cost of the product sold, the amount of the sale, and (for an order paid by credit) how much the customer owes must be reflected in the general ledger. If a subsystem is allowed to enter this information directly into the general ledger, it may be aware of the internal workings of the general ledger. With such an arrangement, whenever the general ledger changes, all subsystems dependent on it are affected.

Consider the following situation:

Food Warehouse records all changes of financial status in its general ledger. Other subsystems never need to retrieve the financial status from the general ledger. (In other words, from the outside the general ledger appears to be a write-only subsystem.) FW has an existing general ledger application that it does not want to replace at this time, and when it does replace the existing general ledger, it does not want the warehouse management subsystem (or any other subsystems of the application) to be affected.

In this case the Facade pattern of *Design Patterns* could be used to isolate the external subsystems from the general ledger. The Journal in the general ledger provides a JournalFacade that, as Figure 12.1 shows, can be used to enter information in the general ledger.

This approach works well when the user is disciplined. However, when a particular function or piece of information is not provided by the facade, programmers are often tempted to ignore the facade and go directly to the class (or classes) hidden by the facade. For example, if the JournalFacade did not allow setting of the date attribute on the Journal, then, as Figure 12.1 shows, many developers would use the setDate method provided on the Journal itself. In addition, when an existing general ledger is being used, the facade may be more like an adapter, mapping from an object-oriented design to a procedural design. In these cases, going past the JournalFacade means you are directly using support in the existing (soon to be replaced) system.

To gain the benefits of a facade without tempting the user to bypass it, we combine the Facade pattern of *Design Patterns*, the Class Replacement pattern (see Chapter 3), and a specific partitioning into packages into the Generic Interface pattern. The Facade pattern is used to define a facade called GenericBusinessObject. GenericBusinessObject exposes the methods that are available to other subsystems. The target class, called ActualBusinessObject, either directly implements the support targeted by the facade or acts as an adapter and indirectly implements the support via other classes or an existing system.

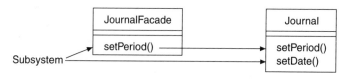

Figure 12.1. Using a Facade to Work with a General Ledger Journal

As we have seen, this alone is not enough; the addition of the Class Replacement pattern makes the GenericBusinessObject independent of the ActualBusinessObject. That is, the GenericBusinessObject does not need to know anything about the ActualBusinessObject. Thus, the GenericBusinessObject can be partitioned into one package and the ActualBusinessObject into another.

Why does this partitioning help? In the Facade pattern, the facade is supplied either in the same package as the target or in a package dependent on the target's package. In either case, because of the need to see the facade, the user also can see the actual object(s). In the Generic Interface pattern, the GenericBusinessObject is also provided in a package that is visible to all subsystems that will be using it. Because it is not directly dependent on the ActualBusinessObject, however, the ActualBusinessObject's package does not need to be exposed (or even available) for the subsystems to use the GenericBusinessObject.

Figure 12.2 shows the relationships between the packages. The Generic Interface to the General Ledger package provides the facade (GenericJournal) that is used by the Warehouse Management package. The support targeted by the facades (ActualJournal) is provided as part of the General Ledger package. Thus, from the perspective of the user of the generic interface (ClassInWarehousePackage in this case), only the GenericJournal is visible, as Figure 12.3 shows.

Figure 12.4 shows the perspective of the target (ActualJournal) that inherits from the GenericJournal and implements its methods. In this case the ActualJournal is providing the support, so the setGenericPeriod method of GenericJournal can be mapped to the setPeriod method of ActualJournal.

Why is the method on the GenericJournal called setGenericPeriod when the method on the ActualJournal is called setPeriod? Why not use the same

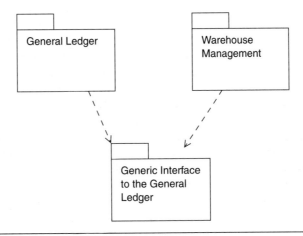

Figure 12.2. Package Partitioning

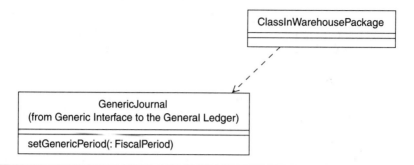

Figure 12.3. The Generic Interface from the User's Perspective

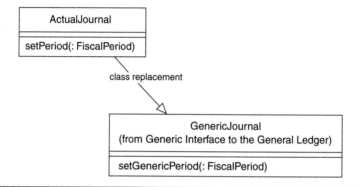

Figure 12.4. The Generic Interface from the Target's Perspective

method name? The main reason is that the contract (what the method requires and what it promises) for the method on the GenericBusinessObject usually differs from the contract for the method on the ActualBusinessObject. For example, the return values and parameters for the GenericBusinessObject's methods may be other GenericBusinessObjects. In addition, exceptions that are thrown by a method on the ActualBusinessObject may be unique to its package; thus, they have to be converted into exceptions supported in the GenericBusinessObject's package. Finally, using unique names makes it easy to identify which methods are introduced as part of the GenericBusinessObject, thereby ensuring that other classes in the ActualBusinessObject's package are using not the methods supporting the facade, but the actual methods directly.

Let's revisit the Food Warehouse example. FW needs to tie its new order management system into an existing general ledger system. It can do this by replacing GenericJournal with an ExistingJournal subclass that understands how to use the application program interfaces provided by its current system. When

FW brings in a new general ledger system during the next phase of its application modernization plan, it will change the class replacement configuration of its order management system to replace GenericJournal with ActualJournal (the live Journal object provided by the new system). The ExistingJournal class is now obsolete and can be removed from FW's system installation if desired.

In most cases the Generic Interface described here is sufficient; however, a few situations have additional requirements. FW, for instance, needs only to write to the general ledger, so a write-only generic interface is provided. If the subsystem using the general ledger's generic interface was accounts receivable rather than warehouse management, the interface would also need to support get methods, so it would be a read-write generic interface. For example, a payment received by accounts receivable must be reflected on the same account to which the bill was originally posted in the general ledger. Accounts receivable thus holds on to the Journal it originally used and retrieves the account from it.

The ability to retrieve information from the interface also means that in some cases a GenericBusinessObject will be returned from a method. In such instances the returned object is not being created, but is only being used as the GenericBusinessObject. Thus, the ActualBusinessObject simply needs to inherit from the GenericBusinessObject so that it can be cast to the GenericBusinessObject and returned from the interface; it does not need to replace the GenericBusinessObject.

Applicability

Consider using the Generic Interface pattern when any of the following criteria apply:

- Independence between two subsystems is needed or desirable. The Generic Interface pattern allows an existing system to be gradually upgraded or replaced without impact on dependent subsystems. It also allows compile-time enforcement of subsystem independence.

- Simplification of the interface to the subsystem is desirable. The Generic Interface pattern exposes only the portion of the interface that is needed outside of the subsystem, and thus it minimizes dependencies on the target subsystem.

Structure

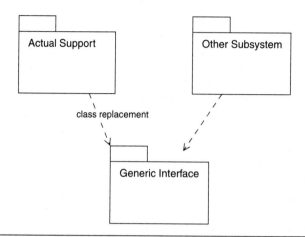

Figure 12.5. Generic Interface Package Structure

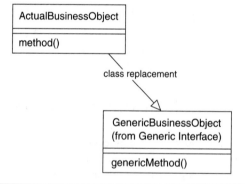

Figure 12.6. Generic Interface Class Structure

Participants

- **Actual Support package** (General Ledger package). A package that contains the ActualBusinessObjects that directly or indirectly support the GenericBusinessObjects. The use of the Class Replacement pattern means that this package, although it supports the Generic Interface package, does not need to be exposed when the Generic Interface package is used.

- **Generic Interface package** (Generic Interface to the General Ledger package). A package that contains the GenericBusinessObject facades that other subsystems should use to enter information in the Actual Support package.

- **Other Subsystem package** (Warehouse Management package). A package that represents the users of the Generic Interface package. This package cannot see or use classes in the Actual Support package.

- **GenericBusinessObject** (GenericJournal). One of potentially many classes that make up the facade that the other subsystems will use. The GenericBusinessObject is available in a package common to all subsystems that use it. It does not directly depend on the Actual Support package or the target subsystem.

- **ActualBusinessObject** (ActualJournal, ExistingJournal). The class that provides support for the GenericBusinessObject. It may be implemented to use the application program interfaces of an existing system, or it may be the actual class in the target subsystem.

Collaborations

- When a class in the Other Subsystem package needs to use the Actual Support package, it will work with the GenericBusinessObjects in the Generic Interface package.

- A GenericBusinessObject will be class-replaced (by the ActualBusinessObject in the Actual Support package) to provide support for setting and possibly getting the information in the target subsystem.

Consequences

The Generic Interface pattern has the following tradeoffs, benefits, and drawbacks:

Tradeoffs

- **Complexity versus independence.** Adding generic interfaces increases complexity.

- **Functionality versus coupling.** As more interface is exposed, more function is provided by the generic interface; however, it also exposes more of the underlying support. This exposure increases the coupling between the dependent subsystem and the target subsystem, which increases the complexity of providing an alternative subsystem. On the other hand, exposing too little function will create an unusable generic interface. This tradeoff includes making decisions on issues such as whether the GenericBusinessObjects are persistent and whether the interface is read-only or read-write.

Benefits

- **Object-oriented interface.** The Generic Interface pattern provides an object-oriented interface to a subsystem, rather than the typical set of application program interfaces.

- **Enforcement of independence.** Because only the generic interfaces are available, there is no possibility of going past them and coding to the actual supporting system. This restriction ensures that the subsystems are independent of the actual supporting system and will not be affected if the supporting system changes.

- **Support of many target subsystems.** Any system that can fulfill the interface of the generic interface can be used. The generic interface can be replaced with adapters that adapt it to the supporting system.

- **Combination of target and facade.** When a system directly supports the generic interface, such as the ActualJournal described above, the facade objects and the objects of the supporting system are the same. This overlap eliminates the need to manage the facade objects separately. It also eliminates any performance overhead that otherwise would have been introduced by a separate facade object.

Drawbacks

- **Prevention of temporary bypassing of facade.** Only what is exposed on the generic interface is available. Thus, you cannot temporarily use a method on the ActualBusinessObject while waiting for it to be put on the GenericBusinessObject. In other words, you must wait for the updates.

Implementation

Consider the following implementation issues for the Generic Interface pattern:

- **Developing the interface iteratively.** If you have the time, consider developing the generic interface iteratively. Start as small as possible and grow it as you explore the different uses of the interface. If you take this approach, however, be prepared to add things to the interface rapidly as they are needed.

- **Deciding between read-only and read-write.** The support provided by the generic interface does not have to be limited to write-only, as described in the "Motivation" section of this chapter. Methods that return information can also be provided. Note that adding read-style methods to the interface increases the complexity needed in the ActualEntity class replacement provided by the target subsystem.

- **Deciding if a target subsystem must be present.** In some cases the generic interface does not have to have a supporting subsystem. For example, you may not require a general ledger application to be present (such as during development). In this case you want the generic interface to react as if it works, but really just to discard the information. What the generic interface does when no support is provided (i.e., it is not class-replaced) depends on the particular requirements. In this case the GenericBusinessObject is implemented rather than just being an interface.

- **Isolating the generic classes from the actual classes.** To isolate generic classes from actual classes, you can add an intermediate adapter class. This adapter class introduces the methods of the actual class as abstract methods and implements the methods of the generic class that use them. Thus, the actual class does not have to be concerned (or cluttered) with the details of supporting the generic class.

  Figure 12.7 shows an example of using a JournalAdapter class between the GenericJournal and the ActualJournal. This intermediate adapter class introduces abstract methods for the methods on the ActualJournal that map to the generic methods. In the example, JournalAdapter implements the setGenericPeriod method (inherited from the GenericJournal) by delegating to the abstract setPeriod method it introduces. The ActualJournal provides the implementation for the abstract methods and does not have to do anything with the generic methods. Thus, use of the adapter isolates the generic class from the actual class. An example of the benefit of this isolation is that generic facade classes throw exceptions that differ from those thrown by the actual supporting classes. The adapter provides an

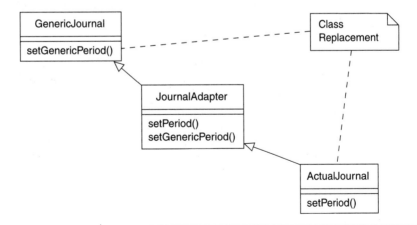

Figure 12.7. Using an Adapter

ideal place to catch the actual exceptions and transform them into the appropriate generic exceptions. Adapters can also transform parameters or return values from actual to generic interface items.

- **Generic Interface as a true facade.** A GenericBusinessObject may also act as a facade for more than one class in the target package. In this case the ActualBusinessObject acts more like an adapter from the GenericBusiness-Object to the supporting objects or to the existing (procedural) target.

Sample Code

Continuing with the example of the GenericJournal in the generic interface for the general ledger, the GenericJournal defines a method setFiscalPeriod:

```
public void setGenericFiscalPeriod(FiscalPeriod fiscalPeriod) {
    return;
}
```

This method is intended to be overridden via class replacement, so it could simply be an abstract method on the GenericJournal. In this case a default implementation is provided that does nothing. We might use such an implementation when we want the interface to appear to work when it has not been class-replaced.

Now let's look at the adapter implementation. Remember that an adapter isolates the generic classes from the actual classes.

```
public abstract FiscalPeriod setFiscalPeriod(FiscalPeriod);

public void setGenericFiscalPeriod(FiscalPeriod newPeriod) {
    setFiscalPeriod(newPeriod);
}
```

In this case the abstract method setFiscalPeriod (eventually to be implemented by the actual class) is defined. The generic method setGenericFiscalPeriod delegates to this abstract method. Note that as part of this delegation, we would normally catch exceptions from the ActualJournal and turn them into the appropriate generic exceptions. In addition, if the parameter or return value is another generic item in the interface, this method will transform it from generic to actual or actual to generic as appropriate. In this case, the FiscalPeriod is provided as part of the lower layer and does not require translation.

Finally, the ActualJournal implements the setFiscalPeriod method:

```
public void setFiscalPeriod(FiscalPeriod fiscalPeriod) {

    // Update the fiscal period
    ivFiscalPeriod = fiscalPeriod;
}
```

This is the actual method that sets the journal's fiscal period attribute to the passed-in fiscal period.

Known Uses

SanFrancisco uses the Generic Interface pattern to provide interfaces to the General Ledger Core Business Process (the primary example in this chapter) and the Accounts Payable/Accounts Receivable Core Business Process.

Related Patterns

- **Facade.** The Generic Interface pattern is a variation of the Facade pattern of *Design Patterns.*
- **Adapter.** The Adapter pattern of *Design Patterns* (in its class adapter form) can be used by the target subsystem when supporting the GenericBusiness-Object. It can also be used when the ActualBusinessObject acts as an adapter to multiple objects or an existing system.
- **Class Replacement.** The Class Replacement pattern (see Chapter 3) is used to allow the GenericBusinessObject classes in the generic interface to be replaced by the ActualBusinessObject.

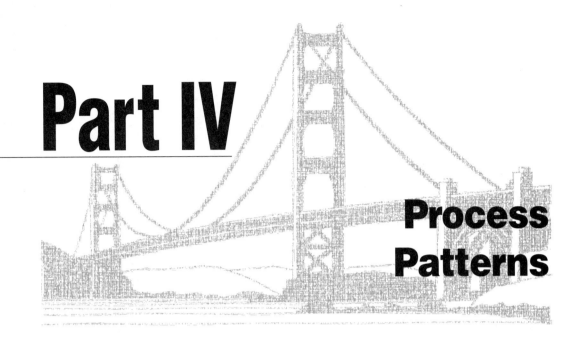

Part IV

Process Patterns

SanFrancisco's process patterns are concerned with how businesses organize and process information. The process patterns do not identify the information involved, but rather define *how* businesses work with that information. Process patterns can be applied in many business situations. The use of these patterns provides consistency for the same types of processes, allowing the user to grasp more quickly the mode of information processing and the flexibility provided as part of that processing.

The Cached Aggregate pattern (Chapter 13) provides a means of managing, maintaining, and retrieving cached information. This pattern is often needed when results that could be retrieved by a query need to be cached for fast access.

The Keyed Attribute Retrieval pattern (Chapter 14) is used when information must be defined and retrieved in a very flexible manner. This pattern offers flexibility in defining both the business attributes used to identify the retrieved information and the business policies used to prioritize how those attributes are used during retrieval.

The List Generation pattern (Chapter 15) describes how to generate and work with a list. This kind of processing is common when building lists of items to work with or to take action on. As each item on the list is processed, the processing is often reflected back on the items used to generate the list.

13

Cached Aggregate

Intent

Provide an encapsulated way of storing, updating, and retrieving the results of an aggregation, or a derivative of the aggregation, for a set of criteria, and do so in a manner that provides a configurable means of effectively maintaining and using a cache of aggregations that require fast access.

Motivation

When processing a customer's order on credit,[1] the last thing we want to have to say is, "Please hold while I see if you have enough credit." We could assume that the customer's credit is good, take the order, and then, after hanging up, check the customer's credit. Although this approach solves one problem, it creates another one: If we discover a credit problem, what do we do? Do we hold the order? What if the order we are holding is critical to the customer? What if part of the order is crucial and part is not? It would be much better if we could immediately see that a customer will exceed the credit limit and take care of it while the customer is on the phone—for example, by offering the customer a

---

1. This discussion is about credit extended by a company, not the use of credit cards. In the case of credit cards we would access the credit card company's approval process. Within their approval process, however, they would have issues similar to those described here.

193

cash on delivery (COD) order, seeing if the customer would like to hold one of his or her other orders, or modifying the order to remove the noncritical items until the amount of the order falls within the credit limit.

How do we check that a customer has not exceeded his or her credit limit? To check the credit limit, we first determine the current credit balance, then add the value of the new order and check this value against the credit limit assigned to this customer. If the total is greater than the credit limit, placing the order will put the customer over the credit limit.

How do we get the current credit balance? In the simplest case this balance is the value of all of the customer's orders on credit that have not yet been paid. To get this balance, we must go through all the customer's orders and total all the orders on credit. Then we must go through all the payments and total all those that were for an order on credit. Finally, we must combine these two values (credits minus payments) to get the balance. For an active customer, this process can mean having to add up a lot of things to get the final value.

Figure 13.1 shows an example of calculating the credit balance. In this case there are five orders and two payments. Four of the orders are orders on credit, and one is a COD order. The amount of credit is the total of the four orders on credit: 920. The total payments add up to 125. Thus, the customer's current credit balance is 795.

In most cases, going through all of the customer's orders and payments is too slow a process. How can we speed up these calculations so that we don't have to defer the credit check until after the phone call? The first possibility is

Orders

Number	Payment Method	Period	Amount
1	Credit	1	50
2	COD	1	200
3	Credit	1	75
4	Credit	2	95
5	Credit	2	700

920 on credit

Payments

Order Number	Period	Amount
1	1	50
3	1	75

125 in payments

920 − 125 = 795 in outstanding credit

Figure 13.1. Determining a Customer's Credit Balance

to delegate selection of the orders on credit and the credit payments to the database.[2] However, although this approach reduces the number of items we must handle, we still have to retrieve information from each of the selected items and perform a calculation. For a large number of orders, this modified process still won't be fast enough.

If we can't make the calculation faster, what can we do? The other option is to spread out the calculation. To do this, we calculate the starting amount for the customer's credit balance; then as new orders are taken their values are added, and as new payments are taken their values are subtracted. In this way the customer credit balance is always up-to-date. These calculations are not free, however. We are paying a little bit of overhead each time we do something that affects the balance. But when we need the balance, we can get it immediately. This technique is typically called *caching,* so the results are commonly referred to as *cached aggregates* or *cached balances.*

Let's look at Food Warehouse's specific situation:

Case Study

Food Warehouse needs to carefully manage the credit it extends to its customers. Two scenarios are possible: First, every time an order on credit is taken, part of accepting the order is ensuring that the customer has enough credit to cover the order. FW performs this check while the customer is waiting so that if the credit is exceeded, the customer can help determine what action should be taken. In the second scenario, just before shipping an order on credit to a customer, FW performs a credit check against a different balance and credit limit. In this case only the unpaid orders that have been shipped to the customer are included in the check. This check allows FW to manage the amount of credit that has been irrevocably committed to the customer. If this check fails, FW has several options. For example, one option is to repeat the check periodically, delaying shipment of the order until the check passes. In both scenarios FW allows the check to be overridden. In such cases a supervisor looks at other factors, such as the payment history of the customer, to determine if the customer should be allowed to exceed the credit limit.

In other words, Food Warehouse doesn't always need to retrieve customer credit balances quickly. In some cases, speed is not important. Why not just cache them all anyway? As we stated earlier, caching a balance is not free. It requires additional processing to maintain the cache, as well as additional storage. These

2. We may do this by using support in the infrastructure that transforms an object query into a database query or by executing a query directly against the database.

two factors have to be weighed against the increase in retrieval speed. That is, we must have a cache of the credit balances needed during order entry (while the customer is waiting), but for credit checking as part of shipping, we could calculate the credit balance from the raw objects (as a background job) each time we need it. This does not mean that our less urgent needs should always go to the raw objects. We should always try to fulfill requests from the cache and go to the raw objects only as a last resort.

Not only does FW need to be able to decide what to cache and what not to cache, it also needs to do this dynamically. Say, for example, that as FW processes orders on credit, it finds that in certain cases the supervisors are always approving exceptions to the customer's credit limit. Once FW recognizes this pattern, it wants to be able to update its automated credit-checking policy to add a check for this new case (only after the original check fails). However, this new check requires additional information that may not have been cached. Now that this new information is used during order taking, it must be retrieved quickly (and thus must be dynamically added to the cache).

Just as the less urgent requests we have mentioned should take advantage of the cache whenever possible, so also should ad hoc requests. For example, suppose that FW is concerned about the payment practices of one of its customers. A supervisor is assigned to look at the customer's payment history and decide if action needs to be taken, such as decreasing the amount of credit FW will extend to this customer.

Are these really all of FW's requirements? Yes and no. FW wants the behavior described here, but another unspoken requirement is the ability to ask for the credit balance without regard to how it is calculated (or where it comes from). That is, when FW wants a credit balance, it wants to have to go to only one place for it.

How do we fulfill these requirements? The first thing is to encapsulate the management and retrieval of balances in a central class. This class, CustomerBalanceManager, supports any request for a balance. Using this class requires no knowledge of the source of the balance. CustomerBalanceManager also supports the ability to identify which balances should be cached. Internally, the class consists of two pieces, as Figure 13.2 shows.

One piece encapsulates the cached balances. This class, CachedBalances, provides the ability to fulfill requests for balances, update balances, and manage which balances are cached. CustomerBalanceManager delegates all requests related to cached balances to the CachedBalances class. The other piece of CustomerBalanceManager encapsulates getting the balance from the raw objects. This object, called Query, does a query on the controllers[3] of the objects involved in calculating the balances (a function typically relegated to an underlying database). It uses the results of these queries to calculate the requested balances. In our example, Query works with the OrderController to get the orders on

---

3. For more information on controllers, see Chapter 10.

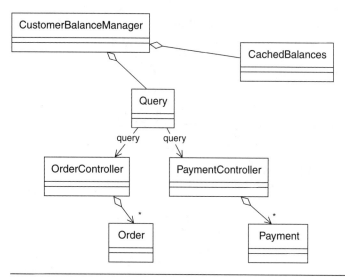

Figure 13.2. CustomerBalanceManager

credit for this customer and with the PaymentController to get the payments from this customer.

CustomerBalanceManager, as shown in Figure 13.3, fulfills a balance request by going first to the CachedBalances and, if it cannot fulfill the request, then to the Query. If the request is made to the Query, this object queries each of the controllers and uses the results to calculate the requested balance.

Now that we know where to go to get the balances, how do we identify which balance we want? We have a set of criteria over which we want to retrieve balances. For example, for Food Warehouse the criteria are as follows:

- The **customer,** so that we can look at just those items related to the customer. Usually this criterion is not explicitly part of the criteria. Instead each customer has his or her own CustomerBalanceManager, which manages only that customer's balances. For our example, we will assume this is the case.

- The **fiscal period,** so that we can look at customer history over time. In our example, we will assume that the fiscal periods are set up to match each month. Thus, fiscal period 1 represents 1 January through 31 January.

- A **sequence value** that defines the stage with which the balance is associated. In our example, these stages are as follows:

  - Order taken

  - Order shipped

  - Order paid

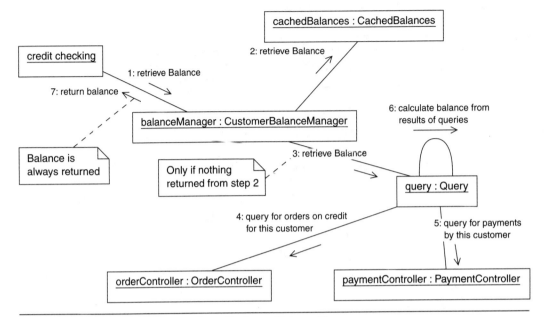

Figure 13.3. Retrieving Balances from CustomerBalanceManager

- A **payment method** that defines how the order has been or will be paid. In our example, these stages are as follows:
  - Cash
  - Cash on delivery
  - Credit

The sequence value allows us to get the balances for different stages of the order. Figure 13.4 shows how this value is used as the order is processed.

When an order is created, an entry is created that contains the sequence value "order taken." When the order is shipped, the entry is removed from

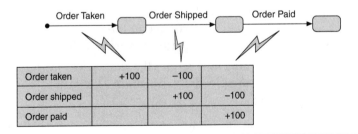

	Order Taken	Order Shipped	Order Paid
Order taken	+100	−100	
Order shipped		+100	−100
Order paid			+100

Figure 13.4. Sequence Values

"order taken" and added to "order shipped." Finally, when the order is paid, the entry is removed from "order shipped" and added to "order paid." In this way, the total of all entries associated with a sequence value represents the total value of all orders at that particular point of order processing. Thus, the total of all entries associated with the "order shipped" sequence value is the total of orders that have been shipped and have not been paid for; and the total of all entries associated with the "order taken" sequence value is the total of orders that have been taken but have not been shipped or paid for. The credit check done during order taking would use the sum of both of these totals ("order taken" and "order shipped"), and the check during shipment would use only the "order shipped" total.

Although these criteria are sufficient for our example, there will be more criteria. In fact, even if Wondrous Functions[4] thinks it has identified all the criteria needed by all of its customers, when it consults a particular customer, such as Food Warehouse, that customer will want something unique. For example, FW could be trying to become an organic food supplier and want to encourage customers that are supermarkets to purchase its organic food. To do this, FW wants to allow these customers separate organic food credit limits in addition to their current credit limits. Extending a customer's credit in this way requires the addition of an indicator to identify whether or not the order on credit is associated with organic food. In other words, adding this function means adding a new criterion.

To allow the criterion to be specified and still to be modified for a particular Wondrous Functions customer, CustomerBalanceManager is designed to use a CustomerBalanceAccessKey to retrieve a balance. The CustomerBalanceAccessKey is a usage-specific subclass of the AccessKey from the Key/Keyable pattern (see Chapter 11). This subclass allows the criteria to be encapsulated in a way that the CustomerBalanceManager can work independently of the actual criteria. In our example, the CustomerBalanceAccessKey contains a keyable for the period, a keyable for the sequence value, and a keyable for the payment method. Thus, as each order is processed, each stage is associated with a key.

Figure 13.5 shows the orders that were introduced in Figure 13.1 as they are being processed; each step is associated with the appropriate CustomerBalance-AccessKey. Order 1, an order on credit for period 1, has five entries associated with it: one entry when the order was taken, two entries when it was shipped (one subtracting it from the "order taken" sequence value), and two entries when it was paid (one substracting it from the "order shipped" sequence value).

Note that two orders on credit (orders 1 and 3) were taken in period 1. Order 1 was fully paid by the end of period 1, but order 3 (value 75) has not

---

4. The fictitious application provider Wondrous Functions is providing a framework that is being used to develop various applications, including FW's application; thus, its concerns are broader than those of FW.

Order	Period	Sequence	Payment Method	Amount
1	1	Order taken	Credit	50
2	1	Order taken	COD	200
3	1	Order taken	Credit	75
1	1	Order shipped	Credit	50
1	1	Order taken	Credit	–50
4	2	Order taken	Credit	95
2	1	Order shipped	COD	200
2	1	Order taken	COD	–200
1	1	Order paid	Credit	50
1	1	Order shipped	Credit	–50
4	2	Order shipped	Credit	95
4	2	Order taken	Credit	–95
5	2	Order taken	Credit	700

Figure 13.5. Order Processing with Associated CustomerBalanceAccessKeys

been paid. So if we build a CustomerBalanceAccessKey containing period 1, order taken, and credit, and use it to retrieve a balance from the CustomerBalanceManager (containing the data shown in Figure 13.5), it will return 75. Figure 13.6 shows how this key is matched with each entry to determine which entries are included in this balance. It also shows which entries would be used to calculate the balance for the CustomerBalanceAccessKey containing period 2, order taken, and credit.

In addition, the CustomerBalanceAccessKey can be used to specify that we want to collapse all values of a particular keyable. To get the total balance for orders on credit associated with the "order taken" sequence value, we would use the BalanceAccessKey containing *ignore, order taken, and credit. This key would ignore the period and in our example would return 775.

So far we have described what the Query portion of CustomerBalanceManager does. When a balance is requested, the key can be used to generate a query. The results of this query can then be used to calculate the balance.

The CachedBalances piece of CustomerBalanceManager does not keep each of these entries; instead it keeps the final balance or intermediate balances. Although we could use CustomerBalanceAccessKeys to specify the balances we want to keep, it is much better to use a CustomerBalanceSpecificationKey, which is a usage-specific subclass of the SpecificationKey class from the Key/Keyable pattern (see Chapter 11).

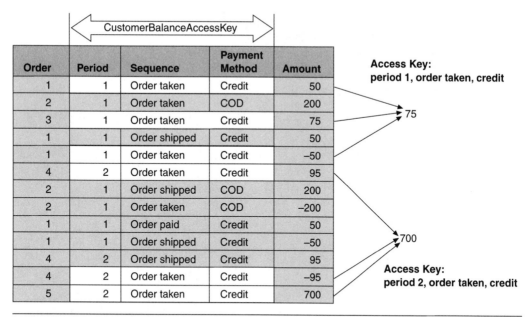

Figure 13.6. Balances for CustomerBalanceAccessKeys

CustomerBalanceSpecificationKeys allow us to specify groups of balances we want to cache. For example, we could define a CustomerBalanceSpecificationKey indicating that we want to keep balances for all periods, all order types, and all sequence values. Thus, an entry for each permutation of the criteria would be kept, but entries for the same criteria would be combined. Figure 13.7 shows the result of telling the CustomerBalanceManager (and thus the CachedBalances) to cache the balances for the CustomerBalanceSpecificationKey just described.

Use of a SpecificationKey as a filter was described at length in the Key/Keyable pattern (see Chapter 11), so it will not be described here. However, this type of filtering is central to the requirements for caching balances. A class called CachedBalanceSet encapsulates a map from an access key to a cached balance, as well as a specification key that defines the filter used to populate this map. Thus, in Figure 13.7 the resulting map from CustomerBalanceAccessKey to balance, combined with the CustomerBalanceSpecificationKey, could be implemented by a CachedBalanceSet.

CachedBalanceSet also provides methods for working with the map. The method retrieveBalance takes an access key and returns either the balance or null if the balance cannot be retrieved from the CachedBalanceSet. This retrieval does not have to be a direct lookup in the map; it can be done by the combining of elements of the map. A direct lookup occurs when there is an exact match for the access key in the map—for example, in requesting the balance for the

Order	Period	Sequence	Payment Method	Amount
1	1	Order taken	Credit	50
2	1	Order taken	COD	200
3	1	Order taken	Credit	75
1	1	Order shipped	Credit	50
1	1	Order taken	Credit	–50
4	2	Order taken	Credit	95
2	1	Order shipped	COD	200
2	1	Order taken	COD	–200
1	1	Order paid	Credit	50
1	1	Order shipped	Credit	–50
4	2	Order shipped	Credit	95
4	2	Order taken	Credit	–95
5	2	Order taken	Credit	700

CustomerBalanceSpecificationKey:
*all, *all, *all

Period	Sequence	Payment Method	Amount
1	Order taken	Credit	75
1	Order shipped	Credit	0
1	Order paid	Credit	50
1	Order taken	COD	0
1	Order shipped	COD	200
2	Order taken	Credit	700
2	Order shipped	Credit	95

Figure 13.7. Balances for CustomerBalanceSpecificationKeys

CustomerBalanceAccessKey "period 1, order taken, credit" with the Cached-BalanceSet shown in Figure 13.8. In this case the value 75 would be returned.

Figure 13.9 shows an example of getting a balance indirectly. In this case, a CustomerBalanceAccessKey containing *ignore, order taken, and credit is used. This key causes the period to be collapsed, so the two entries ("period 1, order taken, credit" and "period 2, order taken, credit") are combined to return the requested balance.

We can determine if retrieveBalance will return a balance from a CachedBalanceSet by seeing if the CachedBalanceSet's specification key includes the balance's access key. If it does, the balance can be retrieved either directly or indirectly.

Specification Key: *all, *all, *all

Period	Sequence	Payment Method	Amount
1	Order taken	Credit	75
1	Order shipped	Credit	0
1	Order paid	Credit	50
1	Order taken	COD	0
1	Order shipped	COD	200
2	Order taken	Credit	700
2	Order shipped	Credit	95

Access Key: period 1, order taken, credit

75

Figure 13.8. CachedBalanceSet retrieveBalance Method: Direct Lookup

Specification Key: *all, *all, *all

Period	Sequence	Payment Method	Amount
1	Order taken	Credit	75
1	Order shipped	Credit	0
1	Order paid	Credit	50
1	Order taken	COD	0
1	Order shipped	COD	200
2	Order taken	Credit	700
2	Order shipped	Credit	95

Access Key: *ignore, order taken, credit

775

Figure 13.9. CachedBalanceSet retrieveBalance Method: Combining Elements

The other method that CachedBalanceSet provides is the condense method. This method encapsulates the process of filtering the CachedBalanceSet to create a new CachedBalanceSet based on a filtering specification key. For example, if we had a CachedBalanceSet for the specification key "*all, *all, *all," as shown in Figure 13.9, and we called the condense method, passing the specification key "*ignore, *all, *all" (which means that we want to ignore the period), we would get the five balances shown in Figure 13.10. As described in the Key/ Keyable pattern (see Chapter 11),[5] we can condense information whenever we are condensing to a specification key that is a subset of the CachedBalanceSet's specification key.

---

5. CachedBalanceSets are not introduced as part of the Key/Keyable pattern, but the function encapsulated by CachedBalanceSet is described in the section titled "Filtering" in Chapter 11.

Specification Key: *all, *all, *all

Period	Sequence	Payment Method	Amount
1	Order taken	Credit	75
1	Order shipped	Credit	0
1	Order paid	Credit	50
1	Order taken	COD	0
1	Order shipped	COD	200
2	Order taken	Credit	700
2	Order shipped	Credit	95

condensation

Specification Key: *ignore, *all, *all

Period	Sequence	Payment Method	Amount
*	Order taken	Credit	775
*	Order shipped	Credit	95
*	Order paid	Credit	50
*	Order taken	COD	0
*	Order shipped	COD	200

Figure 13.10. CachedBalanceSet condense Method

CachedBalanceSets are interesting, but what do they have to do with the CustomerBalanceManager? The CustomerBalanceManager works with the CachedBalanceSet in two ways: (1) to support requests for sets of balances, and (2) via CachedBalances, to manage and maintain the cached balances.

Why might we request a set of balances? In our example, a supervisor looking at the customer's history needs to look at a set of balances rather than a single balance. The supervisor could retrieve each of these balances individually, but it is more convenient to get them all at once. Thus, the CustomerBalanceManager, in addition to supporting the retrieveBalance method that takes a CustomerBalanceAccessKey and returns a single balance, supports a retrieveBalances method that takes a CustomerBalanceSpecificationKey and returns a CachedBalanceSet.

The other use of CachedBalanceSets is to manage the cached balances. Why use CachedBalanceSets? The advantage is that balances can be derived from them according to well-defined rules. If a single balance is requested, each specification key held by a CachedBalanceSet (in other words, every cached combination managed by the set) can be checked for one that best includes the access key of the requested balance. If multiple balances are requested, then the specification key of each cached CachedBalanceSet can be checked for one that is a superset of the specification key of the requested balances.

The SpecificationKeyMap, described in the Key/Keyable pattern (see Chapter 11), is ideally suited for this checking. We use it by mapping from the CachedBalanceSet's specification key to the CachedBalanceSet itself. The SpecificationKeyMap supports methods that can then be used for finding the best CachedBalanceSet to use when retrieving single or multiple balances. Note that "best" in this case is defined as requiring the least amount of work to calculate the requested balance or balances. Thus, the CachedBalances portion of the CustomerBalanceManager contains a SpecificationKeyMap that it uses to fulfill requests and manage the cached balances.

How do the CachedBalanceSets become part of the SpecificationKeyMap? They are added and removed just like elements in any other map. However, the CustomerBalanceManager usually has methods that allow specification keys to be added and removed to control caching. When a specification key is added, the associated CachedBalanceSet is built[6] and then added to the SpecificationKeyMap. When a specification key is removed, the CachedBalanceSet associated with that specification key is removed from the SpecificationKeyMap. In this manner, we can dynamically control what is cached.

Now that the balance is cached, how do we update it? The CustomerBalanceManager must be notified of any change that could affect the cached balances. This notification can take the form of a reference to the updated item, such as an order, or it could be a CustomerBalanceAccessKey and the amount by which the balance needs to be changed. If the item (order) is passed, the CustomerBalanceManager uses it to create the appropriate CustomerBalanceAccessKey and amount. These pieces of information are passed to the CachedBalances, which iterates through the SpecificationKeyMap and for each entry uses the specification key to convert the access key. If the key is not converted, the entry is skipped (because the access key does not pass the filter). If the key is converted, the converted access key is used to retrieve and update an existing entry or used to add a new entry to the CachedBalanceSet.

What if we want to cache something other than a simple integer? In our example, a simple integer will do the job, but in other situations more complex things will need to be cached. For example, we might want to cache the objects that would result from a particular query. The CachedBalanceSet needs to be able to work abstractly with whatever is being cached so that it can combine those objects when calculating a balance or when updating the cached balance. We achieve this capability by introducing an interface called CachedBalance, which introduces an addTo method (that takes a CachedBalance). The CustomerBalanceManager provides an implementation, CreditBalance, for what it wants

---

6. This retrieval is done as if the user had requested the CachedBalanceSet. First the cache is checked, and if the CachedBalanceSet is not available there, a query is done.

to cache. In this case CreditBalance contains a single integer, the balance. It supports addTo by taking the value out of the other CreditBalance and adding that value to itself.

For the more complex case of caching the objects associated with a balance, the implementation could, in addition to the integer value, include a collection of objects associated with the value. The addTo method not only would add to its own value the value from the passed-in CreditBalance, but also would add to its own collection the entries in the collection from the passed-in CreditBalance.

For example, if we have a CreditBalance with a value of 5 that is the result of adding up the values for objects A, B, and C, the CreditBalance will contain the value 5 and a collection of references to A, B, and C. When this CreditBalance is updated to include an object D, a new CreditBalance for D will be created. For this example, the object D contains the value 2 and a collection that contains a reference to D. Thus, when the original CreditBalance is updated by a call to the addTo method that passes in the CreditBalance created for D, the result is that the original CreditBalance now contains the value 7 and a collection of references to A, B, C, and D.

Applicability

Consider using the Cached Aggregate pattern when any of the following criteria apply:

- Rapid access to the result of an aggregation (or calculation) over a large number of objects is needed. The process could be a simple calculation, such as a summation, or an aggregation, such as the collection of objects that would result from a query.

- Dynamic control of the tradeoff between rapid access and storage is needed.

Structure

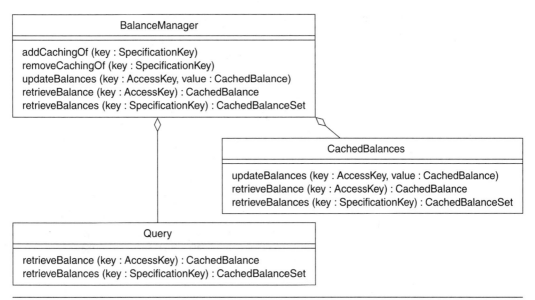

Figure 13.11. BalanceManager Structure

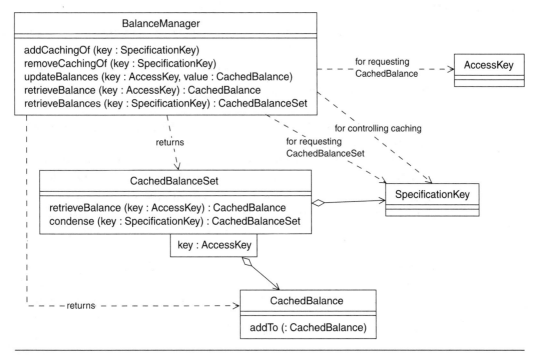

Figure 13.12. BalanceManager Usage

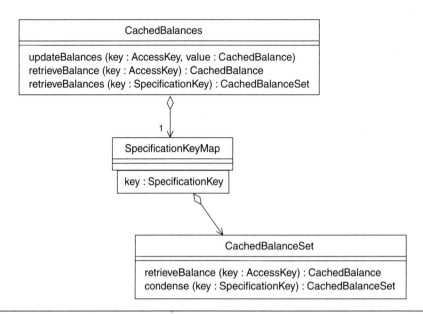

Figure 13.13. CachedBalances Structure

Participants

- **BalanceManager** (CustomerBalanceManager). A class that provides support for retrieving balances and controlling which balances are cached.

- **CachedBalances.** A class that encapsulates the cached balance support.

- **Query.** A class that encapsulates the code used to retrieve a balance from the raw objects.

- **AccessKey** (CustomerBalanceAccessKey). A class (or a usage-specific subclass) that encapsulates the criteria associated with a balance. It is used in retrieving a single balance from the BalanceManager and when updating the BalanceManager because of a change that affects the cached balances.

- **SpecificationKey** (CustomerBalanceSpecificationKey). A class (or usage-specific subclass) that encapsulates the specification of a set of AccessKeys. It is used to retrieve a CachedBalanceSet from the BalanceManager and to identify the balances that should be cached.

- **CachedBalanceSet.** A class that maps AccessKeys to their associated balances. The content of a CachedBalanceSet is defined by an associated SpecificationKey. CachedBalanceSet supports the retrieval of balances, including balances that can be calculated from its contents, as well as condensation into other CachedBalanceSets.

- **CachedBalance.** An interface that allows the application to work abstractly with what is being cached. Specific implementations will be created for the particular application of the pattern.
- **SpecificationKeyMap.** A class, introduced in the Key/Keyable pattern (see Chapter 11), that is a special map providing additional functions because it requires that the key be a SpecificationKey.

Collaborations

- When clients need a CachedBalance, they create an AccessKey containing the criteria for which they want the balance. This key is passed to the BalanceManager, which first tries to fulfill the request from its cache via the CachedBalances and, if that fails, from the raw objects via Query.
- Similarly, when a set of balances is needed, a SpecificationKey is used to retrieve a CachedBalanceSet.
- What is cached is dynamically controlled by the addCachingOf and removeCachingOf methods on the BalanceManager. The addCachingOf method creates the CachedBalanceSet associated with the given SpecificationKey and adds it to CachedBalances (which adds it to its SpecificationKeyMap). The removeCachingOf method removes the CachedBalanceSet associated with the SpecificationKey from CachedBalances (which removes it from its SpecificationKeyMap).
- When something that affects the balances changes, an updateBalances method is called on the BalanceManager. Either this method can take the raw object that changed and convert it into the appropriate AccessKey and CachedBalance, or it can take them directly. BalanceManager delegates this function to CachedBalances, which iterates through its SpecificationKeyMap, updating the contained CachedBalanceSets as needed.

Consequences

The Cached Aggregate pattern has the following tradeoffs, benefits, and drawbacks:

Tradeoffs

- **Cost of caching versus querying.** When there is little data, doing a query for each request may cost less in terms of performance than caching does. Each specification key over which balances are cached requires additional storage and a slight increase in the amount of time required for a change that affects the balances to take effect. This amount of time increases because the BalanceManager needs to be notified so that it can update the appropriate cached balances. In addition, as more specification keys are added to the cache, more CachedBalanceSets are added to the SpecificationKeyMap, so there is more to iterate through, and in most cases another update will be necessary.

- **One versus many BalanceManagers.** Having one BalanceManager makes sense when there is no logical partitioning of the data, especially with respect to the information that will be requested. For example, when caching account balances in a general ledger, the criteria over which balances will be requested are diverse enough that no appropriate partitioning can be done. Having multiple BalanceManagers does not mean that composite information cannot be determined; it just means that the results of the multiple BalanceManagers will have to be combined. If determining composite information is a common occurrence, consider having one BalanceManager.

  Having one BalanceManager creates a bottleneck during updates. All updates, for various reasons, must go to the BalanceManager. Although providing support for asynchronous update can help ease this problem, multiple BalanceManagers provide partitioning of the updates and reduce the bottleneck.

  In our example, the balances are always retrieved in the context of a particular customer, so having one BalanceManager per customer is the best choice. On the other hand, when dealing with account balances in the general ledger, requests will span everything, so any division would not make sense.

Benefits

- **Encapsulation of how balances are retrieved and cached.** This encapsulation makes the client code independent of the choices made in the tradeoff between the cost of caching versus querying and allows this tradeoff to be considered on a real-time basis instead of being fixed.
- **Encapsulation of the criteria used with the BalanceManager.** This use of keys allows the criteria to change without the BalanceManager or its parts having to be modified.

Drawbacks

- **Increased complexity.** The encapsulation and flexibility of the Cached Aggregate pattern increase the complexity of the application.

- **Increased storage usage.** Because the cached balance information is new, it requires additional storage. This storage need increases with the amount of cached information.

- **Reduced performance.** Cached balances are updated whenever an item is changed in a way that affects the balance. Thus, performance is reduced during these operations. We can minimize this reduction by updating the balances asynchronously.

Implementation

Consider the following implementation issues for the Cached Aggregate pattern:

- **Providing reusable implementations.** Implementations for the core elements of this pattern, listed here, can be provided:

  - **AccessKey, SpecificationKey, and SpecificationKeyMap.** The Key/ Keyable pattern (see Chapter 11) describes implementations for the AccessKey, SpecificationKey, and SpecificationKeyMap classes used in this pattern.

  - **CachedBalanceSet.** The CachedBalanceSet can be provided in a reusable implementation that would work with AccessKeys, SpecificationKeys, and CachedBalances, each of which would be subclassed and specialized for the particular use.

  - **CachedBalances.** A reusable implementation of the CachedBalances class can be provided that would use a SpecificationKeyMap to manage CachedBalanceSets. This reusable class is provided by SanFrancisco as the CachedBalanceSetCollection class.

  - **BalanceManager.** The BalanceManager should not be provided in a reusable manner. It should expose the usage-specific subclasses of the AccessKey, SpecificationKey, and CachedBalances classes, thereby isolating the user from the details of the implementation and making the BalanceManager easier to use.

  - **Query.** The Query portion of the BalanceManager should not be provided in a reusable manner, because this class needs to know what it must query and how to query it. On the other hand, the Query class can be written so that it uses the keys to help generate the actual query. Methods would be added to the usage-specific subclasses of the keys to return an appropriate query statement. Thus, when the keys changed, the Query class would not need to change.

- **Deciding what to cache.** CachedBalance is an interface that provides support for aggregation. It supports an addTo method that takes another

CachedBalance. The usage-specific implementation defines what this interface actually does. In our example, the CreditBalance subclass simply contains an integer, and the addTo method is implemented to add the values. The implementation of CachedBalance does not have to be limited to holding just a simple value. It could have as complex a function as keeping a collection of references to the orders included in a balance (possibly in addition to the integer balance value). This collection is essentially caching a query result—that is, the orders that would be returned for the access key associated with the CachedBalance.

- **Deciding which cached CachedBalanceSet to use.** The SpecificationKeyMap provides support for getting the best CachedBalanceSet. The algorithm for determining what is best is based on the difference between the two keys. For example, given two SpecificationKeys— "*all, *all, *all, *all" and "*ignore, *ignore, *all, *all"—the best fit for a specification key request using "*ignore, *ignore, *ignore, *all" would be the second specification key because this key has fewer entries that need to be condensed to get the required result.

  When complex specifications are involved, it is sometimes impractical to determine which one is best. For example, given two specification keys— one containing "A, B, C" and "1, 2, 3" and the other containing "B, C, D" and "2, 3, 4"—the best fit for a specification key request containing "B, C" and "2, 3" is both keys. If the first specification key had contained "A, B, C, D" and "1, 2, 3" instead, the second key would have been best. However, if it takes us too long to determine which specification key is best, we will spend more time finding the best key than it would have taken simply to use one that was "good enough."

  The designers of SanFrancisco decided to solve this problem by calculating a value for each specification key based on heuristics related to the number of potential elements in an associated CachedBalanceSet. This number is then used to determine the best specification key. Note that this calculation is applied after it is determined that the access key is included or the specification key is a subset, so even if the specification key is not the best, it is guaranteed to work.

- **Saving storage in CachedBalanceSets.** The CachedBalanceSet can be configured so that it saves storage by not retaining initial values—for example, not keeping an entry if the balance is zero. Values are evaluated by the method isInitialValue on the CachedBalance interface. If after aggregation the target's isInitialValue method returns true, the value is not put into the CachedBalanceSet. Use of this method depends on the particular requirements. If you need to be able to tell the difference between a zero because there has been no activity and a zero because everything canceled out, you should not use this method. Support for this function can be provided in the reusable implementation of CachedBalanceSet. We can turn the support on by coding the isInitialValue method appropriately and turn it off by coding the method to always return false.

- **Managing which balances are cached.** Consider the following issues:

  - **Caching the right set of CachedBalances.** When registering for caching (in our example), the BalanceManager always created and added the CachedBalanceSet to the CachedBalances. Users need to strike a balance between maintaining too few and maintaining too many cached balances. For example, if users blindly add all specification keys they think they might want, in some situations it will have been better not to add one and simply to use the condensation support to get the balance(s) from an already cached CachedBalanceSet.

    For example, given two SpecificationKeys—"*all, *all, *all, *all" and "*ignore, *ignore, *all, *all"—the CachedBalanceSet of the second specification key can be condensed from the CachedBalanceSet of the first. So it appears that it would be best to register the first specification key and not the second.

    Unfortunately it isn't simple to determine when condensation is the right choice. In our example, if the first two keyable positions don't contain a large number of entries (say 10 possibilities each: 1 through 10 and A through J), then this approach makes sense. If, on the other hand, they contain thousands of entries, this approach might be the wrong choice because depending on the requirement, condensation might not be fast enough.

    How we determine what to cache depends on the particular use of the pattern. In some cases, the application will define a fixed set of balances to cache that can be condensed to fulfill all requests. In others, the registration process can optimize the registrations by using knowledge of the nature of the different keyables (or a best guess). Finally, the choice can be left to the users, possibly with utilities to help them evaluate what they have and what adding a new cached CachedBalanceSet will do.

  - **Deferring registration of a CachedBalanceSet.** Specification keys can be registered immediately, or registration can be deferred. If deferred, registration is done in two parts. The first part indicates that the specification key should be cached; the second generates the CachedBalanceSet and adds it to the CachedBalances (SpecificationKeyMap). This partitioning of registration allows deferral of the more expensive generation of CachedBalanceSets from the raw objects until nonpeak times, such as at night for a business that operates only during the day.

We can evaluate when to register the specification keys in various ways. One approach is first to see if the new CachedBalanceSet can be retrieved from the cache. If it can, we do it immediately; if not, we defer. Another approach is to defer the registration of all specification keys, but if that CachedBalanceSet is requested—that is, if we're going to do the query anyway—we should add it immediately.

- **Handling values not in the cache.** As already discussed, the specific balances that are registered for caching can affect the time it takes to retrieve a balance. If the cache is set up correctly, balances that need to be retrieved quickly will always be retrieved quickly. However, when quick retrieval is crucial (in our example possibly during order taking), and you cannot guarantee that the correct balances are or will continue to be cached, you should consider either adding a warning to the retrieveBalance method of BalanceManager or providing an additional method to be used in this case.

  The warning could be in the form of a warning exception that would be thrown when the retrieveBalance method was called and could not retrieve the balance from the cache. We can skip this check by turning off warnings. The additional method could be retrieveCachedBalance on BalanceManager, which would only use the CachedBalances. This method will return null when the balance cannot be retrieved from the cache rather than going to the Query. This approach would allow the credit check to be handled interactively during order taking only if the balance was available from the cache (the retrieveCachedBalance method returns a non-null value), and it would defer the check until after the phone call if the balance was not available. Similar actions could be taken for the retrieveBalances method.

- **Synchronous versus asynchronous updates to the cache.** BalanceManager can be updated synchronously or asynchronously, depending on your particular needs. If you use the asynchronous approach, you must provide a way of resynchronizing. Asynchronously updated caches cannot be used for real-time information retrieval, so in some cases business requirements force the synchronous approach to be used.

- **Ownership of the raw objects.** BalanceManager can manage the raw objects that the balances represent. For example, when managing product balances, ProductBalanceManager manages the inventory records, as well as the cached balances over those records. This additional management is typical when the raw objects are not part of another object. For example, this management would not be done in the general ledger, where the balances are over the journal entries, which are part of the journals. When the BalanceManager also owns the raw objects, the BalanceManager will update the collection of objects. The collection may be implemented by a controller owned by the BalanceManager, or the BalanceManager may itself be a controller (for more on controllers, see Chapter 10).

- **Working with multiple BalanceManagers.** When caching is partitioned into multiple BalanceManagers, usually the domain class over which they are partitioned is the natural place, from a domain perspective, to work with balances. The domain class can expose methods for retrieving, managing, and updating balances. In our example, where caching is partitioned into one BalanceManager per customer, the Customer class should expose the retrieveBalance and retrieveBalances methods. It may or may not expose the balance management and update methods.

- **Defining the keys.** When creating the usage-specific key subclasses, the number and kind of keyables are crucial. Adding a new criterion to a key after the balances are cached can require all the balances to be regenerated. The specification key supports the ability to ignore a criterion; thus, criteria that may be needed can be added to the key and simply ignored. This feature is not free, however; it increases the size of the key and slightly increases the processing time. Adding a few keyables that are very likely to be needed is worth the additional cost.

Sample Code

The main use of the Cached Aggregate pattern is to support the retrieval of balances. The following code snippets highlight the retrieveBalance support.

A client who wants to get a balance creates the CustomerBalanceAccessKey that contains the criteria for the desired balance. Then the client requests the balance from the Customer object:

```
CreditBalance theBalance =  customer.getBalance(
                          customerBalanceAccessKey);
```

The getBalance method on Customer then locates the CustomerBalanceManager (in this case CustomerBalanceManager is one of Customer's attributes) and delegates the request to it:

```
public CreditBalance retrieveBalance(CustomerBalanceAccessKey key) {

  // Pass request to CustomerBalanceManager
  Return ivCustomerBalanceManager.retrieveBalance(key);
}
```

Within the CustomerBalanceManager, the retrieveBalance method first tries to get the balance from the cache (the CachedBalances instance it contains), and if that fails, it uses the raw data (via the Query instance it contains):

```
public CreditBalance retrieveBalance(CustomerBalanceAccessKey key) {

    // See if request can be filled from cached balances
    CachedBalance result = ivCachedBalances.retrieveBalance(key);

    if (result != null) return (CreditBalance)result;    // It was

    // It wasn't, so go to the raw data
    return ivQuery.retrieveBalance(key);
}
```

The retrieveBalance method of CachedBalances finds the best cached CachedBalanceSet to use to fulfill the request. If one of them contains the access key exactly, it is used. If none do, then the one that will require the least amount of calculation is used. The search for this instance is supported by the SpecificationKeyMap, which the CachedBalances class uses to hold and manage its cached CachedBalanceSets.

```
public CachedBalance retrieveBalance(CustomerBalanceAccessKey key) {

    // Find the best cached CachedBalanceSet to use
    CachedBalanceSet balanceSet =
        (CachedBalanceSet)ivSKMap.getObjectWhoseKeyMostCloselyIncludes(
                                                              key);

    if (balanceSet == null) return null;    // One wasn't found

    // Get balance from cached CachedBalanceSet
    return balanceSet.getBalance(key);
}
```

If none of the cached CachedBalanceSets can be used, then null is returned and the retrieveBalance method of CustomerBalanceManager uses the Query instance to retrieve the balance from the raw data.

To keep the balances up-to-date, the CustomerBalanceManager must be notified when something occurs that will affect the balances. In this example, a new order on credit has been taken. As part of the order entry processing (after the customer has hung up), the CustomerBalanceAccessKey is created and, along with the value of the order, is used to update the CustomerBalanceManager associated with the customer placing the order. As was done with the retrieveBalance method, the update method is exposed on the Customer.

In this case the method takes an Order. It creates the CustomerBalanceAccessKey and CreditBalance and calls the update method on the CustomerBalanceManager. A similar update method that takes a Payment would also be provided.

```
public void updateBalances(Order order) {

    // Create the CustomerBalanceAccessKey from the Order
    CustomerBalanceAccessKey key = new CustomerBalanceAccessKey(order);
```

```
    // Create the CreditBalance from the Order
    CreditBalance updateValue = new CreditBalance(Order);

    // Update the CustomerBalanceManager, which is an attribute
    ivCustomerBalanceManager.updateBalances(key, updateValue);
}
```

The update request is immediately delegated to the CachedBalances by the CustomerBalanceManager:

```
public void updateBalances(CustomerBalanceAccessKey key,
                           CreditBalance value) {

    // Update the cached balances
    ivCachedBalances.updateBalances(key, value);
}
```

Note that if the CustomerBalanceManager also managed the items represented by the balances—Orders and Payments in this case—the CustomerBalanceManager would support an update method that takes the item (or information to create the item) and would update its collection (or controller) for that item in addition to updating the CachedBalances.

Continuing with our example, the updateBalances method of CachedBalances goes through all the cached CachedBalanceSets and updates those affected by the update:

```
public void updateBalances(BalanceAccessKey key, CachedBalance value) {

    // Get the keys from the SpecificationKeyMap
    Enumeration keys = ivSKMap.getKeys();

    // Loop through the keys
    while (keys.hasMoreElements()){

        // Get the SpecificationKey
        SpecificationKey specKey = (SpecificationKey)keys.nextElement();

        // Use the SpecificationKey to convert the passed AccessKey
        AccessKey convertedKey = specKey.convert((AccessKey)key);

        // If it could be converted, continue,
        // else no update needed for this element
        if (convertedKey != null) {

            // See if there is an existing entry for this key
            CachedBalance balanceValue =
              (CachedBalance)ivSKMap.getObjectBy(convertedKey);
```

```
        if (balanceValue != null){

            // If one exists, add the update
            balanceValue.addTo(valueToAdd);
        }

        // Otherwise, add this as a new entry
        else ivSKMap.addObjectBy((AccessKey)key, (Object)valueToAdd);
        }
    }
}
```

The casts are necessary because we are reusing the CachedBalanceSet and SpecificationKeyMap. These classes work with abstract items, which the CachedBalances class turns into the concrete items of the particular usage. In other words, the CachedBalances class encapsulates the fact that this reuse is occurring. In fact, in some cases it can translate CachedBalanceSets into a CachedBalanceSet subclass or wrapper class that works with the concrete items. In this way, the client is protected from doing the casts.

To have a reusable CachedBalanceSet, we must create an implementation of the CachedBalance interface for each use of the Cached Aggregate pattern. In the example given earlier, a simple integer balance value was needed. The following code shows a sample implementation that supports this example.

```
public class CreditBalance implements CachedBalance {

  public CreditBalance(int value) {
     ivBalanceValue = value;
  }

  public void addTo(CachedBalance valueToAdd) {
     ivBalanceValue += ((CreditBalance)valueToAdd).getBalanceValue();
  }

  public int getBalanceValue() {
     return ivBalanceValue;
  }

  private int ivBalanceValue;
}
```

In the addTo method shown here, the downcast to CreditBalance is safe because it is the only implementation of CachedBalance being used.

Known Uses

SanFrancisco uses the Cached Aggregate pattern to handle the following functions:

- Managing customer financial balances (the primary example in this chapter). This function is supplied as part of the Common Business Object layer. It allows information from both the Order Management and the Accounts Payable/Accounts Receivable subsystems (and any other appropriate subsystems) to be included.

- Managing product balances to support product availability checking. This function is supplied as part of the Warehouse Management Core Business Process.

- Managing account balances in the General Ledger Core Business Process.

Related Patterns

- **Key/Keyable.** The criteria for the Cached Aggregate pattern are encapsulated by use of the Key/Keyable pattern (see Chapter 11). In addition, the SpecificationKeyMap support is used.

14

Keyed Attribute Retrieval

Intent

Provide a way of retrieving values of an attribute on the basis of a set of criteria. How the criteria are used is encapsulated in a policy to allow easy customization.

Motivation

Defining the discounts you give your customers directly affects your business. Getting it wrong costs you either money or customers. You want to give appropriate discounts at the right time. You want to discount products that are not selling well or are discontinued. You want to discount seasonal products in the off-season. You want to give your best customers discounts to encourage them to keep buying from you.

In addition, more than one discount may apply at any one time. You have to be able to decide if discounts accumulate additively (two 5 percent discounts become a 10 percent discount) or multiplicatively (two 5 percent discounts become a 9.75 percent discount), or if you use the best discount (8 percent when both a 6 percent and an 8 percent discount apply). Even your way of handling multiple discounts might vary.

Case Study

Food Warehouse requires a very flexible pricing and discount system:

- Certain customers receive special prices and discounts, some that apply only for certain days and others that always apply.
- Products go on sale during certain dates. Such sales are handled by the use of discounts.
- The best discount is always used.
- At any time FW may need to adapt to the changing business environment, so it must be able to change how it determines discounts.

The first possible solution is to create a new class that references a customer and a product, called CustomerProductLink, which contains the appropriate discount. However, if the same discount applies to every product for every customer, a link class will needlessly be created for each combination. In addition to this combinatorial explosion, some discounts are based on criteria other than just product and customer. For example, the product group or customer group could be used. In such a case we would have to add a ProductGroupProductLink and a CustomerGroupProductLink. The creation of link classes quickly gets out of hand.

How do we avoid this explosion? A better solution is to have a central definition of the discounts based on the different criteria. This centralization still allows discounts to vary depending on the customer purchasing the product and the particular product being purchased, but it allows other criteria, such as the time of purchase, the product group, the customer group, and so on, to be added.

There are many ways to find the discount. We can first determine if there is a discount for the particular set of criteria, such as George, pencils, and today. If a discount is not found with those criteria, the algorithm can then see if there is a discount for a subset of the criteria, such as one that applies to this customer (George) at this time no matter what product the customer is purchasing. Other algorithms might try to find all discounts for various combinations of the criteria and accumulate the discounts or take the best discount found. Each company will define the criteria used to define the discounts and the algorithm used to look up the discount(s) that should be applied.

For example, when Food Warehouse defines discounts, it uses several different criteria: product, customer, and time period (see Table 14.1; the first column is included only for ease of reference). As already described, with this definition we can retrieve discounts in various ways, and we can find exact matches or partial matches.

In an *exact match,* there is an entry for a particular product, customer, and date. For example, if Anne wants to buy lettuce on 30 December, we would try

Table 14.1. Sample Discount Definitions

	Product	Customer	Time Period	Discount (%)
1	Lettuce	Anne	1 Jan–31 May	10
2	Lettuce	Anne	1 Jun–2 Jun	3
3	Lettuce	Anne	3 Jun–31 Dec	24
4	Any product	Anne	1 Jan–31 Jul	7
5	Any product	Anne	1 Aug–31 Dec	6

to find an exact match for "lettuce, Anne, 30 December." Line 3 in Table 14.1 is an exact match in this case, so a discount of 24 percent would be returned. However, if Anne wants to buy a peach on 21 March, we would not find an exact match for "peach, Anne, 21 March."

In a *partial match*, not all the available criteria are used in the search. In the case of discounts, we want to find out if a customer receives any particular discounts on all products he or she purchases (i.e., we ignore the specific product being purchased when searching for discounts). In the preceding example in which no exact match was found, we would do a minimum match search; that is, we would look for "any product, Anne, 21 March." In this case line 4 of Table 14.1 returns a discount of 7 percent.

A partial match can also be used to find all applicable discounts for a particular subset of the criteria. Again, our search for discounts ignores the specific product being purchased. So if Anne wants to buy lettuce on 2 June, a search for the applicable discounts will yield both 3 percent (from line 2 of Table 14.1) and 7 percent (from line 4). We can then determine the discount either by taking the best one available (7 percent in this case) or by accumulating the discounts additively (10 percent in this case) or multiplicatively (9.79 percent).[1] Although these examples are over a limited set of criteria, the methods of determining discounts can be extended to any number of criteria.

The Keyed Attribute Retrieval pattern captures the solution to this problem. Figure 14.1 shows how the pattern would be applied to discounts. The discount definition is encapsulated in a DiscountDefinition class, and the central place for managing and retrieving discounts is the DiscountDefinitionController (see Chapter 10 for more information on controllers). The criteria associated with each discount are encapsulated in keys from the Key/Keyable pattern (see Chapter 11). Thus, the criteria can change with minimal (or no) impact on the lookup algorithm. In addition, the Key/Keyable pattern defines relationships between the keys that can be leveraged by this pattern. In fact, the DiscountDefinitionController can effectively be implemented by a SpecificationKeyMap, in which the specification key encapsulates the criteria and maps them to DiscountDefinition instances.

---

1. That is, $100 - (93 \times .97)$ or $100 - (97 \times .93)$.

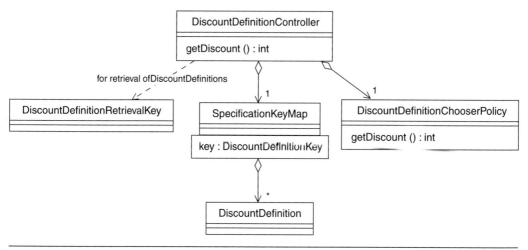

Figure 14.1. Applying the Keyed Attribute Retrieval Pattern to Discounts

Retrieving the discount to use for a particular situation is a process supported by the getDiscount method on the DiscountDefinitionController. The business logic for determining which discount to use, as described earlier, varies. To support this variation, the Simple Policy pattern (see Chapter 7) is used to encapsulate determination of the discount in the DiscountDefinitionChooserPolicy. As Figure 14.2 shows, when the controller is asked for a discount, it delegates the request to the policy. In this example, the policy tries to find first an exact match and then a partial match. If either search returns a set of DiscountDefinitions, the policy uses them to calculate the discount and returns the result. If neither search returns any DiscountDefinitions, the policy returns zero.

Why are there two different keys in Figure 14.1? Shouldn't there just be one usage-specific subclass of SpecificationKey? Figure 14.3 shows the two usage-specific subclasses. These two types of keys are defined because they are used differently. The DiscountDefinitionKey is used when DiscountDefinitions are being added to the controller. Usually this key can be directly created from DiscountDefinition and thus does not have methods for manipulating the individual keyables. Note that the DiscountDefinition can specify discounts for groups of criteria. For example, it can specify that customers Anne, Joseph, and Barbara (a set of criteria) receive a 12 percent discount from 1 January to 1 July (a range of criteria).

On the other hand, the DiscountDefinitionRetrievalKey is used to retrieve discounts. The client uses this key to define the criteria for which it is requesting the discount, so the key must support working with the individual keyables (through usage-specific methods). In fact, the DiscountDefinitionRetrievalKey

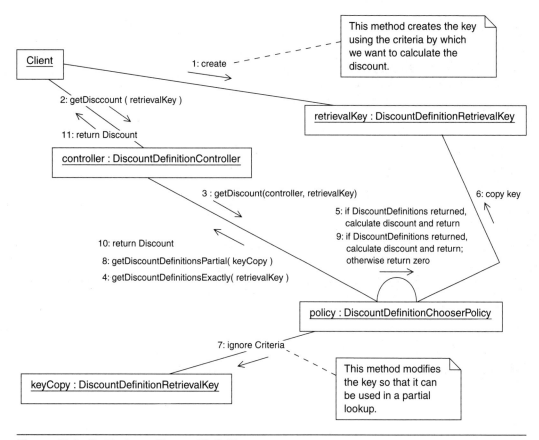

Figure 14.2. Retrieving a DiscountDefinition

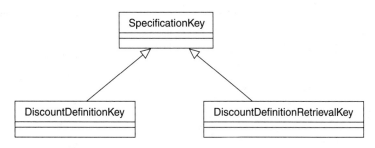

Figure 14.3. Usage-Specific Subclasses of SpecificationKey

looks more like an AccessKey than a SpecificationKey. It supports only specific values in each keyable position. A SpecificationKey is used because of the function it provides over the AccessKey: It allows for easier implementation of the exact and partial lookups. Another reason this key is unique is that it must support being changed so that it can be used for partial lookups. The key is modified for partial lookup by any of a group of usage-specific ignoreCriteria methods (see step 7 in Figure 14.2)—for example, ignoreCustomer.

Applicability

Consider using the Keyed Attribute Retrieval pattern when you need to look up a value on the basis of a variable set of criteria in a flexible way. The pattern is useful when the following circumstances apply:

- The criteria must be customizable.
- The lookup may be done multiple times using different aspects of the supplied criteria.
- The algorithm for lookup must be customizable.

Structure

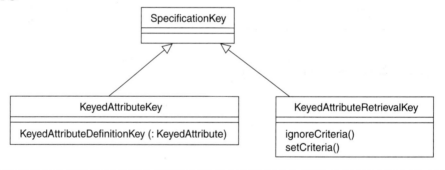

Figure 14.4. Key Structure

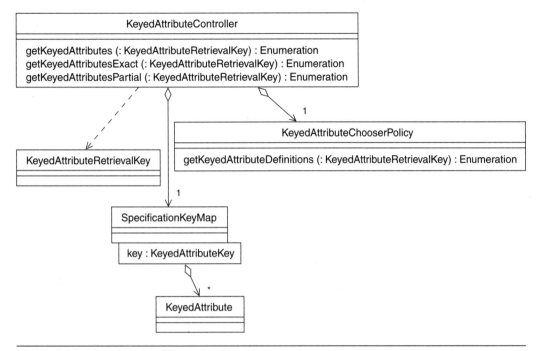

Figure 14.5. KeyedAttributeController Structure

Participants

- **KeyedAttribute** (DiscountDefinition). A class that defines the attribute being enabled for keyed retrieval. Usually this class also contains the criteria used for mapping the attribute, since often these criteria are of interest as a snapshot of the information used to determine the attribute value.

- **KeyedAttributeController** (DiscountDefinitionController). A class that manages the KeyedAttributeDefinitions and provides a method to retrieve a KeyedAttributeDefinition on the basis of a set of criteria using the KeyedAttributeRetrievalKey.

- **KeyedAttributeChooserPolicy** (DiscountDefinitionChooserPolicy). A policy that uses a KeyedAttributeRetrievalKey to determine the KeyedAttribute(s) to retrieve. This policy can return either a single value or a set of values, depending on the requirements. The example given in the "Motivation" section returned a single value. Returning multiple values is discussed in the "Implementation" section later in this chapter.

- **KeyedAttributeRetrievalKey** (DiscountDefinitionRetrievalKey). A key that encapsulates the criteria used to look up KeyedAttributes.

- **KeyedAttributeKey** (DiscountDefinitionKey). The key that is created from the criteria in the KeyedAttribute when the KeyedAttribute is added to the KeyedAttributeController.

Collaborations

- KeyedAttributes are created and added to the KeyedAttributeController. The controller creates the appropriate KeyedAttributeKey from information in the KeyedAttribute and adds the KeyedAttribute to its Specification-KeyMap.

- The customer retrieves one or more KeyedAttributes via the getKeyed-Attributes method on the KeyedAttributeController. This method is supported by the KeyedAttributeChooserPolicy. The criteria to use in choosing are encapsulated in a KeyedAttributeRetrievalKey.

- The KeyedAttributeChooserPolicy uses the KeyedAttributeRetrievalKey to find the correct KeyedAttribute(s) to return. This search may involve modifying the key and using it to do partial lookups, then resetting it and repeating the process. It may also involve combining the KeyedAttributes it finds.

Consequences

The Keyed Attribute Retrieval pattern has the following tradeoffs, benefits, and drawbacks:

Tradeoffs

- **Flexibility versus performance.** The Keyed Attribute pattern provides a lot of flexibility. Because it is accompanied by increased complexity, this flexibility increases the performance overhead.

Benefits

- **Flexible retrieval.** Very complex algorithms can be defined for retrieving the keyed attributes. Any criteria can be used, and in multiple ways. The retrieval algorithm (chooser policy) can easily be adapted as the business environment changes.

Drawbacks

- **Increased complexity.** If both the criteria and the retrieval algorithm are permanently fixed, this approach is unnecessarily complex.

Implementation

Consider the following implementation issues for the Keyed Attribute Retrieval pattern:

- **Retrieving more than one attribute.** Although our discussion of this pattern has focused on the return of a single KeyedAttributeDefinition, a set of definitions could be returned. Because it is easier to add this support when the pattern is first applied, it should be considered right away. Sometimes returning a set of definitions makes sense from a business perspective (e.g., when retrieving all applicable discounts), and sometimes it doesn't (e.g., when retrieving a product price based on specified criteria). One factor is the processing encapsulated in the chooser policy. If the policy encapsulates all the logic necessary to determine the result, only a single attribute needs be returned. However, if the logic is encapsulated in a command that uses the the controller to get the attributes and then determine the result, multiple attributes will need to be returned.

- **Determining the type of chooser policy.** The KeyedAttributeDefinition-ChooserPolicy can be an object-specific policy or a chain of responsibility-driven policy (see Chapters 7 and 8). For example, the chain of responsibility-driven policy could support looking for the policy on first the product, then the customer, and finally the controller. In this manner the policy could change depending on the participants.

- **Adding new criteria.** When extending the KeyedAttributeDefinition to add new criteria, you need to subclass it and two other classes: Keyed-AttributeRetrievalKey and KeyedAttributeDefinitionKey. This subclassing allows usage-specific methods for the new criteria to be added. Although KeyedAttributeChooserPolicy probably also should change, it does not have to change immediately. Until it is changed, it will simply assume that the new criteria are an exact match (or subset).

- **Retrieving attributes.** For the retrieval of KeyedAttributeDefinitions from the KeyedAttributeDefinitionController, typically two different methods are provided:

    1. The **getKeyedAttributeDefinitionsUsingExactKey** method returns the KeyedAttributeDefinitions associated with KeyedAttributeDefinitionKeys that exactly match the passed-in KeyedAttributeRetrievalKey. Note that a date specified in the KeyedAttributeRetrievalKey is considered an exact match when it is either identical to or within a date range contained in the KeyedAttributeDefinitionKey.

    2. The **getKeyedAttributeDefinitionsUsingMinimumKey** method returns the KeyedAttributeDefinitions associated with KeyedAttributeDefinition-Keys that match the passed KeyedAttributeRetrievalKey. However,

keyable positions that are cleared in the KeyedAttributeRetrievalKey are treated as matching anything (wild cards) in comparisons of the keys.

- **Choosing the type of controller.** The controller is usually a root controller (see Chapter 10). An aggregating controller would be a possibility, but this complexity should be avoided unless it is absolutely necessary; it makes things very messy. For example, with an aggregating child controller, any request for minimal matches goes to the parent, gets the partial matches there, and then finds its own partial matches. Another aggregating child controller of the same parent does the same. It is difficult to define the KeyedAttributes in the parent controller so that they are appropriate in both situations. In addition, defining the overriding behavior of an aggregating child controller can be quite complex. In a partial match, when should the entry in the parent be overridden—when only the partial portion of the key matches or when the entire key matches?

- **Going directly to an underlying database.** The controller implementation may support going directly to the underlying database for the retrieval of a definition. This support is necessary when the number of definitions is large. We can go directly to the database by mapping the parts of the key into columns of the database table so that efficient query mechanisms can be used. SanFrancisco provides generic classes in its Common Business Objects layer that support such behavior.

- **Taking a snapshot of a result.** Sometimes a retrieved value should no longer change. In such cases, a snapshot must be taken of the value to ensure that it is not changed as the definitions in the controller are updated. For example, when the price is retrieved and quoted to a customer, the quoted price may need to be kept (rather than a reference maintained to the original price definition) so that the price does not change when the customer decides later to accept the quote.

Sample Code

In the example from the "Motivation" section, the DiscountDefinitionController supported the getDiscountDefinitionsUsingExactKey method. This method is used by the DiscountDefinitionChooserPolicy when it is looking up the DiscountDefinitions. (Note that in Java this method has to be made public or package-protected, even though it should not be used directly by clients of the controller, but rather only by the policy. C++ has an advantage here because of its ability to establish friendship between classes.) The code for this method looks like this:

```
public Hashtable getDiscountDefinitionsUsingExactKey
            (DiscountDefinitionRetrievalKey discountKey) {
```

```
return ivSpecificationKeyMap.getObjectsForKeysThatAreASupersetOf
                                                 (dDiscountKey);
}
```

The getObjectsForKeysThatAreASupersetOf method will return all DiscountDefinitions that are associated with DiscountDefinitionKeys that are a superset of the DiscountDefinitionRetrievalKey. To be a superset, the specification key must contain at least the same information. It can contain more. Supersets are described as part of the Key/Keyable pattern (see Chapter 11).[2]

The getDiscountDefinitionsUsingExactKey method is used by the getDiscount method of DiscountDefinitionChooserPolicy. The method tries to find the discount using different variations of the passed-in key. First it ensures that the key contains a time stamp, adding the current time stamp if one is not present. Then it tries to locate, using exact matching, DiscountDefinitions associated with each of the following in turn:

1. At least all of the passed-in criteria (including the time stamp)

2. At least the product and the time stamp

3. At least the customer and the time stamp

As soon as DiscountDefinitions are located during any of these steps, the best discount is determined and returned.

Assume that we have the DiscountDefinitionController entries shown in Table 14.2 (the first column is included only for ease of reference). In this table we have defined discounts that apply when Joseph buys lettuce and discounts that apply when Joseph buys any product. In addition, we always discount spinach. The product, customer, and time period make up the DiscountDefinitionKey.

If we want the discount for Joseph buying lettuce on 30 December, we build a DiscountDefinitionRetrievalKey and call the getDiscount method on the controller. The controller delegates the request to the policy, which first sees if an entry contains at least all the criteria. In this case only entry 3 does, so its discount (24 percent) would be returned.

If we want the discount for Joseph buying spinach on 30 December, we follow the same procedure. However, no entry contains at least these criteria; that is, no entry contains both Joseph and spinach. We then reduce the key to just the product (spinach) and the time stamp and try again. This time entry 6 is found and its discount (95 percent) returned.

---

2. The Key/Keyable pattern actually talks about subsets. However, the discussion of subsets applies to supersets as well, since the ability to determine if something is a subset can be used to determine if something is a superset. In other words, "specificationKey1.isSupersetOf(specificationKey2)" is equivalent to "specificationKey2.isSubsetOf(specificationKey1)."

Table 14.2. Sample DiscountDefinitionController Entries

	Product	Customer	Time Period	Discount (%)
1	Lettuce	Joseph	1 Jan–31 May	10
2	Lettuce	Joseph	1 Jun–2 Jun	3
3	Lettuce	Joseph	3 Jun–31 Dec	24
4	Any product	Joseph	1 Jan–31 Jul	7
5	Any product	Joseph	1 Aug–31 Dec	6
6	Spinach	Any customer	1 Jan–31 Dec	95

Finally, if we want the discount for Joseph buying peaches on 1 September, we follow the same procedure. In this case again, no entry contains at least these criteria; that is, no entry includes peaches and Joseph. We then reduce the key to the product and the time stamp, but still we find no entry that contains at least these criteria (there still is no entry for peaches). Finally we reduce the original key to just the customer and the time stamp. In this case entry 5 is found and its discount (6 percent) returned.

In these examples, none of our requests returned more than one Discount-Definition. If the policy did the search in a different order (for example, trying just the customer first), then when we requested the discount for Joseph buying lettuce on 4 June, we would get back two DiscountDefinitions, those for entries 3 and 4. The discount returned would be the larger of the two, which in this case is 24 percent.

The following code shows the implementation of this policy. Note that the numbered steps defined earlier are identified in the comments.

```
public int getDiscount
            (DiscountDefinitionController controller,
             DiscountDefinitionRetrievalKey discountKey) {

    // Create a place to put the DiscountDefinitions
    Enumeration discountDefinitions;

    // Copy the key so that we can change it without affecting
    // the original
    DiscountDefinitionRetrievalKey oDiscountKey =
        new DiscountDefinitionRetrievalKey(discountKey);

    // If the time stamp isn't set, use the current time
    if (oDiscountKey.getTimeStamp() == null)
        oDiscountKey.setTimeStamp( new Timestamp());
        // This constructor uses the current date and time
```

```
    // create a working copy of the key
  DiscountDefinitionRetrievalKey dDiscountKey =
    new DiscountDefinitionRetrievalKey(oDiscountKey);

// Step 1:
// Try finding an exact match for everything
discountDefinitions =
     controller.getDiscountDefinitionsUsingExactKey(dDiscountKey);

// Step 2:
// If no match was found in step 1 and the product is specified in
// the key, try finding an exact match for just the product
if ((discountDefinitions == null) &&
    (dDiscountKey.getProduct() != null)) {

  // Because the key has not changed, it is not necessary
  // to make a new copy of it

  // Clear everything except product and time stamp
  dDiscountKey.clearCustomer();

  // See if there is an exact match
  discountDefinitions =
     controller.getDiscountDefinitionsUsingExactKey(dDiscountKey);
}

// Step 3:
// If no match was found in step 2 and the customer is specified in
// the key, try finding an exact match for just the customer
if ((discountDefinitions == null) &&
    (dDiscountKey.getCustomer() != null)) {

// Make a new copy of the key
dDiscountKey = new DiscountDefinitionRetrievalKey(oDiscountKey);

 // Clear everything except product and time stamp
  dDiscountKey.clearProduct();

  // See if there is an exact match
  discountDefinitions =
     controller.getDiscountDefinitionsUsingExactKey(dDiscountKey);
}

// Go through the DiscountDefinitions and find the
// largest discount

// Set up the result. If nothing is found, return zero.
int discount = 0;

If (discountDefinitions != null) {

  // There are DiscountDefinitions; loop through them
  While (discountDefinitions.hasMoreElements()) {
```

```
        // Get the discount from the DiscountDefinition
        int newDiscount =
          ((DiscountDefinition)discountDefinitions.nextElement())
          .getDiscount();

        // Keep the larger of what we've found so far and the new one
        discount = Math.max(discount, newDiscount);
      }
    }
    // Else there weren't any, so return 0;

    return discount;
  }
```

Known Uses

SanFrancisco uses the Keyed Attribute Retrieval pattern for discounts (the primary example in this chapter) and prices in the Order Management Core Business Process, as well as for lead times and transport times in the Warehouse Management Core Business Process.

Related Patterns

- **Key/Keyable.** The criteria for the Keyed Attribute Retrieval pattern are encapsulated by the Key/Keyable pattern (see Chapter 11), and the mapping is done by a SpecificationKeyMap.

- **Simple Policy.** The Simple Policy pattern (see Chapter 7) is used to define the retrieval policy.

- **Controller.** The definitions are controlled objects (see Chapter 10).

15

List Generation

Intent

Define a consistent way of generating a list from a set of input items and working with the list and its entries. List entries are composed of one or more input items with common characteristics that are selected by policy.

Motivation

To fill customer orders quickly and efficiently, we must be able to retrieve the items ordered from the warehouse so that they can be shipped. This retrieval is referred to as *picking*. To maximize efficiency, often we pick more than one order at a time. We pick multiple orders by creating one or more pick lists. Then employees called pickers (or machines in automated warehouses) use the lists to pick the number of items specified from the indicated zones and locations in the warehouse.

When generating a pick list, typically we want to optimize the list according to many different criteria. One simple criterion is to combine picking of the same product from all the outstanding orders into a single entry on one pick list. This approach prevents the picker from going to a zone and location, picking one of an item for a particular order, bringing it to the shipping department, and then having to go back to the same zone and location to pick up another one of the same item for a different order.

We might also want to organize pick lists on the basis of zones within the warehouse, building a separate pick list for each zone and assigning each pick list to a different picker. More sophisticated policies might even sort the goods being picked by other criteria, such as their fragility, and place the most fragile goods last in the pick list (so that the picker doesn't throw the can of baked beans on top of the egg carton, for example).

Just the fact that an item is on the pick list doesn't mean there will be enough of that item when the picker goes to pick it. For example, the picker might go to pick light bulbs and find that 50-pound bags of sugar were accidentally stacked on top of them. Normally this won't be the case, but when it is, the orders whose items were being picked must be updated to reflect this status. Once the items are picked, the picker confirms the items on the pick list; that is, the picker confirms that all the items could be picked or indicates how many of the items could be picked. If all the items could be picked, the orders can be shipped. If only some of the items could be picked, some decisions need to be made.

Remember that an entry on a pick list may actually be for more than one order, so when only some of the requested quantity can be picked, we have to decide which order(s) should be filled first. Orders whose requested amount has been met can be shipped. Orders that have received some (or none) of what they need are then processed to handle the shortage. For example, the customer may have agreed to accept a partial shipment, or a substitute product may be available.

Case Study

Food Warehouse generates pick lists for each warehouse every two hours during the workday, starting one hour before the warehouse opens and stopping one hour before the warehouse closes. Pick lists are generated for all the orders that have picking details (requests for a particular quantity of a particular item) that are not in a previous pick list. FW's requirements for their pick lists are the following:

- One pick list is generated for each picker available during the current time period for that particular day. Each picker is assigned stock zones within the warehouse from which he or she is responsible for picking. Thus, the list of picking details is divided by stock zone.

- A pick list entry is created for the total number of items at a particular location. (FW's policy is never to mix products in a single location.)

- The pick list entries are ordered to optimize the picker's traversal of the warehouse. That is, the picker will go from location to location in the most efficient manner possible.

- After a picker picks an item, he or she delivers it to the shipping location (where a ship list will be used to collect all the items for an order) and notifies the system of the number of items that were picked.

- If the number of items matches the pick list entry, inventory for the item is updated to record this fact, and all of the associated picking details are made shippable.

- If the number of items does not match the pick list entry, FW's policy is to fill the pickable details starting with the first one and completely filling each detail in turn until the item runs out. Any picking details that cannot be completely filled are handled by FW's order management system. For example, FW might ship a partial order and place on back order the item(s) that could not be shipped, it might hold an order (e.g., if the customer refused to accept a partially filled order), or it might use substitute items to complete the order (e.g., using a name brand in place of a generic).

As Figure 15.1 shows, the pick list is represented by the PickList class. This class contains PickListDetails, which represent the entries on the list. The PickListDetails cover one or more PickingDetails of an order. The PickLists are naturally owned by the company, so they follow the Controller pattern (see Chapter 10) and are controlled by the PickListController.

We create PickLists by creating a set of PickingDetails (by querying the pickable orders and retrieving their pickable details) and calling the generatePickLists method on the PickListController, passing the set of PickingDetails on the call.

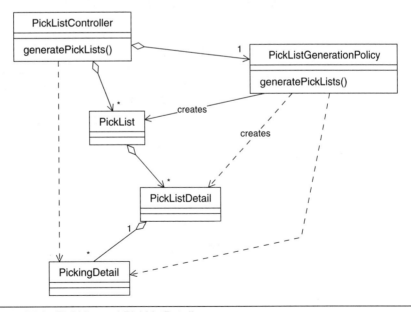

Figure 15.1. PickList and PickListDetails

This method is supported by an object-specific policy (see Chapter 7) called the PickListGenerationPolicy. In this case the policy determines the number of pickers and the stock zones to which they are assigned. It creates a PickList for each picker. One PickListDetail is created for all items of the same product in the same stock zone and location. Each PickListDetail records which PickingDetails it covers. (This information allows later processes to find the appropriate PickingDetails.) Each PickListDetail is added, according to zone, to the appropriate picker's PickList.

Figure 15.2 shows an example of generating a pick list. In this example there are three picking details from three different orders. It is assumed that all three picking details are for the same product and that they are all in the same zone, so the product and zone are not included in the figure. Order 1's picking detail specifies a quantity of 3 from bin 4, and because this order is the only request for bin 4, a list detail for just this single item is created. On the other hand, the picking details for orders 2 and 3 are for the same bin, so they can be combined into a single list detail, with the combined quantity of 42.

After the pick lists have been generated, each list is sent to the handheld device used by the appropriate picker. After picking an item and bringing it to the shipping location, the picker enters on the pick list how many of each item could be picked. This function is supported by the confirm method, which takes a number. The confirm method is supported by a policy called PickListDetail-ConfirmationPolicy (see Figure 15.3).

This policy looks at the value passed, and if it matches the amount that was supposed to be picked, it notifies the picking details that they have been picked

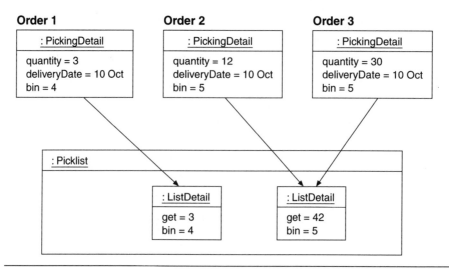

Figure 15.2. Generating a Pick List

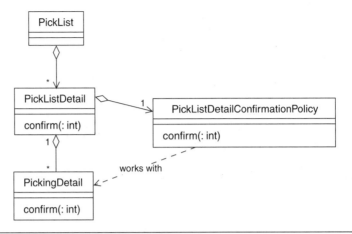

Figure 15.3. PickListDetailConfirmationPolicy

(thereby making them shippable). If the amount does not match, the policy goes through the associated picking details and completely fills them until it runs out of the particular item. Then it uses the remaining items (which may be 0) on the next picking detail, and confirms 0 for the rest.

If an order's request is completely filled, then the picking detail is notified (thereby making the order shippable). On the other hand, if only some (or none) of the amount was provided, the picking detail is notified of the amount assigned to it. The order is then processed by Order Management to determine how to handle the shortage. For example, a partial order may or may not be acceptable; the customer may have requested that only a complete order be shipped.

Applicability

Consider using the List Generation pattern when any of the following criteria apply:

- A list must be generated from a set of items and those items handled as part of the generated list. We can think of this new list as another view over the original items.
- Flexibility in how the list is generated is needed.
- Flexibility in how the items in the list are processed is needed—in particular, the processing when multiple items are associated with a single list entry, as well as processing that applies to the entire list.

Structure

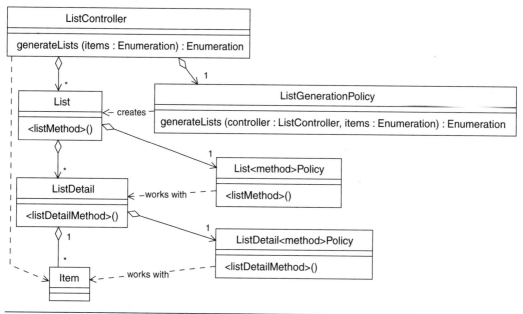

Figure 15.4. List Generation Structure

Participants

- **ListController** (PickListController). The class that follows the Controller pattern (see Chapter 10). The ListController manages the lists and provides the method for generating the lists.

- **List** (PickList). The class that contains the list. It consists of ListDetails that represent the entries on the list. It may provide methods for manipulating all ListDetails. These methods may be supported by a List<method>Policy.

- **List<method>Policy** (ListConfirmAllPolicy). A policy that encapsulates the operation of a method on the List, such as a confirmAll method. See the "Implementation" section later in this chapter for details.

- **ListDetail** (PickListDetail). A class that represents the entries on the List. ListDetails know which Items they are associated with. This class supports methods that will affect the items associated with it, such as the confirm method. These methods may be supported by a ListDetail<method>Policy.

- **ListDetail<method>Policy** (PickListDetailConfirmationPolicy). A policy that encapsulates the impact of a ListDetail method on its associated items.

- **Item** (PickingDetail). A class that represents the items over which the list is to be generated.
- **ListGenerationPolicy** (PickListGenerationPolicy). A policy that controls how many Lists are generated, which ListDetails are part of each List, and which Items each ListDetail covers.

Collaborations

- The user collects the set of Items to be used to generate one or more Lists. These Items are passed to the generateLists method on the ListController. This method is supported by an object-specific policy, ListGenerationPolicy, to which processing is delegated.
- ListGenerationPolicy takes the input Items, determines how many Lists to create, and creates them. It determines how the Items will be combined into ListDetails and to which List these ListDetails will be assigned.
- In some situations—for example, moving a ListDetail to another List or creating a new List—once created, the List(s) can be manually updated.
- Methods can be supported on the List for working with all the ListDetails. These methods can be supported by List<method>Policy classes, which are object-specific policies.
- As a result of working with a List, a business processing method of some kind is typically called on a ListDetail. This method is supported by an object-specific policy, ListItem<method>Policy, to which processing is delegated.
- The ListItem<method>Policy deals with the fact that the processing of one ListDetail affects one or more Items. It may simply invoke a method on each of the Items, or it may do additional processing to determine which methods to invoke on which items.

Consequences

The List Generation pattern has the following tradeoffs, benefits, and drawbacks:

Tradeoffs

- **Flexibility versus performance.** Policies can be added for all methods supported on the List or ListDetails. We must consider on a method-by-method basis the tradeoff between having these methods supported by policies and having them hard-coded. If they are supported by a policy, one aspect of this tradeoff is determining which type of policy to use—that is, deciding among the Simple Policy, the Chain of Responsibility-Driven Policy, and the Token-Driven Policy. These patterns are discussed in Part II, "Behavioral Patterns."

Benefits

- **Business-oriented manipulation of items.** Providing the policies for the methods on the List or ListDetails allows the natural manipulation of the List or ListDetails to affect the associated Items appropriately.

Drawbacks

- **Unnecessary complexity for simple cases.** If compound lists are not typical for a business process, the List Generation pattern may be overkill. Simple, direct processing of the items may be sufficient in this case.

Implementation

Consider the following implementation issues for the List Generation pattern:

- **List generation policy.** The ListGenerationPolicy may be a chain of responsibility-driven policy. In the pick list example, we may have a default policy on the company and specific policies on various warehouses.
- **List generation using keys.** The ListGenerationPolicy can use the keys from the Key/Keyable pattern (see Chapter 11). One of the examples in Chapter 11 describes using keys to generate pick lists.
- **Item manipulation policies.** The methods on the List and ListDetail may be supported by policies. Sometimes methods on the List are simply convenience methods that call the same method on each of the ListDetails. For example, a confirmAll method could be provided on the PickList that simply confirms that all the PickListDetails were completely picked. This method probably would not be associated with a policy; instead its behavior would be hard-coded in the PickList class.

Sample Code

In the PickList example, the pick list is generated by the generatePickList method of the PickListGenerationPolicy. In this example, multiple PickLists are generated. However, all PickingDetails for the same product in the same zone and location are combined into a single PickListDetail. One PickList is generated for each picker. Pickers are assigned to particular zones in the warehouse, so the zone is used to assign PickListDetails to the appropriate picker's PickList:

```
public class PickListGenerationPolicy {

  public PickList[] generatePickLists(PickListController controller,
                                      Enumeration pickingDetails) {

    // Create an array of empty PickLists
    PickList[] pickLists =
        new PickList[controller.getNumberOfPickers()];

    // Create a Hashtable to use while creating the PickListDetails
    Hashtable pickListDetails = new Hashtable();

    // Create a key for consolidating the PickingDetails
    PickListGenerationKey key = new PickListGenerationKey();

    // Consolidate the PickingDetails into PickListDetails
    while (pickingDetails.hasMoreElements()) {

      // Get the PickingDetail to work with
      PickingDetail pickingDetail =
          (PickingDetail)pickingDetails.nextElement();

      // Set the key for this particular PickingDetail
      key.setFromPickingDetail(pickingDetail);

      // Use the key to retrieve PickListDetail from Hashtable
      PickListDetail pickListDetail =
       (PickListDetail)pickListDetails.get(key);

      // If found, then combine PickingDetail into existing
      // PickListDetail
      if (pickListDetail != null)
        pickListDetail.addPickingDetail(pickingDetail);
      else {
        // If not found, then create a new PickListDetail and add
        // to Hashtable
        pickListDetail = new PickListDetail(pickingDetail);
        pickListDetails.put(key, pickListDetail);
      }
    }

    // Put the PickingDetails into the PickList for the picker assigned
    // to the zone in which they are located
    Enumeration pickDetailsToIterate = pickListDetails.elements();

    while (pickDetailsToIterate.hasMoreElements()) {

      // Get the PickListDetail to work with
      PickListDetail pickListDetail =
          (PickListDetail)pickDetailsToIterate.nextElement();
```

```
        // Get the zone and picker number for that zone
        int pickerNumber =
            controller.getPickerNumberForZone(pickListDetail.getZone());

        // Add the PickListDetail to that picker's PickList
        pickLists[pickerNumber].addPickListDetail(pickListDetail);
    }

    // Return the array of PickLists
    return pickLists;
  }
}
```

After the pickers have picked the items on their PickLists and delivered them to shipping, they confirm which items they were able to pick. In this example, if everything was picked, then the confirm method on the PickingDetail that does not take a parameter is used. This method is used to confirm the entire quantity. If the full amount could not be picked, then the other confirm method, which takes an amount, is used to tell the PickingDetail how many of the items were picked.

If everything cannot be picked, we completely confirm PickingDetails until we run out of the item. For example, assume we have five PickingDetails with quantities of 2, 3, 2, 5, and 1, respectively. If the confirmed amount is 6, we would completely confirm the first and second PickingDetails for 2 and 3, respectively, the third partially for 1 (it required 2), and the fourth and fifth for 0.

```
public class PickListDetailConfirmationPolicy {

  public void confirm(PickListDetail pickListDetail,
                      int numberConfirmed) {

    // See if everything could be picked
    if (numberConfirmed == pickListDetail.getQuantity()) {

      // Everything could be picked, so go through the PickingDetails
      // and confirm them all
      Enumeration pickingDetails = pickListDetail.getPickingDetails();

      while (pickingDetails.hasMoreElements()){
        PickingDetail pickingDetail =
                  (PickingDetail)pickingDetails.nextElement();

        // Use the confirm method without parameters, thus confirming
        // the entire quantity
        pickingDetail.confirm();
      }
    }
    else {
```

```
    // Some items were not available to be picked
    // Completely fill as many PickingDetails as possible
    Enumeration pickingDetails = pickListDetail.getPickingDetails();

    // Keep track of how many we have left that we can confirm
    int leftToConfirm = numberConfirmed;

    while (pickingDetails.hasMoreElements()) {
        PickingDetail pickingDetail =
                    (PickingDetail)pickingDetails.nextElement();

        // Assume we cannot confirm any
        int canConfirm = 0;

        // See if any are left
        if (leftToConfirm != 0) {

            // Some left, so confirm what we can

            // We can confirm the smaller of the amount needed and what
            // we have
            canConfirm = Math.min(pickingDetail.getAmount(),
                                  leftToConfirm);

            // Update what's left
            leftToConfirm -= canConfirm;
        }
        // Else none left, so canConfirm = 0, which is its initial
        // value

        // Confirm what we can
        pickingDetail.confirm(canConfirm);
    }
  }
 }
}
```

Known Uses

SanFrancisco uses the List Generation pattern for the following:

- Pick lists (the primary example in this chapter), which are provided as part of the Warehouse Management Core Business Process.

- Other lists resulting from order processing (e.g., ship lists, invoices), which are provided as part of the Warehouse Management and Order Management Core Business Processes.

- Payment runs—that is, determining which suppliers you wish to pay (or which customers you want to refund)—which are provided as part of the Accounts Payable/Accounts Receivable Core Business Process.

Related Patterns

- **Controller.** The lists are managed by a controller (see Chapter 10).

- **Simple Policy.** The list is generated by a policy (see Chapter 7), and the processing of items in the list can be supported by policies.

- **Chain of Responsibility-Driven Policy.** Use of the Simple Policy pattern may be replaced by use of the Chain of Responsibility-Driven Policy pattern (see Chapter 8) as needed.

- **Key/Keyable.** The Key/Keyable pattern (see Chapter 11) can be used in the ListGenerationPolicy to determine which Items should be consolidated into ListDetails.

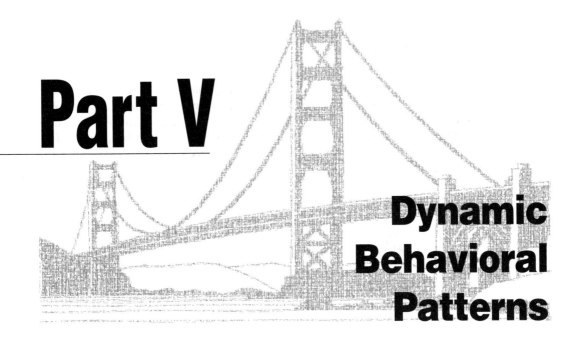

Part V

Dynamic Behavioral Patterns

SanFrancisco's dynamic behavioral patterns describe object-oriented approaches for modeling entities in the business domain that exhibit behavioral changes throughout their existence—not only changes to existing behavior, but also changes to the set of behaviors (responsibilities) supported by the business entity at any given time. The patterns in Part V build on the general concepts described in the State pattern of *Design Patterns* and on one another.

The Extensible Item pattern (Chapter 16) is the core pattern in this section. It describes a means of designing business objects that support dynamic behavioral changes.

The Hierarchical Extensible Item pattern (Chapter 17), as the name implies, builds on the Extensible Item pattern and describes an approach for modeling hierarchical business entity structures with ExtensibleItems.

The Business Entity Lifecycle pattern (Chapter 18) also builds on the Extensible Item pattern, by describing how the occurrence of dynamic behavioral changes on an ExtensibleItem can be automated and configured. In other words, this pattern allows a developer to isolate the state machine controlling a business object's dynamic behavior from that business object.

The Hierarchy Information pattern (Chapter 19) combines the Hierarchical Extensible Item and Business Entity Lifecycle patterns to describe a mechanism for encapsulating behavioral aspects of a hierarchy of lifecycle-based business entities.

Finally, the Decoupled Processes pattern (Chapter 20) introduces an approach for representing individual business processes targeted at a given business entity. The pattern allows the processes to be reused in different orderings for different business contexts in which the target business entity is used. This pattern is closely tied to the Business Entity Lifecycle and Hierarchy Information patterns.

16

Extensible Item

Intent

Allow an object to support dynamic changes in behavior and data, simulating dynamic inheritance. The mechanisms defined by this pattern include adding, removing, or overriding supported methods and adding or removing data attributes as necessary to model a business object correctly at different stages of its existence.

Motivation

Certain entities in the business domain may change their behavior during their lifetimes. A person, for example, may start out as a customer of the Food Warehouse company, later be hired as an FW employee, and once employed, take on different roles or positions within the company. Although the application developer can define the set of roles that are valid under these circumstances, only the application user can specify the roles a specific instance will play over its lifetime. When such an entity is modeled in an object-oriented software application, the business object that represents the business entity must be able to change its behavior over its lifetime to simulate the business entity it represents.

One simple solution to this requirement is to define a set of interfaces representing the different roles of various business objects, then implement these interfaces as appropriate in each class. However, effective modeling of such behavioral changes may require the business object to allow the changing of supported interfaces and of implementations of interfaces, as well as the addition and removal of attributes. These changes must be accomplished at runtime—during the life of the business object. Given the constraints of strongly typed object-oriented languages like Java or C++, it is difficult for a single object instance to support runtime behavioral change to this extent.

In solving the problem of representing a dynamically changing business object, note that the data and behavior a business object acquires or relinquishes over its lifetime tend to come in packages. In the example just given, when a person becomes an employee, he or she acquires a package of behavior (methods) and information (attributes) necessary for being an employee. Similarly, person roles such as customer or manager can also be represented as packages of behavior and information. The Extensible Item pattern models the business object (person) as an ExtensibleItem and the packages of behavior and information (roles) as Extensions. Each ExtensibleItem contains a collection of Extensions that can be added or removed from the ExtensibleItem throughout its lifetime.

Unfortunately, simply adding and removing Extensions from an ExtensibleItem does not give us the required dynamic behavioral changes to the ExtensibleItem: Adding an Extension with a given method does not expose this method on the ExtensibleItem itself. The next step is to introduce a method on the ExtensibleItem base class that allows clients to invoke methods generically on the Extensions or the ExtensibleItem subclass itself. Called invokeMethod, this method takes a method name that is represented as a String, and an array of parameter objects to be passed into the target method. The return value of invokeMethod is an object that represents the return value (if one exists) of the target method. The ExtensibleItem base class provides an implementation of invokeMethod that binds the client's invokeMethod call to an actual method on the ExtensibleItem itself or on an Extension.[1]

The implementation of invokeMethod should account for overriding of the behavior of existing methods. For example, when a person who has the role of employee takes on the additional role of manager, his or her job responsibilities change. Using the Extensible Item pattern, we would make this transition by adding a ManagerExtension to a Person ExtensibleItem that already contains an EmployeeExtension (see Figure 16.1). If both the EmployeeExtension and ManagerExtension introduce a getJobResponsibilities method, the newer ManagerExtension's implementation of the method should be given preference over the older EmployeeExtension's implementation.

---

1. You may notice the similarity between the syntax of invokeMethod and Java's Method.invoke. This similarity is deliberate, given the similar semantics of these methods. However, the method invocation support provided in Java's Reflection package does not offer the same functionality as invokeMethod does. The invokeMethod method can be used to invoke a method that was not present at the time the ExtensibleItem instance was created; Java's Reflection support cannot. In the "Implementation" section later in this chapter we discuss how Java's Reflection support can be used in the implementation of the Extensible Item pattern.

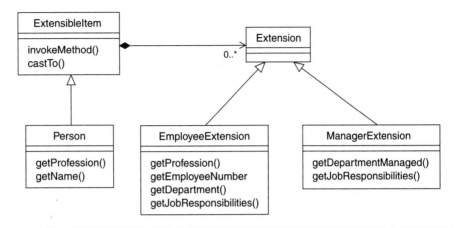

Figure 16.1. Extensible Item Pattern Used to Represent a Person with Employee and Manager Roles

To provide this sort of intuitive method-overriding behavior, the invokeMethod implementation uses a priority for ordering that is the reverse of the order in which the Extensions were added to the ExtensibleItem. Methods on the ExtensibleItem subclass itself should be given the lowest priority, allowing baseline implementations of methods to be placed directly on the ExtensibleItem subclass.

Remember that throughout this pattern, the goal is to simulate dynamic inheritance. Another aspect of dynamic inheritance is the ability of a subclass to delegate part of the implementation of a particular method to one or more of its base class implementations (e.g., the Java super.<methodName> call). ExtensibleItem provides this support through its base class implementation, allowing Extensions to delegate portions of their responsibility to other Extensions residing on the ExtensibleItem, or to the ExtensibleItem itself. The Extension doing the delegating does not know to whom it is delegating; the target of delegation is controlled by the order in which Extensions have been previously added to the ExtensibleItem.

Through the use of Extensions and the invokeMethod interface, an ExtensibleItem can now support the dynamic addition, removal, and overriding of methods. Unfortunately, the Extensible Item pattern, as described to this point, still has a significant drawback. Consider the following example that expands on our case study from Chapter 2:

The Food Warehouse application has a routine that allows the price of a product to be overridden for a specific order. FW's business rules dictate that no such change can be made without the authorization ID of a manager.

Within the FW application, this routine may be implemented as an overridePrice method on an OrderDetail that takes an instance of the Manager interface. If, within the FW application, a manager is implemented as a Person ExtensibleItem with a ManagerExtension, a strongly typed language (such as Java) will not allow a Person to be passed into the overridePrice method, even if all the methods of the Manager interface are supported through the invokeMethod interface.

How are we going to allow a properly typed object to be passed on this interface? We can solve this problem by using the Adapter pattern of *Design Patterns*. Remember that Extensions are packages of behavior, which represent roles that the ExtensibleItem can adopt. These roles commonly are associated with an interface, as in the Manager example. When an ExtensibleItem is to be treated as an instance of an interface that it supports through the invokeMethod method, an adapter object is substituted for the ExtensibleItem. The adapter object is an instance of an adapter class that implements or extends the required interface in a true compile-time sense. The adapter class contains a reference to the ExtensibleItem that it represents, and it implements each inherited method by invoking it on the associated ExtensibleItem through the invokeMethod interface (see Figure 16.2).

Continuing with the Manager example, a ManagerAdapter class would be introduced that contains a reference to the Person ExtensibleItem and implements inherited Manager methods such as getDepartmentManaged by calling invokeMethod on the associated Person, passing "getDepartmentManaged" as the target method name.[2]

Using adapters with ExtensibleItems gives us the ability to use an ExtensibleItem as a true instance of an interface it supports, but how does a client obtain a specific adapter for an ExtensibleItem? Since an ExtensibleItem may support a given interface for only part of its lifetime, how does a client know that the ExtensibleItem can support a specific adapter at any given time? The answers to these questions lie in adding a castTo method to the ExtensibleItem class.

Coming back to our goal of emulating dynamic inheritance, what we want is the capability to cast the ExtensibleItem. With traditional inheritance, an object that implements multiple interfaces can generally be cast to any of the supported interfaces. Introduction of the castTo method allows similar behavior for an ExtensibleItem. The castTo method takes a String that represents the class (or interface) name to which the ExtensibleItem is to be cast and returns an

---

2. Note that we did not suggest having the ManagerExtension also implement the Manager interface, for two reasons: First, the ManagerExtension will never be used polymorphically as a Manager, and second, the Extensible Item pattern does not require that an Extension class implement all the methods introduced by its corresponding interface; some of the methods may be delegated to other Extensions or to the ExtensibleItem itself.

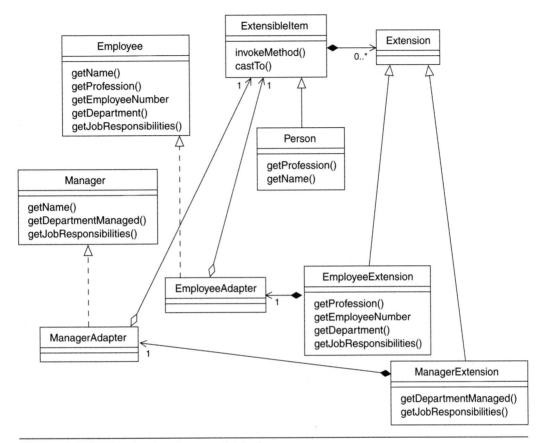

Figure 16.2. Introducing Interfaces and Adapters

object that can then be cast (a real cast) to an instance of the requested interface. If the requested interface is not supported by the ExtensibleItem, no object is returned.

The ExtensibleItem base class implements the castTo method by checking each of its contained Extensions for one that supports the requested interface: It asks each Extension to produce an adapter object that implements the given interface. An Extension that is responsible for enabling the requested interface on the ExtensibleItem will return an adapter object that supports the interface. Other Extensions will not return an adapter. Once an adapter is returned from an Extension, that adapter is returned to the client. If no Extension returns an adapter, no object is returned to the client.

Figure 16.3 shows how a call to castTo would work on the Person ExtensibleItem shown in Figures 16.1 and 16.2. Note that in this example each Extension holds on to an instance of the adapter it supports.

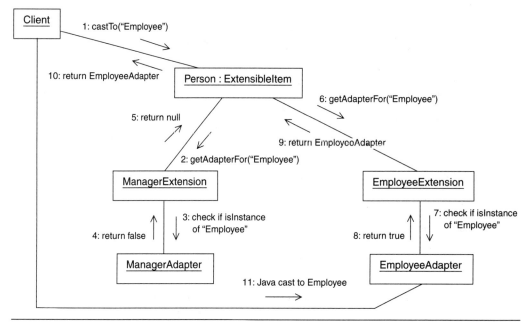

Figure 16.3. Casting a Person to an Employee Using castTo

Now we have a complete solution for emulating dynamic inheritance. With the Extensible Item pattern, we can do all of the following:

- Dynamically add and remove behavior and attributes to and from a class
- Delegate responsibility for part or all of a particular method to the "dynamic superclasses" of the object
- Cast an object to any of the dynamically inherited interfaces it supports

Applicability

Consider using the Extensible Item pattern when any of the following criteria apply:

- Business objects need to take on varying sets of roles throughout their lifetimes.
- The interfaces and behavior of a business object will change depending on which roles are currently supported.

The Person object from the preceding example is one case that meets these criteria. Here are some other examples:

- A business document such as an invoice may support a role of "receivable" and later have a role of "received."

- A warehouse may support roles of "order target" and "order source" when used with purchase orders and sales orders, respectively.

- An order and its order details may take on roles such as "plannable," "pickable," "shippable," and so on.

Structure

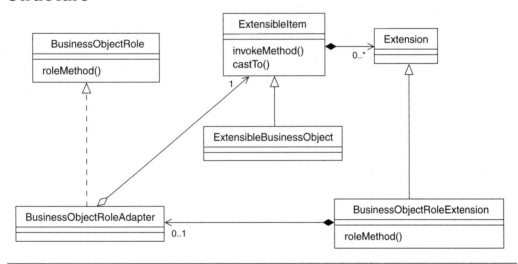

Figure 16.4. Extensible Item Structure

Participants

- **ExtensibleItem.** The primary participant in this pattern. The ExtensibleItem class or subclass represents the business object that is being modeled. ExtensibleItem objects contain Extensions and are responsible for introducing and implementing the invokeMethod and castTo methods.

- **ExtensibleBusinessObject** (Person). A subclass of ExtensibleItem representing a particular business entity that exhibits dynamically changing behavior.

- **Extension.** A package of behavior and data representing a role that an ExtensibleItem can take on. The Extension class is a base class that is inherited by specific Extension subclasses. Extension subclasses enable a set of methods on the ExtensibleItem to which they are added. If an Extension subclass enables an ExtensibleItem to support an interface (e.g., Employee), the Extension class should be able to return an adapter object that implements that interface.

- **BusinessObjectRoleExtension** (CustomerExtension, EmployeeExtension, ManagerExtension). A subclass of Extension that provides the behavior and data for the particular role a business object is to play.

- **BusinessObjectRoleAdapter** (CustomerAdapter, EmployeeAdapter, ManagerAdapter). The adapter class that follows the standard Adapter pattern by implementing a specific interface (shown as BusinessObjectRole) through calls to the ExtensibleItem's invokeMethod method. Instances of the adapter class will be produced by their associated Extension when the implemented interface is specified in a call to the ExtensibleItem's castTo method. An adapter object represents its associated ExtensibleItem when the ExtensibleItem is to be treated as an instance of the implemented interface.

- **BusinessObjectRole** (Customer, Employee, Manager). A Java interface that declares the behavior (the supported methods) for the particular role a business object is to play.

Collaborations

- An ExtensibleItem contains an ordered collection of Extension objects to which (in addition to itself) it will bind method calls invoked through invokeMethod.

- An ExtensibleItem delegates the retrieval of an adapter for an interface requested through the castTo method to its contained Extensions.

- An Extension enables a set of its own methods on the ExtensibleItem (through invokeMethod) when it is added to the ExtensibleItem.

- An Extension may override methods that were enabled on the ExtensibleItem either by a previously added Extension or by the ExtensibleItem itself.

- An Extension must produce an adapter for its associated interface (if one exists) when asked by the ExtensibleItem to do so.

- An adapter object references an ExtensibleItem and delegates all supported methods to the ExtensibleItem.

Consequences

The Extensible Item pattern has the following tradeoffs, benefits, and drawbacks:

Tradeoffs

- **Performance versus flexibility.** As the benefits and drawbacks that follow indicate, the Extensible Item pattern provides a powerful and flexible approach to modeling business objects with changing roles, but it does not come without performance cost. In deciding whether to use this pattern for a business object, it is important to consider whether or not the roles supported by a business object will change over its lifetime. For instance, Food Warehouse may consider all its warehouses capable of shipping customer orders as well as receiving incoming orders for the duration of their existence. Given this requirement, it is more practical to build the "order target" and "order source" roles into the interface of the Warehouse object.

Benefits

- **Correct modeling of changing roles.** The Extensible Item pattern allows a business object to correctly model the changing roles and behavior of the business entity it represents. Unlike the basic State pattern of *Design Patterns*, methods associated with a given role are enabled only when the Extension representing the role is present. This restriction means that the role method implementations do not need to be concerned with whether the ExtensibleItem was in the proper state for the method to be called.
- **Support for newly defined roles.** An ExtensibleItem can support roles that were not known at the time it was implemented. For example, when the Food Warehouse application was designed and implemented, it was determined that a Person object was needed and that the Person object should be able to support the roles of Employee and Manager. Later, after the FW application had been in use for some time, it was decided that it would be useful for a Person object to support the role of OrderTaker as well. To support this function, all that is required is the introduction of an OrderTaker interface, an OrderTakerExtension, and an OrderTakerAdapter. The Person class and its existing instances do not need to be altered.

Drawbacks

- **Increased method call overhead.** When a method is called on an ExtensibleItem through invokeMethod, its performance will not match that of a method called directly, regardless of the implementation of invokeMethod.

- **Increased complexity.** When a business object is modeled as an Extensible-Item, more objects are involved than if a single object that incorporated the data and behavior of a given set of roles had been used.

Implementation

Consider the following implementation issues for the Extensible Item pattern:

- **Implementing invokeMethod.** The implementation of invokeMethod is probably the most complex and performance-critical aspect of implementing the Extensible Item pattern. This pattern does not specify whether binding of methods called through invokeMethod should be based on method name alone or on the entire signature of the requested method (allowing support for overloaded methods). The SanFrancisco implementation of the Extensible Item pattern supports the former approach in order to minimize complexity and increase performance. Here are some possible approaches for the invokeMethod implementation:

  - Introduce a handleInvokeMethod method on both the ExtensibleItem and the Extension base classes that would be responsible for binding the passed method name and parameter array to an actual method on that Extension or ExtensibleItem object. Some means of indicating to the ExtensibleItem that the requested method was not supported would be necessary. We could handle this requirement by having handle-InvokeMethod return a ReturnValue that would have both the result object from the called method and a flag indicating whether the Extension had supported the method. The ExtensibleItem would walk its ordered collection of Extensions from last added to first added, calling handleInvokeMethod on each Extension until a ReturnValue was returned indicating that the method was actually invoked. If no Extensions supported the requested method, handleInvokeMethod would be called on the ExtensibleItem itself. When a valid ReturnValue was returned, the ExtensibleItem would extract the result object from within and return it to the client. If neither the Extensions nor the ExtensibleItem supported the requested method, an exception would be thrown. The handleInvokeMethod method either could be left abstract, requiring each ExtensibleItem or Extension subclass to override it with a switchlike implementation that would be specific for that subclass, or it could be implemented in a generic (but slower) fashion in the base class by use of Java's Reflection support.

    This approach minimizes Extension add times, as well as the footprint of an ExtensibleItem object, but because of the sequential checking of the existing Extensions, the resulting performance of invokeMethod is not optimal.

   – Have the ExtensibleItem keep a "map" of requested method name or
     signature to the most recently added Extension (or the ExtensibleItem
     itself) that supports the method. Extensions would add entries to the
     ExtensibleItem map for their supported methods as they were added
     to the ExtensibleItem. ExtensibleItems and Extensions would support
     a handleInvokeMethod as already described. The ExtensibleItem's
     implementation of invokeMethod would find the entry for the requested
     method in the map and then call handleInvokeMethod on the
     ExtensibleItem or Extension associated with that map entry. This ap-
     proach optimizes the invokeMethod performance but increases both
     the time required to add an Extension to an ExtensibleItem and the
     ExtensibleItem's footprint.

- **Implementing castTo.** As described earlier, to implement the castTo
  method, ExtensibleItem walks through its contained Extensions, asking
  each to produce, if possible, an adapter object that supports the requested
  interface. It is beneficial to have the Extension subclass contain an instance of
  its associated adapter class. This arrangement minimizes the cost of producing the adapter on request. Another advantage of holding the adapter
  object is that, in a language such as Java, the adapter object itself can be
  used in the determination of whether or not it implements a given interface.

- **Managing adapter behavior.** Because adapters represent an ExtensibleItem
  to the objects with which they collaborate, they must be managed properly with respect to the object lifecycle of the underlying ExtensibleItem.
  In particular, consideration must be given to what should happen when
  an ExtensibleItem is to be deleted. Should the ExtensibleItem even be allowed to be deleted if any of its adapters are currently referenced by other
  objects? Should the ExtensibleItem be responsible for cleaning up all its
  associated adapters at delete time? Or should the adapters gracefully
  handle the dangling adapter case? This issue also applies to the creation
  and deletion of specific Extensions within an ExtensibleItem. When an
  Extension is deleted from an ExtensibleItem instance, that instance is
  dynamically "losing" inheritance of the interfaces represented by that
  Extension; thus, the adapter associated with that Extension is no longer
  valid.

- **Supporting interfaces with multiple Extensions.** The set of methods introduced by an interface and implemented through an adapter may be supported by more than one Extension or by the ExtensibleItem itself. For example,
  methods introduced by the Manager interface are supported by the Person
  (e.g., getName) and the ManagerExtension (e.g., getDepartmentManaged,
  getJobResponsibilities) objects.

- **Supporting multiple adapters per Extension.** In some cases, it may be
  useful for a single Extension subclass to enable multiple interfaces on its
  associated ExtensibleItem. In these cases we can simply implement the

Extension subclass so that it is able to produce (or contain) adapters for each of the supported interfaces.

- **Supporting an adapter on the ExtensibleItem.** Although we have limited our discussion on the support of interfaces and their adapters primarily to Extension objects, ExtensibleItem subclasses themselves can also be allowed to support interfaces through adapters. Because it allows Extensions to provide or override the implementation of the methods introduced on the interface, rather than limiting such capability to the ExtensibleItem subclass itself, this approach may be preferable to having the ExtensibleItem subclass extend an interface directly.

- **Checking if a method is supported.** Since, by design, the set of methods supported through invokeMethod on an ExtensibleItem may change throughout the life of the object, allowing a user to check if a method is supported on an ExtensibleItem before invoking that method can be useful. In SanFrancisco, a method called checkIfMethodSupported provides this function. The implementation of this method is similar to the invokeMethod implementation and is shown in the sample code that follows.

Sample Code

This sample implementation of invokeMethod on the ExtensibleItem base class uses the first implementation approach described in the previous section:

```
public Object invokeMethod(String methodName,
                           Object[] parameterList) {

    // Walk through the Extensions
    for (int i = 0;i<ivExtensions.size();++i) {
        // Get the next Extension from the collection
        // (this assumes that collection is ordered from newest
        // Extensions to oldest)
        Extension ext = (Extension)(ivExtensions.elementAt(i));

        // Try invoking the requested method on it
        ReturnValue retVal = ext.handleInvokeMethod(methodName,
                                                    parameterList);

        // Check the ReturnValue object to see if the
        // method was invoked; if it was, return the result
        // object to the caller and we're done
        if (retVal.methodInvoked()) {
            return retVal.getMethodResult();
        }
```

```
        // Otherwise, continue to the next Extension
    }

    // If we get here, no Extension was found that supported the
    // requested method, so try calling it on the ExtensibleItem
    // itself
    ReturnValue retVal = handleInvokeMethod(methodName,
                                            parameterList);

    // If the method was successfully invoked, return
    // the result to the caller
    if (retVal.methodInvoked()) {
      return retVal.getMethodResult();
    }

    // Otherwise, this is an error case because the method
    // was not supported by the ExtensibleItem or its Extensions
    throw new MethodNotFoundException(methodName);
}
```

Here's a sample implementation of the castTo method on the ExtensibleItem base class:

```
public Object castTo(String interfaceName) throws
    ClassNotFoundException {

    // Walk through the Extensions
    for (int i = 0;i<ivExtensions.size();++i) {
      // Get the next Extension from the collection
      Extension ext = (Extension)(ivExtensions.elementAt(i));

      // See if the Extension can produce an
      // Adapter that supports the requested interface
      Object adapter = ext.getAdapterFor(interfaceName);

      // If we got an adapter back, return it to the
      // caller and we're finished
        if (adapter!= null) {
            return adapter;
        }

    // Otherwise, continue to the next Extension
    }

    // At this point we know that that no Extension supports
    // the interface, so return null to the client
    return null;
}
```

The following block of code shows the checkIfMethodSupported method described earlier, in the "Implementation" section. Our implementation of this method depends on a supportsMethod helper method that indicates whether a method is supported on a specific Extension or ExtensibleItem object. Subclasses of Extension and ExtensibleItem provide specific implementations of this method:

```
public boolean checkIfMethodSupported(String methodName) {

    // Walk through the Extensions
    for (int i = 0;i<ivExtensions.size();++i) {
        // Get the next Extension from the collection
        Extension ext = (Extension)(ivExtensions.elementAt(i));

        // See if the Extension supports the method
        if (ext.supportsMethod(methodName)) {
            return true;
        }
        // Otherwise, continue to the next Extension
    }

    // If we get here, no Extension was found that supported the
    // requested method, so check the ExtensibleItem itself
    return supportsMethod(methodName);
}
```

Here's the Person class implemented as a subclass of ExtensibleItem:

```
public class Person extends ExtensibleItem {

    // Constructor
    public Person(String name) {
        ivName = name;
    }

    // This is an example of a fixed method that will
    // probably not be overridden by an Extension
    public String getName() {
        return ivName;
    }

    // This is an example of a baseline implementation
    // of a method that will likely be overridden by
    // Extensions such as EmployeeExtension
    public String getProfession() {
        return "none";
    }

    // A simple, nongeneric implementation of handleInvokeMethod
    public ReturnValue handleInvokeMethod(String methodName,
                                          Object[] parameterList) {
```

```
        // Hold the result as an Object
        Object result = null;
        if (methodName.equals("getName")) {
            result = getName();
        }
        else if (methodName.equals("getProfession")) {
            result = getProfession();
        }
        else {
            // At this point we know that the method
            // was not supported by this ExtensibleItem,
            // so return a ReturnValue indicating this
            return new ReturnValue(null,false);
        }

        // If we get here, a method was called,
        // so put the result in a ReturnValue,
        // indicate that the method was invoked,
        // and return the result to the caller
        return new ReturnValue(result,true);
    }

    // A nongeneric implementation of the supportsMethod
    // helper method called from checkIfMethodSupported
    public boolean supportsMethod(String methodName) {
        if (methodName.equals("getName") ||
            methodName.equals("getProfession")) {
            return true;
        }
        else {
            return false;
        }
    }

    protected String ivName = null;
}
```

What follows is a generic implementation of the getAdapterFor method from the Extension base class. This implementation assumes that Extensions that support interfaces will cache their adapters in an attribute (ivAdapter) in the Extension base class.

```
public Object getAdapterFor(String interfaceName) throws
    ClassNotFoundException {

    // Check if the Extension has an adapter at all;
    // if not, return null, indicating that the given
    // interface is not supported
    if (ivAdapter == null) {
        return null;
    }
```

```
    // Convert the given interface name to a Class
    Class requestedClass = Class.forName(interfaceName);

    // Now see if the adapter is an instance of the Class;
    // if so, return the adapter
    if (requestedClass.isInstance(ivAdapter)) {
        return ivAdapter;
    }

    // Otherwise, return null, indicating that the given
    // interface is not supported
    return null;
}
```

Here's the Employee interface:

```
public interface Employee {
    public String getName();
    public String getEmployeeNumber();
    public String getProfession();
    public String getDepartment();
}
```

and the following shows the EmployeeAdapter class:

```
public class EmployeeAdapter implements Employee {

    // Constructor
    public EmployeeAdapter(Person person) {
        ivPerson = person;
    }


    public String getEmployeeNumber() {
        // Delegate the method call to the associated
        // ExtensibleItem through the invokeMethod interface
        return
            (String)(ivPerson.invokeMethod("getEmployeeNumber",null));
    }

    public String getProfession() {
        return (String)(ivPerson.invokeMethod("getProfession",null));
    }

    public String getDepartment() {
        return (String)(ivPerson.invokeMethod("getDepartment",null));
    }

    public String getName() {
        // Here we call getName through the invokeMethod
        // interface, even though we might have called it
```

```
        // directly against Person. Using invokeMethod
        // allows for the possibility of an override by
        // an Extension; a direct call does not.
        return (String)(ivPerson.invokeMethod("getName",null));
    }

    Person ivPerson = null;
}
```

Now let's look at the EmployeeExtension class. EmployeeExtension is a concrete Extension subclass. The nongeneric implementation of handleInvoke-Method shown here keys off of the method name rather than the complete method signature. Note that EmployeeExtension does not introduce a getName method. The getName method on the Person class will be sufficient to fulfill the Employee interface.

```
public class EmployeeExtension extends Extension {

    // Constructor (The Person parameter is the Person to which this
    // Extension will be added. It is necessary in this implementation
    // to allow full construction of the contained adapter.)
    public EmployeeExtension(String employeeNumber,
                             String profession,
                             String department,
                             Person person) {
        ivEmployeeNumber = employeeNumber;
        ivProfession = profession;
        ivDepartment = department;

        // Set the parent class adapter attribute
        ivAdapter = new EmployeeAdapter(person);
    }

    // A simple, nongeneric implementation of handleInvokeMethod
    public ReturnValue handleInvokeMethod(String methodName,
                                          Object[] parameterList) {

        // Object to hold result
        Object result = null;
        if (methodName.equals("getEmployeeNumber")) {
            result = getEmployeeNumber();
        }
        else if (methodName.equals("getProfession")) {
            result = getProfession();
        }
        else if (methodName.equals("getDepartment")) {
            result = getDepartment();
        }
        else {
            // At this point we know that the method
            // was not supported by this Extension,
```

```
                    // so return a ReturnValue indicating this
                    return new ReturnValue(null,false);
            }

            // If we get here, a method was called,
            // so put the result in a ReturnValue,
            // indicate that the method was invoked,
            // and return the result to the caller
            return new ReturnValue(result,true);
    }

    // A nongeneric implementation of the supportsMethod
    // helper method called from checkIfMethodSupported
    public boolean supportsMethod(String methodName) {
        if (methodName.equals("getEmployeeNumber") ||
            methodName.equals("getProfession") ||
            methodName.equals("getDepartment")) {
            return true;
        }
        else {
            return false;
        }
    }

    // Implementations of Employee methods

    public String getEmployeeNumber() {
        return ivEmployeeNumber;
    }

    public String getProfession() {
        return ivProfession;
    }

    public String getDepartment() {
        return ivDepartment;
    }


    // Data added by the Extension
    public String ivEmployeeNumber;
    public String ivProfession;
    public String ivDepartment;

}
```

Known Uses

The Extensible Item pattern is used in the SanFrancisco Common Business Objects to implement the Initials class. An Initials object can be thought of as a responsible party for a given business process. Initials support roles such as Salesman, OrderTaker, or WarehouseEmployee.

The Extensible Item pattern is also used in the implementation of orders and order details within the Order Management Core Business Process and of collection documents in the Combined Ledger Core Business Process.

Related Patterns

- **Adapter.** Adapter objects (as defined in *Design Patterns*) are used to adapt an ExtensibleItem to an interface that it supports through an Extension.

- **State.** ExtensibleItem is a more flexible approach to meeting many of the requirements that the State pattern of *Design Patterns* also addresses.

17

Hierarchical Extensible Item

Intent

Provide a flexible, loosely coupled mechanism for arranging business objects in a tree structure that naturally reflects the structure and behavior of hierarchies of entities found in many business domains, and allow those entities to emulate dynamic inheritance.

Motivation

Let's continue with the Person example from Chapter 16. In the real world, it is quite common for a person to belong to a group or organization, such as a family, a club, or a fitness class. In the business world, a person who is an employee in a company is probably a member of a group called a department. A department, in turn, is part of an organization, which may be part of a division, and so on. Persons, departments, organizations, and divisions within a company form a treelike hierarchy (see Figure 17.1).

The fact that business objects such as Persons and Departments form hierarchies is not particularly interesting in itself. What is interesting about these objects and their structure is the delegation of behavior within the structure. Some reasonable questions to ask of a person in a department are what her department number is and who her manager is. Although we would expect to be able to retrieve this information directly from a Person, things like department number and manager name are attributes of the department itself. So in

269

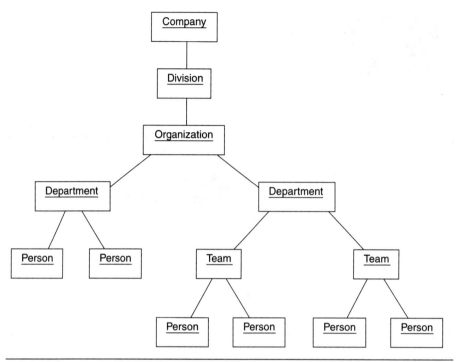

Figure 17.1. Organizational Hierarchy

this case, the Person object delegates the responsibility of producing a department number and manager name up to its hierarchical parent: the Department object.

In this instance, the delegation of responsibility proceeds upward through the business object hierarchy, but this isn't always the case. Consider a typical Department responsibility, such as producing the department's travel expenses for the year. The actual travel expenses may be associated directly with the persons who incurred them. In this case the Department object delegates the production of a travel expense total down to its hierarchical children: the Person objects.

The simplest way to design the Person and Department objects is to add a Department relationship to Person and a collection of Persons to the Department object. This approach is adequate if the Person-Department relationship is fixed and unchanging throughout the application. However, organizational levels may vary across different areas of a company. For instance, persons in the sales department may lie directly below the department in the organizational structure, and persons in the engineering department may be members of teams, which themselves are organizational children of the department. In both cases, Persons delegate requests for their managers' names to their immediate hierarchical parents. In the latter case, the Team object must continue the delegation upward to the parent Department. This example shows that a simple design that tightly couples the Person and Department objects is not sufficient. What's needed is a more generic, less strongly typed way of coupling objects that allows for a generic delegation of methods upward and downward through an object hierarchy.

Now let's look at the Extensible Item pattern (which we discussed in Chapter 16). The invokeMethod interface on a business object implemented as an ExtensibleItem is quite close to the type of generic method delegation interface that is needed for business objects within a hierarchy. Adding parent and child links to the ExtensibleItem class would allow us to place ExtensibleItems into object hierarchies. Using linked ExtensibleItems, we could implement the Person-Department hierarchy in such a way that the Person could implement its getManagerName method by simply calling getManagerName on its hierarchy parent through the invokeMethod interface. This approach works well when Person is an immediate child of Department, but it is less than ideal when a Team object lies between Person and Department (see Figure 17.2). This approach forces the Team class to implement somewhat unnatural getManagerName and getTravelExpenses methods simply to allow the wire-through behavior that is necessary to support the delegation of methods between the Person and Department objects.

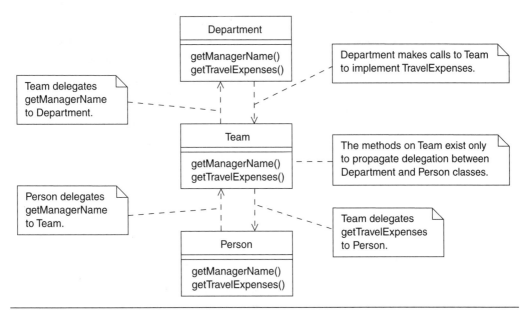

Figure 17.2. Simple Fixed Hierarchy Implementation

The solution to this dilemma is to introduce variations of invokeMethod to ExtensibleItem that automatically support upward and downward delegation of method calls. The first of these methods, which we'll call invokeMethod-UsingDrillup, is responsible for delegating a method call upward through the object hierarchy until an object is found that supports the requested method. The implementation of invokeMethodUsingDrillup is quite simple (see Figure 17.3):

1. Determine if the method is supported on this object (the different ways of making this check vary depending on the implementation chosen for the Extensible Item pattern).

2. If the method is supported, invoke it through the standard invokeMethod interface and return the result.

3. If the method is not supported, call invokeMethodUsingDrillup on the parent object and return the result (in this case, if there were no parent the result would be an error).

Note that the search for a method to invoke within invokeMethodUsingDrillup follows a Chain of Responsibility (see *Design Patterns*) that proceeds upward through the hierarchy of related business objects.

Next we address downward method delegation by introducing the method invokeMethodUsingDrilldown. Downward and upward method delegation are not entirely symmetric: Whereas upward delegation follows a linear path, downward delegation does not. For a Department to produce a travel expense total, getTravelExpenses must be called on each descendant Person and the results of those calls accumulated into a sum. To accommodate this nonlinear method

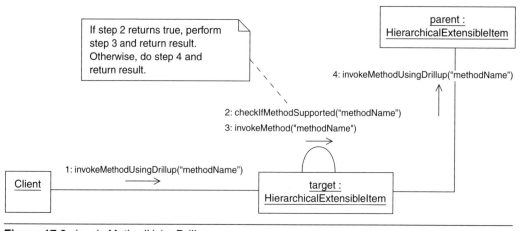

Figure 17.3. invokeMethodUsingDrillup

invocation behavior, we use the following implementation approach for invokeMethodUsingDrilldown (see Figure 17.4):

1. Determine if the method is supported on this object.

2. If the method is supported, invoke it through the standard invokeMethod interface and return the result. (Note that the implementation of the method being invoked on this object may choose in turn to delegate part or all of its responsibility to child objects by invoking the drilldown method on each of its children.)

3. If the method is not supported, call invokeMethodUsingDrilldown on each child object, accumulate the results, and return the final accumulated result.

Let's go into the "accumulate results" part of step 3 in a little more detail. We need a generic way to accumulate the results from the invokeMethodUsing-Drilldown calls that does not require the parent object to be aware of the specific type of results being returned. We create this means of accumulating results by introducing a CumulativeResult interface that provides an accumulateResult method. This method takes another CumulativeResult object as a parameter and "accumulates" that object into the target object. Objects as simple as a representation of a decimal value or as complex as an ordered or unordered collection

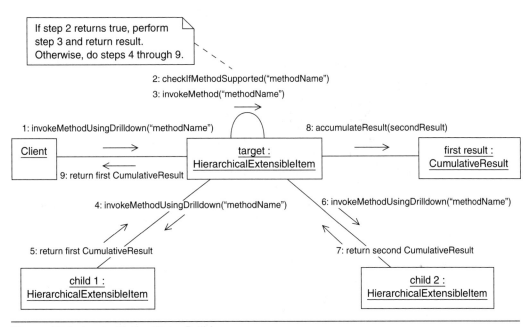

Figure 17.4. invokeMethodUsingDrilldown

can implement this interface. In the SanFrancisco framework, for instance, the CurrencyValue class is a type of CumulativeResult that implements accumulateResult by adding the value of the passed CurrencyValue object to itself.

Now let's revisit the Person-Department example we introduced earlier and assume that Person, Team, and Department are implemented by means of the Hierarchical Extensible Item pattern we have just discussed. A client (typically the ExtensibleItem's adapter) can now call the getManagerName or get-DepartmentNumber methods on Person through the invokeMethodUsing-Drillup method. These calls will be delegated upward through the object hierarchy to the Department object without requiring either the Person or Team classes to provide any sort of implementation of these methods.

Similarly, a client can get the total travel expenses for a Department by calling getTravelExpenses through the invokeMethodUsingDrilldown method on Department. This call will be delegated downward to all descendant Person objects regardless of whether the hierarchy includes intermediate Team objects. Note that Person objects can now be moved from under a sales Department to a Team in an engineering Department without any of the classes involved having to be modified.

Applicability

Consider using the Hierarchical Extensible Item pattern when any of the following criteria apply:

- The business entities being modeled exist in hierarchies within the business domain.

- The business entities being modeled meet the applicability requirements for ExtensibleItems as laid out in Chapter 16.

- The structure of the business entity hierarchies is not rigidly fixed. In other words, the types of a business entity's parent and children may vary depending on the specific hierarchy instance in which the entity is placed.

In the previous section, the sample business hierarchy was the organizational structure of a company. Here are some other hierarchy examples in which this pattern may apply:

- **Sales order.** A sales order, its order lines, and their subsequent details (picking, shipping, invoicing, and so on) form a hierarchy that requires both upward and downward method delegation.

- **Product assembly from a manufacturing system.** Product assemblies consist of a hierarchical structure of subassemblies and individual parts.

Structure

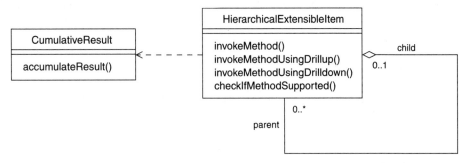

Figure 17.5. Hierarchical Extensible Item Structure

Participants

- **HierarchicalExtensibleItem** (Person, Team, Department). A specialized ExtensibleItem that is the primary participant in this pattern. The HierarchicalExtensibleItem class or subclass represents the hierarchical business entity that is being modeled. In addition to standard ExtensibleItem behavior and relationships, HierarchicalExtensibleItem objects contain a single, optional reference to a parent Hierarchical-ExtensibleItem object and a collection of references to child Hierarchical-ExtensibleItem objects. The HierarchicalExtensibleItem class enhances standard ExtensibleItem behavior by introducing invokeMethodUsing-Drillup and invokeMethodUsingDrilldown to allow upward and downward delegation of methods, respectively. HierarchicalExtensibleItem objects use the CumulativeResult interface in the implementation of invokeMethodUsingDrilldown.

- **CumulativeResult** (CurrencyValue). An interface implemented by classes whose instances will be used as return values from a method that may be called through invokeMethodUsingDrilldown. Classes that implement the CumulativeResult interface must implement the abstract accumulateResult method to combine a passed CumulativeResult (of the same class) to the target object. Likely implementers of the CumulativeResult interface are unit-style classes such as CurrencyValue, Decimal, Quantity, and so on. Another possible type of CumulativeResult would be a class that contains a Boolean attribute. This class could implement accumulateResult in such a way that a sum of instances of the class would be true only if all in-stances were true, or vice versa. This type of CumulativeResult would be useful for determining whether a certain condition holds for all children of a HierarchicalExtensibleItem. Collection classes could also implement this interface, allowing the CumulativeResult to be a composite of numerous business objects, which could then be manipulated individually by the caller of the method.

Collaborations

Methods invoked on HierarchicalExtensibleItem objects through invokeMethodUsingDrillDown return CumulativeResult objects.

Consequences

The Hierarchical Extensible Item pattern has the following benefits and drawbacks:

Benefits

- **Support for loosely coupled business object hierarchies.** The Hierarchical Extensible Item pattern allows business objects to be placed in hierarchies without requiring the objects to have specific knowledge of the objects above or below them in the hierarchy. This loose coupling of hierarchical business objects allows the objects to be moved between hierarchies and the hierarchies themselves to be modified at runtime.

- **Built-in support for method delegation.** Business objects implemented as hierarchical ExtensibleItems benefit from having built-in support for delegating methods upward and downward through the hierarchy. The class of a business object need not explicitly introduce a method that is to be delegated to a parent or child.

Drawbacks

- **Additional performance overhead.** The performance considerations for the ExtensibleItem pattern (see Chapter 16) apply to this pattern too. The dynamic binding of method calls that characterizes these patterns is inherently slower than a direct call.

- **Client awareness of delegation behavior.** To properly invoke a method that will be delegated, a client must be aware that the method is supported through delegation and know the direction in which the delegation should proceed. This information allows the client to select correctly among invokeMethodUsingDrillup, invokeMethodUsingDrilldown, and the standard invokeMethod. We can alleviate this problem by using adapters (as described in Chapter 16) that encapsulate this knowledge, allowing clients to call methods directly through the adapter interface without knowledge of what type of delegation (if any) is used to support the method.

- **Restriction on methods called through invokeMethodUsingDrilldown.**
  Methods that are to be called through invokeMethodUsingDrilldown are restricted to returning objects that implement the CumulativeResult interface. The SanFrancisco framework addresses this restriction by having all unit-style classes implement the CumulativeResult interface.

Implementation

Consider the following implementation issues for the Hierarchical Extensible Item pattern:

- **Implementing InvokeMethodUsingDrilldown.** In the invokeMethod-UsingDrillup implementation described earlier, we stated that an error would be thrown if the requested method was not supported by the target object or any of its ancestors. Implementing invokeMethodUsingDrilldown in a similar fashion is a little more difficult. A more straightforward approach—that used in the SanFrancisco framework—is simply not to require that the method be supported by the object (or its descendants). This approach is quite reasonable if you consider that invoking a modifier method through invokeMethodUsingDrilldown is a broadcast-style call. On the other hand, if a retrieval method is invoked, the fact that no CumulativeResult object was returned tells the caller that the method was not supported.

- **Traversal approaches in invokeMethodUsingDrilldown.** The algorithm that was described earlier for invokeMethodUsingDrilldown stops delegating downward when a descendant object is found that supports the requested method. In this implementation approach, usually the hierarchy of descendants of the target object is only partially traversed. You may choose to modify this implementation so that all descendants are traversed by simply calling invokeMethodUsingDrilldown on the children of a target object regardless of whether the target object itself handled the method. Such modification might be useful if you are determining whether all details of an order are in a completed, or closed, state before archiving the order. Of course, we could accomplish this task with the original invokeMethodUsingDrilldown implementation by requiring that the target method (e.g., getDetailState) be implemented so that this method itself propagates the invokeMethodUsingDrilldown call to its object's children.

- **Composite effect.** You may have noticed that invokeMethodUsingDrillup allows a HierarchicalExtensibleItem object to present itself as a composite of itself and its ancestors, much as a subclass does with regard to itself and its ancestor classes. This effect can be leveraged to support Java interfaces (through the use of adapters) without unnecessary duplication of methods within an object hierarchy. For example, our Person object could support an Employee interface that introduces (among other person-type methods) a getDepartmentNumber method, by implementing an EmployeeAdapter class that uses invokeMethodUsingDrillup when calling getDepartmentNumber.

- **Multiple delegation hierarchies.** In our description of the Hierarchical Extensible Item pattern, we have limited our business objects to a single hierarchy for method delegation. In many cases this arrangement is sufficient, but sometimes it will be necessary to allow a business object to exist in multiple delegation hierarchies. For example, the Person object we have used in our examples may exist in a business organizational hierarchy, as well as a household hierarchy, which represents the individuals that make up a household. The Hierarchical Extensible Item pattern could be adapted to support multiple delegation hierarchies in a manner similar to that described for PropertyContainers (see Chapter 5).

Following the approach described for multiple PropertyContainer hierarchies, the HierarchicalExtensibleItem class could be implemented to contain a collection of parent HierarchicalExtensibleItem objects keyed by a hierarchy name String, as well as a collection of child collections also keyed by hierarchy name. The invokeMethodUsingDrillup and invokeMethodUsingDrilldown methods could be enhanced to take an additional hierarchy name parameter that would be used in their implementation to select the correct path for method delegation. For instance, if a Person were being considered in the role of Employee, a hierarchy name of "Business Organization" would be passed on calls to invokeMethodUsingDrillup and invokeMethodUsing-Drilldown (see Figure 17.6). If the Person were being considered in the

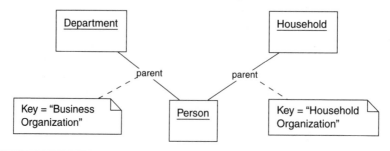

Figure 17.6. Supporting Multiple Hierarchies

role of HouseholdMember, a hierarchy name of "Household Organization" would be passed.

Sample Code

Here's a sample implementation of invokeMethodUsingDrillup on the Hierarchical ExtensibleItem class that uses the algorithm we discussed earlier:

```
public Object invokeMethodUsingDrillup(String methodName,
                                       Object[] parameterList) {

    // If method is supported by this object, invoke it and return
    'if (checkIfMethodSupported(methodName)) {
        return invokeMethod(methodName, parameterList);
    }

    // If a parent is present, delegate the method upward
    if (ivParent != null) {
        return ivParent.invokeMethodUsingDrillup(methodName,
                                                 parameterList);
    }
    else {
      // If no parent, indicate an error
      throw new MethodNotFoundException(methodName);
    }
}
```

Note that this invokeMethodUsingDrillup implementation depends on the checkIfMethodSupported method, which is discussed in the "Implementation" section of Chapter 16.

Here's a sample implementation of invokeMethodUsingDrilldown on the HierarchicalExtensibleItem class that uses the algorithm we discussed earlier. Note that this implementation does not throw an error if the requested method is not supported by this object or its descendants.

```
public CumulativeResult invokeMethodUsingDrilldown(String methodName,
                                       Object[] parameterList) {

    // If method is supported by this object, invoke it and return
    if (checkIfMethodSupported(methodName)) {
        // Note that methods called through invokeMethodUsingDrilldown
        // must return an object of type CumulativeResult
        return (CumulativeResult)invokeMethod(methodName, parameterList);
    }

    // Method not supported at this level, so try children
```

```
    // The accumulatedResult will hold the accumulated results
    // from calls on all children
    CumulativeResult accumulatedResult = null;
    for (int i = 0;i<ivChildren.size();++i) {
        // Get the next child from the collection
        HierarchicalExtensibleItem child =
            (HierarchicalExtensibleItem)(ivChildren.elementAt(i));

        // . . . and get its result
        CumulativeResult childResult -
            child.invokeMethodUsingDrilldown(methodName, parameterList);

        // Accumulate results into the first non-null result
        if (accumulatedResult == null) {
            accumulatedResult = childResult;
        }
        else {
            accumulatedResult.accumulateResult(childResult);
        }
    }
    return accumulatedResult;
}
```

Here's the CumulativeResult interface:

```
public interface CumulativeResult {

    public void accumulateResult(CumulativeResult cumulativeResultObject);
}
```

The following sample unit-style class implements the CumulativeResult interface. This class represents a currency value and has been simplified for this example:

```
public class CurrencyValue implements CumulativeResult {

    // Constructor
    public CurrencyValue(float value,
                         String currencyCode) {
        ivValue = value;
        ivCurrencyCode = currencyCode;
    }

    // Implementation of method from CumulativeResult interface as a
    // wire-through to the addTo method
    public void accumulateResult(CumulativeResult
                                 cumulativeResultObject) {

        if (cumulativeResultObject != null) {
            addTo((CurrencyValue)cumulativeResultObject);
        }
    }
}
```

```
    void addTo(CurrencyValue anotherCurrencyValue) {

        if (!anotherCurrencyValue.getCurrencyCode().
                equals(ivCurrencyCode)) {
            throw new IncompatableCurrencyException();
        }

        ivValue += anotherCurrencyValue.getValue();
    }

    float getValue() {
        return ivValue;
    }

    String getCurrencyCode() {
         return ivCurrencyCode;
    }


    protected float ivValue = 0;
    protected String ivCurrencyCode = null;
}
```

The following is an Employee interface that introduces methods corresponding to those found on the composite Person-Department object we have developed:

```
public interface Employee {
    public String getName();
    public String getEmployeeNumber();
    public String getManagerName();
    public String getDepartmentNumber();
}
```

Finally, the following EmployeeAdapter class adapts our Person object to the Employee interface. Note that some methods are invoked through the standard invokeMethod method, while others—those supported by the Department object—are invoked through invokeMethodUsingDrillup. The type of invocation used for each method is hidden from the user by the adapter.

```
public class EmployeeAdapter implements Employee {

    // Constructor
    public EmployeeAdapter(Person person) {
        ivPerson = person;
    }


    // Call these methods directly on the Person level through
    // the standard invokeMethod method
```

```
    public String getName() {
        return (String)(ivPerson.invokeMethod("getName",null));
    }

    public String getEmployeeNumber() {
        return
            (String)(ivPerson.invokeMethod("getEmployeeNumber",
                                            null));
    }


    // These methods exist at a higher level in the
    // hierarchy than Person, so they are implemented
    // using invokeMethodUsingDrillup
    public String getManagerName() {
        return (String)
            (ivPerson.invokeMethodUsingDrillup("getManagerName",
                                                null));
    }

    public String getDepartmentNumber() {
      return (String)
          (ivPerson.invokeMethodUsingDrillup("getDepartmentNumber",
                                              null));
    }

    Person ivPerson = null;
}
```

Known Uses

The Hierarchical Extensible Item pattern is used within the SanFrancisco framework in the Order Management Core Business Process. Within the Order Management package, the classes Order, OrderPriceDetail, OrderRequestedDetail, OrderPlanningDetail, and many other order detail classes are implemented as HierarchicalExtensibleItems. This pattern is particularly suited to the structure of an order because of the following business requirements:

- Customer information is kept at the order header (Order) level and must be retrievable from order detail objects at any level in the order structure.

- Amount information, such as quantity and value, is held on the individual OrderPriceDetail and OrderRequestedDetail objects. Sums of quantity and value must be retrievable from higher levels of the order.

- Order structures may vary from company to company and even within different order types within a single company. Order detail classes, such as OrderShippingDetail and OrderInvoicingDetail, may be found at different levels in different order structures and must not be tightly coupled with the classes of their parent and child detail objects.

Related Patterns

- **Extensible Item.** HierarchicalExtensibleItems are specialized ExtensibleItems (see Chapter 16).

- **Chain of Responsibility.** The delegation of methods upward within a hierarchy of HierarchicalExtensibleItem objects follows a chain of responsibility (as defined in *Design Patterns*) that extends from the target object upward through the hierarchy.

- **Adapter.** Adapter objects (as defined in *Design Patterns*) are used to adapt a HierarchicalExtensibleItem to an interface that it supports through composition.

18

Business Entity Lifecycle

Intent

Allow a business object to accurately model the various lifecycle paths of the business entity it represents through a decoupled and configurable state management mechanism. State and behavioral changes in the modeled business entity that occur at each stage of its lifecycle are reflected in the associated business object by runtime changes to the object's behavior and data.

Motivation

Let's look a little more closely at the order management aspects of the Food Warehouse application. FW's most common type of order probably is the *remote sales order*. This type of order is initiated remotely by a customer via phone, fax, e-mail, or other means. When a remote sales order request is received by FW, an order taker creates an order in the FW application. Let's assume the FW application uses a simple order structure consisting of an order header (Order) that holds general information about the order, such as customer name and billing address, and order lines (OrderDetails) that contain information such as type of product, quantity, and price.

Once created, the order and its details proceed through a series of processes and states before the order is considered completed. For example, once an order handler has created a remote sales Order and its OrderDetails, the order details will be planned (a source warehouse and lot will be chosen), the ordered

Figure 18.1. Remote Sales Order Lifecycle

items will be picked from a warehouse (a particular stock location in the warehouse from which to pick the goods will be selected) and shipped to the customer, and finally the customer will be invoiced (see Figure 18.1). We'll call this series of states that make up the life of the order detail business entity its *business entity lifecycle.*[1]

However, not all Orders and OrderDetails within the FW application will have the same business entity lifecycle: Suppose FW has a small factory outlet store where it sells certain products directly to the public. Rather than directly picking out items for purchase, a customer starts by selecting items from a catalog or a sale board in the store. The customer places the order with an order taker (cashier), who enters the order, automatically triggering the generation of a pick list for a warehouse stock person. Once the stock person picks the order, the order taker accepts payment from the customer and, finally, issues the customer a receipt. We'll call this type of order a *direct sales order* (see Figure 18.2).

An interesting aspect of the order details in both the remote and direct sales order types is that they change their behavior and data as they progress through the states in their business entity lifecycles. For example, only after a remote sales order detail has been planned will it have information about the warehouse and lot from which the ordered items are to be picked. Only immediately after planning will it be possible to pick the order detail; the order detail cannot be picked before planning or after picking.

Now let's consider implementation of the OrderDetail object within the FW application, taking its business entity lifecycle into account.

Handling Behavioral Change in an OrderDetail

The first challenge is to model the changes in behavior and data that the order detail entity undergoes as it passes through the states of its lifecyle. The Extensible

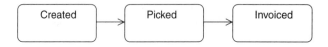

Figure 18.2. Direct Sales Order Lifecycle

---

1. It's important to understand that the business entity lifecycle is the lifecycle of the business entity being modeled, not the "object lifecycle" (in CORBA terms) of the business object.

Thus the classes do not match the Entity Types nor the metaclasses. Thus we have a design detail to capture ie the pattern — which is not needed in the simple impl.

Excellent sentence !!

Item pattern (discussed in Chapter 16) addresses this problem. We can employ the Extensible Item pattern here by implementing OrderDetail as an Extensible-Item and keeping the behavior and data associated with its various business entity lifecycle states as Extension subclasses. We can add and remove Extensions as necessary to place the OrderDetail into various states in its business entity lifecyle.

Capturing the Business Entity Lifecycle

The Extensible Item pattern gives us a means of modeling the different states of an OrderDetail, but something is missing: Where is the knowledge of the ordering of state transitions that make up the business entity lifecyle kept? In other words, which part of the application contains the information that picking follows planning, shipping follows picking, and so on? Requiring clients of the OrderDetail to move the object from one state to another manually would result in spreading the detailed knowledge of the OrderDetail's business object lifecycle throughout the application, effectively unencapsulating knowledge that is logically associated with the order detail itself.

Since unencapsulating the lifecycle knowledge is not desirable, let's consider how we might capture this knowledge within the OrderDetail. One approach is to build the transition knowledge directly into the Extension classes that represent the states of the order detail lifecycle. In this approach, the Extension class that represents the "ready to plan" state would know to add a "ready to pick" Extension to the OrderDetail object once the plan method had been called. Similarly, the "ready to pick" Extension would add the "ready to ship" Extension when the pick method had been called, and so on. This approach succeeds in capturing and encapsulating the business entity lifecycle of an order detail to some extent, but unfortunately it places some limitations on the flexibility of the order detail lifecycle.

We have seen that direct sales order details are different from remote sales order details in that they are simply created, picked, and invoiced; they are neither planned nor shipped. What's interesting here is that although the lifecycles of the remote sales and direct sales order details differ, the order details themselves and their common states—picking and invoicing—may be quite similar. For example, because the same picking process is used for both order types, the behavior and data types associated with the "ready to pick" and "picked" states would be identical. Figure 18.3 shows the picking and invoicing processes shared between two OrderDetail types.

Now the shortcomings of building the business entity lifecycle knowledge directly into the Extensions become apparent: We would like to share the "ready to pick" Extension class between direct sales and remote sales OrderDetails, but such sharing is not possible, because the remote sales "ready to pick" Extension is designed to automatically add a "ready to ship" Extension to the OrderDetail. This behavior is inappropriate for the direct sales OrderDetail, for

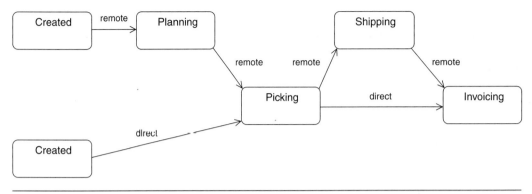

Figure 18.3. Reusing Processes across Different OrderDetail Types

which the "ready to pick" Extension should instead add a "ready to invoice" Extension.

Ideally, we would like to capture and encapsulate the business entity lifecycle within our application in such a way that the lifecycle knowledge is not driven into the participating ExtensibleItem and Extension subclasses. The solution is to introduce a separate class, BusinessEntityLifecycle, that both encapsulates and decouples the business entity lifecycle behavior from the business object.

Defining the BusinessEntityLifecycle Class

Before we discuss the responsibilities of a BusinessEntityLifecycle object, let's define business entity lifecycle behavior a little more formally: A business entity is said to exhibit lifecycle behavior if it traverses a set of distinct behavioral states during its existence. The transition from one state to another is generally triggered by an external stimulus or event, such as the confirmation of an order by an order taker. The graph of acceptable state transitions of such a business entity, the events that trigger each state transition, and the effects of each state transition on the entity itself together make up the lifecycle of the business entity. As we have stated, a BusinessEntityLifecycle instance must encapsulate a business entity lifecycle; that is, it must contain the following:

- A set of the events that trigger lifecycle transitions
- A set of state transitions and the effects of these transitions on the business object
- A mapping of the occurrence of an event in a given state to the appropriate state transition (if any)

The primary responsibility of a BusinessEntityLifecycle object is to use this information to drive the transition of an associated business object through the proper states in the business entity lifecycle in response to transition-triggering events. In simpler terms, the BusinessEntityLifecycle needs to be able to look at the current state of a business object and what just happened to that object, and apply whatever changes are necessary to the object as a result of what just happened.

Examining the State of a Business Object

How does a lifecycle "look" at the current state of a business object? To answer this question we need to define further what is meant by "state." For purposes of clarification, we'll separate the concept of state into object state and lifecycle state. *Object state* is the actual state of a business object in the traditional programmatic sense. The object state of a business object comprises the data logically held by the business object itself, as well as the data held by its contained Extensions. *Lifecycle state* is the current location of the object in its business entity lifecycle.

i.e. status

The concept of lifecycle state is necessary because object state is generally too detailed and has too much extraneous information to be useful as a key for selecting a lifecycle transition. Using object state to determine the position of a business object in its lifecycle is somewhat like determining how many miles a car has on it by examining each of the individual components that make up the car. Because such an approach is not practical, a car uses an auxiliary device called an odometer to track the miles traveled. Similarly, a lifecycle-managed business object uses an auxiliary state-tracking mechanism called a *Condition set* to track lifecycle state.

i.e. Duck = Swan
Even worse!

Conditions are simple identifiers (generally Strings) that represent significant events in the business entity lifecycle of the object. As such, the Condition set of a lifecycle-managed business object represents that object's history (see Figure 18.4).

In addition to the Condition set, a lifecycle-managed business object keeps track of the last-changed Condition. The last-changed Condition can be used to determine which event just occurred. Last event information is especially

which does not show events anywhere!

∴ "condition" is really "status".

This is not true in general if condition = status!

Figure 18.4. Using Conditions in the OrderDetail

significant to many lifecycle configurations because it corresponds to the input associated with an edge in a state transition diagram. The combination of the Condition set (what's happened to the object in the past) and the last-changed Condition (what just happened) determines the lifecycle state of a business object. The use of Conditions provides a quick and easy way for a BusinessEntityLifecycle object to examine the lifecycle state of a business object.

Communicating with the BusinessEntityLifecycle

When does the BusinessEntityLifecycle look at the lifecycle state of a business object? To ensure that the business object progresses through its business entity lifecycle properly, the BusinessEntityLifecycle needs to look at the lifecycle state of the business object after every significant event[2] to determine whether it is necessary to apply any changes to the object. We now need to define a mechanism that allows a significant lifecyle event to trigger the lifecycle to reinspect the lifecycle state of the business object.

Our first inclination might be to add Conditions directly to the business object's Condition set as each method significant to the object's lifecycle is invoked. Unfortunately, this simple approach has a drawback: It places the knowledge of which events are significant to the lifecycle within the business object rather than in the BusinessEntityLifecycle, where the rest of the business entity lifecycle knowledge is encapsulated. Like most challenges in software, this dilemma is solved with a level of indirection. Rather than having methods on the lifecycle-managed business object directly modify the Condition set, we associate event IDs with all methods that could change the object state of the business object.

Like Conditions, event IDs are simple identifiers (generally Strings). When any method that changes object state (such as pick or confirm on an OrderDetail) is called on a lifecycle-managed business object, the object notifies its lifecycle of the method invocation by passing an event ID to a registerEvent method on its associated BusinessEntityLifecycle. The BusinessEntityLifecycle then uses a contained mapping of significant event IDs to Conditions to determine which Condition (if any) to add to the business object's Condition set and last-added Condition field. The use of event IDs allows the lifecycle to filter which events are meaningful and determine how those events are mapped to Conditions.

Now let's return to the original question: When does a BusinessEntityLifecycle look at the lifecycle state of a business object? We have just described how events (method calls) are translated into changes in the business object's Conditions. What remains is for the business object to notify its BusinessEntityLifecycle of a

[2] Significant events in the lifecycle of a business entity, such as the picking or shipping of an order detail, generally correspond to methods on the representative business object that change the object state.

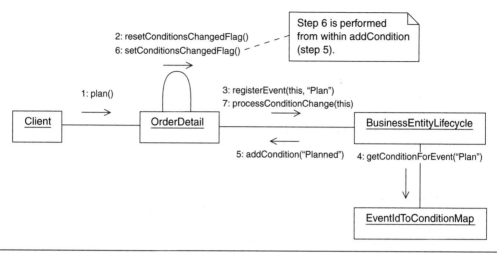

Figure 18.5. Communicating with the BusinessEntityLifecycle

change to its contained Conditions. We handle this notification by adding a transient Boolean attribute to the lifecycle-managed business object that is set to false at the start of each client method invocation and set to true if the object's contained Conditions are changed. At the end of each client method invocation, this attribute is checked to determine if the Conditions have changed. If so, the lifecyle-managed business object calls a processConditionChange method on its associated BusinessEntityLifecycle object, which as a result examines the new lifecycle state of the business object (see Figure 18.5).

Driving the Transition of the Business Object to Its Next State

Now that we have discussed the process for allowing a BusinessEntityLifecycle to look at the current state of a business object, let's examine what the BusinessEntityLifecycle needs to do to drive the transition of the business object to its next state. As a business entity, such as an order detail, progresses through the states of its lifecycle, it may do any of the following:

- **Gain behavior.** An OrderDetail gains the ability to be picked only after it has entered its "ready to pick" state.

- **Lose behavior.** An OrderDetail cannot be picked again after it has entered its "picked" state.

- **Gain information.** An OrderDetail gains planning information, such as the warehouse from which to pick, once it has entered its "planned" state.

- **Lose information.** Selection notes to the stock worker who will pick the order detail may be discarded after the OrderDetail enters its "picked" state.

A BusinessEntityLifecycle can apply all these types of changes to a business object by simply adding and removing Extensions that correspond to the different business entity lifecycle states that the object supports.

In addition to adding and removing Extensions, a BusinessEntityLifecycle may need to invoke methods on the business object. By doing so, the BusinessEntityLifecycle can automatically trigger certain behavior on the business object during a state transition. This automatically triggered behavior may move the business object to yet another state. For example, if Food Warehouse were to support a fully automated process for the planning of its remote sales order details, it could modify its remote sales BusinessEntityLifecycle to invoke the plan method on an OrderDetail automatically after it has entered its "ready to plan" state. Invocation of the plan method would move the OrderDetail to its next state: "ready to pick."

We now have a clear definition of what a BusinessEntityLifecycle can do to a business object while driving the transition of that object to another state:

- Add Extensions
- Remove Extensions
- Invoke methods

How do we store this information in a BusinessEntityLifecycle object? We represent the package of changes associated with a state transition as a StateTransition object. A StateTransition is a type of command (as defined in the Command pattern of *Design Patterns*) that contains a collection of Extensions to remove, a collection of ExtensionCreation objects, and a collection of MethodInvocation objects. The collection of Extensions to remove is simply a collection of IDs (Strings) of the Extensions that are to be removed (for the purpose of supporting removal of Extensions by ID, we insist that Extension classes used with a lifecycle-managed business object support a getId method).

ExtensionCreation objects can be thought of as builder objects (as defined in the Builder pattern of *Design Patterns*) that encapsulate the data and logic needed to create an Extension and add it to a lifecycle-managed business object. ExtensionCreation objects contain a reference to the Class object of the Extension that is to be created, as well as a collection of input parameters to be passed to the create routine of the new Extension object. To support this type of creation, Extension classes used with a lifecycle-managed business object support an initialize method that takes an ordered collection of parameter objects. The ExtensionCreation class declares an apply method that creates and adds its designated Extension to a lifecycle-managed business object that is passed as a parameter to the method.

MethodInvocation objects encapsulate the data and logic needed to invoke a method (through the ExtensibleItem invokeMethod method; see Chapter 16) on a lifecycle-managed business object. MethodInvocation objects contain the method name that is to be invoked (a String), as well as a collection of input parameters to be passed on the method invocation. The MethodInvocation class also declares an apply method that invokes its designated method on a lifecycle-managed business object that is passed as a parameter to the performInvokeMethod method.

The StateTransition class introduces an apply method that takes a lifecycle-managed business object as a parameter. The apply method performs the following steps:

1. It removes Extensions identified in its contained collection from the given lifecycle-managed business object.

2. It iterates through its collection of ExtensionCreation objects, calling apply on each one and passing the given lifecycle-managed business object.

3. It iterates through its collection of MethodInvocation objects, calling apply on each one and passing the given lifecycle-managed business object.

Storing and Retrieving State Transitions

We stated earlier that a BusinessEntityLifecycle must look at the current lifecycle state of a business object and apply the appropriate changes to move the business object to its next lifecycle state. We now have all the necessary pieces for enabling a BusinessEntityLifecycle to support and store a *transition map* of lifecycle states to lifecycle state transitions. The keys for the transition map are the Condition set and the last-changed Condition of a lifecycle-managed business object. The values (results) of the transition map are StateTransition objects. The BusinessEntityLifecycle implements its processConditionChange method by using the Condition set and the last-changed Condition of the given business object to build a ConditionSetKey object that is then used to look up a StateTransition object in the transition map contained in the BusinessEntityLifecycle (see Figure 18.6). Once the appropriate StateTransition object is found, its apply method is called, and the given lifecycle-managed business object is passed in.

Putting It All Together: A Complete State Transition

Now let's look at a complete state transition cycle for a remote sales OrderDetail object. Earlier we stated that, at one point in its lifecycle, a remote sales order detail goes through a planning process and then a picking process. To represent the "ready to plan" state, we'll use a PlannableExtension object that introduces a plan method. To represent the next state, "ready to pick," we'll use a

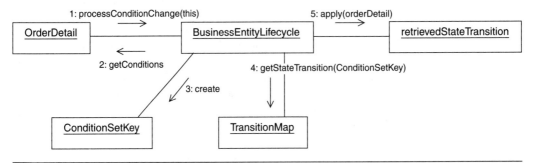

Figure 18.6. Finding a State Transition

PickableExtension object that enables the picking process. We'll assume that the implementer of the PlannableExtension has added to the plan method a call to registerEvent (on the associated BusinessEntityLifecycle) with an event ID of "Plan." We'll set up the remote sales order detail lifecycle to map the "Plan" event ID to a Condition named "Planned." The "Planned" Condition will be used to trigger the state transition to the "ready to pick" state. This state transition will consist of removing the PlannableExtension and adding the PickableExtension. We encapsulate this behavior by creating a StateTransition object that holds the ID of the PlannableExtension in its collection of Extensions to remove and contains an ExtensionCreation object for the PickableExtension. The StateTransition object is added to the lifecycle's transition map with a ConditionSetKey that designates "Planned" as the last-changed Condition.

With the BusinessEntityLifecycle in place, here's what happens when the user calls the plan method on a remote sales OrderDetail (referenced steps refer to Figure 18.7):

1. The plan method performs normal business logic, such as selecting a warehouse from which to pick (step 3).[3]

2. The plan method retrieves the associated BusinessEntityLifecycle from the OrderDetail and calls the registerEvent method on it, passing "Plan" as the event ID (step 4).

3. The BusinessEntityLifecycle maps the "Plan" event ID to the Condition "Planned" (step 5) and adds the Condition to the OrderDetail's Condition

---

3. The plan method probably will create a PlannedExtension object to capture the information produced in the planning process and add it to the OrderDetail. The representation of a process such as planning as the combination of an enabling Extension and a resulting Extension is discussed in Chapter 20.

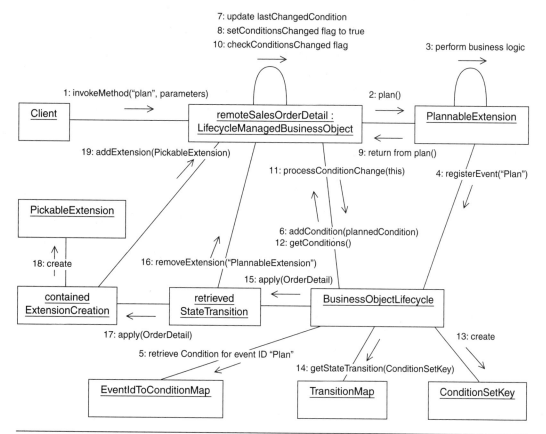

Figure 18.7. A Complete State Transition

set (step 6) and last-changed Condition field (step 7). The OrderDetail's "Conditions changed" flag is set to true (step 8).

4. At the return from the call to plan (step 9), the OrderDetail detects that the "Conditions changed" flag is set to true (step 10) and calls processCondition-Change on the BusinessEntityLifecycle, passing itself (step 11).

5. The BusinessEntityLifecycle retrieves the OrderDetail's Condition set and last-changed Condition field (which is set to "Planned") (step 12) and builds a ConditionSetKey for the transition map from this information (step 13).

6. The BusinessEntityLifecycle uses this ConditionSetKey to retrieve the appropriate StateTransition from its transition map (step 14).

7. The BusinessEntityLifecycle calls the apply method on the retrieved StateTransition, passing the OrderDetail as a parameter (step 15).

8. The StateTransition object removes the PlannableExtension (step 16).

9. The StateTransition object calls the apply method on its contained ExtensionCreation object, passing the OrderDetail (step 17). This object creates the PickableExtension (step 18) and adds it to the OrderDetail (step 19), completing the transition to the "ready to pick" state.

Note that we could change the process that follows planning by simply changing the StateTransition object in the lifecycle's transition map that was triggered by the "Planned" Condition; no change would be necessary for either the OrderDetail class or its Extension classes. We could also change the process ordering by redefining the Condition that is triggered by the "Plan" Condition ID to another Condition (or even to no Condition at all). In general, the configuration of a BusinessEntityLifecycle determines the lifecycle behavior of the business objects that will use that BusinessEntityLifecycle. Similarly, altering the configuration of a BusinessEntityLifecycle results in changes to the lifecycle behavior of associated business objects. By allowing BusinessEntityLifecycles to be configured and subsequently changed at runtime, the Business Entity Lifecycle pattern gives us a free hand to determine the lifecycles of business objects at runtime without necessitating changes to the involved business object or Extension classes.

Applicability

Consider using the Business Entity Lifecycle pattern when any of the following criteria apply:

- The business entity being modeled traverses distinct behavioral states.
- The traversal path through the states may vary for different instances of the business entity depending on the context in which the business entity is used. For example, the lifecycle traversal path for a collection document may vary by company.
- Additional states may be added to the lifecycle of the business entity that were not known or defined at the time of implementation of the corresponding business object.

The order detail in our previous example is an obvious example of a business entity that exhibits flexible lifecycle behavior. Here are some other business entities that could be implemented with the Business Entity Lifecycle pattern:

- **A collection document.** Collection documents progress through distinct states that correspond to events in the collection process such as confirmation and payment. The ordering of these states may vary from company to company, and from country to country (because of varying banking practices).

- **A request generated from a customer contact.** Customer requests progress through different behavioral states as they are evaluated, assigned to a handler, and fulfilled.

Structure

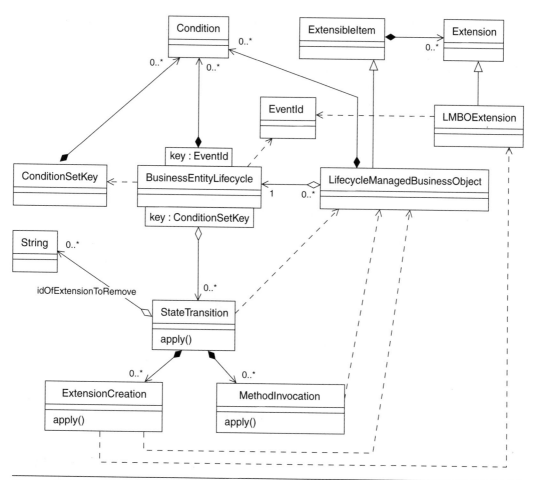

Figure 18.8. Business Entity Lifecycle Structure

Participants

- **LifecycleManagedBusinessObject** (OrderDetail). A business object representing a business entity that exhibits lifecycle behavior. A LifecycleManagedBusinessObject is a type of ExtensibleItem that communicates the occurrence of events to an associated BusinessEntityLifecycle. A LifecycleManagedBusinessObject contains its current lifecycle state in a collection of Conditions.

- **LMBOExtension** (PlannableExtension, PickableExtension). A specialized type of Extension that collaborates with a LifecycleManagedBusinessObject and its associated BusinessEntityLifecycle. Method implementations in an LMBOExtension may register EventIds with the BusinessEntityLifecycle.

- **BusinessEntityLifecycle.** A class that has two primary responsibilities: (1) filtering and interpreting the events that affect an associated LifecycleManagedBusinessObject and modifying the LifecycleManaged-BusinessObject's lifecycle state (Condition set) accordingly, and (2) mapping the current lifecycle state of a LifecycleManagedBusinessObject to a set of changes that need to be applied to that object.

- **EventId** ("Plan," "Pick," "Ship"). A simple identifier associated with an event that occurred to the LifecycleManagedBusinessObject. EventIds are used to communicate the occurrence of an event to the LifecycleManaged-BusinessObject's associated BusinessEntityLifecycle.

- **Condition** ("Planned," "Picked," "Shipped"). A simple identifier used to record the occurrence of a *significant* event in the lifecycle state of a LifecycleManagedBusinessObject. A BusinessEntityLifecycle maps EventIds for significant events to Conditions that represent those events. The set of Conditions that make up a LifecycleManagedBusinessObject's lifecycle state are used by the BusinessEntityLifecycle to build a ConditionSetKey to select an appropriate StateTransition to apply.

- **ConditionSetKey.** An object that holds a set of Conditions and a last-changed Condition that correspond to the Condition set and last-changed Condition of a LifecycleManagedBusinessObject. ConditionSetKey objects form the keys for StateTransitions in the BusinessEntityLifecycle's transition map.

- **StateTransition.** An object that encapsulates a set of changes that need to be applied to a LifecycleManagedBusinessObject. These changes are encapsulated as a collection of ExtensionCreation objects, a collection of MethodInvocation objects, and a collection of Strings that represent the IDs of Extensions to remove. StateTransition objects are held by a

BusinessEntityLifecycle and are applied to a LifecycleManagedBusinessObject as a result of a certain transition-triggering event.

- **ExtensionCreation.** An object that encapsulates the data and logic needed to create an Extension and add it to a LifecycleManagedBusinessObject.

- **MethodInvocation.** An object that encapsulates the data and logic needed to invoke a method (through the ExtensibleItem invokeMethod method) on a LifecycleManagedBusinessObject.

- **ExtensibleItem.** A base class for business object classes that exhibit dynamic behavioral change. See Chapter 16 for additional details.

- **Extension.** A base class for classes that represent packages of data and behavior that can be added to an ExtensibleItem. See Chapter 16 for additional details.

Collaborations

- A LifecycleManagedBusinessObject communicates significant events to its associated BusinessEntityLifecycle (many LifecycleManagedBusinessObjects may reference the same BusinessEntityLifecycle).

- A LifecycleManagedBusinessObject uses EventIds to communicate the occurrence of events to its associated BusinessEntityLifecycle.

- A LifecycleManagedBusinessObject contains a collection of Conditions that represent its lifecycle state.

- A ConditionSetKey contains Conditions that represent a particular lifecycle state of a LifecycleManagedBusinessObject.

- A BusinessEntityLifecycle contains a collection of Conditions keyed by EventIds.

- A BusinessEntityLifecycle contains a collection of StateTransitions keyed by ConditionSetKey objects.

- A StateTransition contains a collection of ExtensionCreation objects.

- A StateTransition contains a collection of MethodInvocation objects.

- StateTransition, ExtensionCreation, and MethodInvocation objects operate on LifecycleManagedBusinessObjects in their apply methods.

Consequences

The Business Entity Lifecycle pattern has the following tradeoffs, benefits, and drawbacks:

Tradeoffs

- **Performance versus flexibility.** Because of the performance overhead of the Business Entity Lifecycle pattern, you should consider carefully whether the points discussed in the "Applicability" section earlier in this chapter warrant the use of this pattern for the business entity you are modeling.

Benefits

- **Correct modeling of behavioral changes.** The Business Entity Lifecycle pattern allows business objects to correctly model the behavioral changes of a business entity as the entity moves through the states in its lifecycle.

- **Decoupling of lifecycle behavior and business logic.** The Business Entity Lifecycle pattern separates business entity lifecycle behavior from the standard business logic of a business object, thereby allowing the methods of the business object to be implemented without dependencies on the lifecycle behavior of the object.

- **Sharing of lifecycles.** The Business Entity Lifecycle pattern encapsulates business entity lifecycle behavior into a BusinessEntityLifecycle object that may be shared by many associated lifecycle-managed business objects of a given type, each of which may be at a different position in its respective business entity lifecycle. This approach allows for the possibility of varying lifecycle behavior for a given type of business object by company, country, or another type of business context.

- **Runtime configuration of significant events.** The Business Entity Lifecycle pattern allows runtime selection of the events that will trigger lifecycle transitions.

- **Runtime configuration of lifecycle behavior.** The Business Entity Lifecycle pattern allows runtime configuration of the business entity lifecycle behavior of a business object, thereby allowing for the possibility of introducing states that were not known when the lifecycle was originally configured.

Drawbacks

- **Performance overhead.** The performance considerations for the Extensible Item pattern (see Chapter 16) apply to this pattern also. The dynamic binding of method calls that characterizes these patterns is inherently slower than a direct call. The mapping of event IDs as described in this pattern also introduces overhead to certain method invocations.

- **Configuration complexity.** The configuration and inspection of a Business-EntityLifecycle may appear complex when done programmatically. This problem may be alleviated through the use of a graphical interface for lifecycle configuration.

- **Dependency on Strings.** A BusinessEntityLifecycle is made up largely of Strings or String-based objects such as method names, parameter types, and so on. Unfortunately, the correctness of these Strings cannot be checked at compile time, leaving errors to be found at runtime. One step that the SanFrancisco framework has taken to alleviate this problem is to add to each interface and class a String constant that contains the fully qualified name of the interface or class. These additions allow the constant Strings to be used in the lifecycle configuration rather than manually typed literal Strings.

Implementation

Consider the following implementation issues for the Business Entity Lifecycle pattern:

- **Registering event IDs.** At the time you implement your lifecycle-managed business object, you may not know which methods will constitute interesting events to the BusinessEntityLifecycle that will control the object. If this is the case, you may need to be quite liberal about placing event ID registrations in your business object methods. The lifecycle that is associated with the business object may then use its map from event IDs to Conditions to filter out event IDs that are not significant. In the SanFrancisco framework, because we could not know the configuration of the lifecycles that would control our OrderDetail objects, we chose to place an event ID registration in each method that changes the object state of the OrderDetail. We assumed that the calling of an observer method that does not change object state would probably not constitute a significant event.

  It may sometimes be useful to use multiple event ID registrations within a method. For instance, a method that toggles a Boolean attribute (such as "approved" or "onHold") may register one event ID when the attribute is set to true and another when the attribute is set to false.

- **Mapping event IDs.** In our discussion of the Business Entity Lifecycle pattern, we have described a simple mapping of event ID registrations to the addition of a Condition to the LifecycleManagedBusinessObject. In the SanFrancisco framework, the mapping of event IDs is enhanced to allow the BusinessEntityLifecycle to map event IDs not only to the addition of Conditions but also to the removal of a specified Condition. This enhancement allows one event ID to cancel out the Condition added by another event ID. We accomplished this feature by mapping EventIds to ConditionAction objects rather than directly to Conditions. The ConditionAction class is an abstract command-type class (as defined in *Design Patterns*) that introduces a performConditionAction method. Subclasses of the ConditionAction class implement the performConditionAction method to modify the Condition set of the LifecycleManagedBusinessObject by either adding or removing a Condition.

- **Conditions.** Earlier in this chapter we stated that the lifecycle state of a LifecycleManagedBusinessObject is represented as a collection of Conditions and a last-changed Condition. The nature of the Condition collection is important in determining how the BusinessEntityLifecycle's transition map will be configured. Using an ordered Condition collection allows a more precise inspection of the lifecycle state of the LifecycleManagedBusinessObject, but for more complex lifecycles it may lead to an explosion of entries in the BusinessEntityLifecycle's transition map. On the other hand, an unordered collection leads to simpler lifecycle transition maps and is generally sufficient for most business entity lifecycle cases.

- **The transition map and ConditionSetKeys.** The implementation of the ConditionSetKey class will also have an effect on the complexity of the lifecycle configuration. The simplest implementation of a ConditionSetKey is one that provides only an equals method that directly compares the state of two ConditionSetKey objects. The BusinessEntityLifecycle's transition map may then be implemented as a simple map (dictionary) with ConditionSetKey objects as keys and StateTransitions as values. Although this approach is straightforward and quite efficient, it may make the transition map difficult to configure when all that matters is the existence of a certain Condition or group of Conditions, regardless of what other Conditions may exist in the LifecycleManagedBusinessObject's Condition set. We have found that, for many simple state transition maps, all that is necessary is to apply a certain StateTransition based solely on a certain last-changed Condition, irrespective of the other Conditions in the Condition set. After all, the last-changed Condition represents the event that just happened to the LifecycleManagedBusinessObject.

To accommodate these situations, SanFrancisco's implementation of the Business Entity Lifecycle pattern employs two subclasses of the ConditionSetKey class: one that does a simple comparison as already described, and one that allows a "subset match" comparison. The "subset match" ConditionSetKey subclass allows a user to specify only the group of Conditions that must be present. This type of key will match another key that has all its specified Conditions, regardless of the additional Conditions the other ConditionSetKey has. For example, a "subset match" key that specifies Conditions "Planned" and "Picked" as present Conditions will match another key that has the Conditions "Confirmed," "Planned," "Picked," and "Shipped." Use of these "subset match" keys allows for a simpler lifecycle configuration but leads to a more complex transition map implementation.

- **Invocation of multiple methods.** In our description of StateTransition objects, we placed no restrictions on how many and what type of methods may be invoked on the target business object through the use of contained MethodInvocation objects. From our experience using BusinessEntity-Lifecycles in the SanFrancisco framework, we have learned to be very careful when calling multiple methods from a StateTransition object that themselves may trigger subsequent state transitions. The reason for this caution is that effects from state transitions triggered by a previous method invocation could cause strange behavior when a method is invoked. In this case, care should be taken to analyze all the potential paths that automated method invocation can take under varying conditions.

- **Use of the Memento pattern.** In our description of the Business Entity Lifecycle pattern, we stated that a LifecycleManagedBusinessObject uses a contained Condition set to capture its lifecycle state. When the processConditionChange method is called on the BusinessEntityLifecycle, the LifecycleManagedBusinessObject is passed as a parameter, allowing the BusinessEntityLifecycle to retrieve the Condition set and build a ConditionSetKey to use in finding a StateTransition. Note that, in the terms of the Memento pattern of *Design Patterns,* a ConditionSetKey is a "memento" of the LifecycleManagedBusinessObject's state. This fact suggests another possible implementation of the Business Entity Lifecycle pattern, one in which the LifecycleManagedBusinessObject contains a ConditionSetKey rather than holding the Condition set and last-changed Condition directly. This approach allows the BusinessEntityLifecycle to use the Lifecycle-ManagedBusinessObject's ConditionSetKey for the StateTransition lookup in the processConditionChange method, eliminating the need to create a new ConditionSetKey object.

- **Use of the Key/Keyable Pattern.** Another possible implementation of the transition map and ConditionSetKey would involve using the Key/Keyable pattern (see Chapter 11). With this approach, ConditionSetKeys could be implemented as SpecificationKeys, making the transition map a map of SpecificationKeys to ConditionChangeResults. The SpecificationKey method isSubsetOf could be used in the selection of a ConditionChangeResult with a key that is included by the key built from the lifecycle state of the LifecycleManagedBusinessObject.

Sample Code

The following sample code shows an OrderDetail implemented as a LifecycleManagedBusinessObject. A BusinessEntityLifecycle is set up to allow the planning of the OrderDetail to trigger the picking process automatically.

Here's the LifecycleManagedBusinessObject base class:

```
public abstract class LifecycleManagedBusinessObject extends
ExtensibleItem {

  // Override of ExtensibleItem's invokeMethod
  public Object invokeMethod(String methodName,
                             Object[] parameterList) {

    // Reset the Conditions-changed flag before invoking method
    ivConditionsChanged = false;

    // Now call the standard invokeMethod method as described
    // in Chapter 16
    Object returnValue = super.invokeMethod(methodName,parameterList);


    // Now check if the Conditions-changed flag has been set;
    // notify Lifecycle
    if (ivConditionsChanged == true) {
       ivLifecycle.processConditionChange(this);
    }

    return returnValue;
  }

  // This method will be used by the BusinessEntityLifecycle
  // to add Conditions to this object
  public void addCondition(Condition condition) {

    // Put the Condition in our collection
    ivConditionSet.addElement(condition);

    // Set it as the last-changed Condition
    ivLastChangedCondition = condition;

    // Set the flag
    ivConditionsChanged = true;
  }

  public Vector getConditionSet() {

    return ivConditionSet;
  }
```

```
    public Condition getLastChangedCondition() {

        return ivLastChangedCondition;
    }

    public BusinessEntityLifecycle getLifecycle() {

        return ivLifecycle;
    }

    // This method is provided to allow a StateTransition object
    // to remove an Extension of a specified ID
    public void removeExtensionBy(String extensionId) {

      // Find the matching Extension and remove it
      Enumeration extensions = ivExtensions.elements();
      while (extensions.hasMoreElements()) {
          LMBOExtension curExt =
              (LMBOExtension)(extensions.nextElement());
          if (curExt.getId().equals(extensionId)) {
              ivExtensions.removeElement(curExt);
          }
      }
    }

    // These attributes make up the OrderDetail's object state
    public Condition ivLastChangedCondition = null;
    public Vector ivConditionSet = new Vector();

    // The reference to the BusinessEntityLifecycle
    public BusinessEntityLifecycle ivLifecycle = null;

    // Flag indicating that the lifecycle state has changed
    public boolean ivConditionsChanged = false;
}
```

Here's the OrderDetail class itself:

```
public class OrderDetail extends LifecycleManagedBusinessObject {

    public OrderDetail(BusinessEntityLifecycle lifecycle) {
        ivLifecycle = lifecycle;

        // Call processConditionChange to trigger any
        // lifecycle behavior that may take place upon creation
        ivLifecycle.processConditionChange(this);
    }

    // These are methods that must be overridden by ExtensibleItem
    // subclasses; they are described in Chapter 16
```

```
    public ReturnValue handleInvokeMethod(String methodName,
                                        Object[] parameterList) {

        // No methods supported through invokeMethod
        return new ReturnValue(null,false);
    }

    public boolean supportsMethod(String methodName) {

        // No methods supported through invokeMethod
        return false;
    }
}
```

Here's the LMBOExtension base class:

```
public abstract class LMBOExtension extends Extension {

    // Subclasses of this class will need to override
    // this method to set the reference to the
    // LifecycleManagedBusinessObject and
    // parse out the parameters in the passed
    // array to complete their initialization
    public abstract void
        initialize(LifecycleManagedBusinessObject businessObject,
                    Object[] creationParms);

    // This method is provided to allow StateTransition objects
    // to identify an Extension that is to be removed;
    // subclasses will need to override this method with a
    // specific implementation
    public abstract String getId();

    // Helper method to get the BusinessEntityLifecycle from
    // the associated LifecycleManagedBusinessObject
    public BusinessEntityLifecycle getLifecycle() {
        return
            ivBusinessObject.getLifecycle();
    }

    // We need to keep a reference to the LifecycleManagedBusinessObject
    // so that event IDs from Extension methods can be registered
    // with the BusinessEntityLifecycle
    public LifecycleManagedBusinessObject ivBusinessObject = null;
}
```

The example that follows uses PlannableExtension and PickableExtension classes to enable the planning and picking processes, respectively, on the OrderDetail. The PickableExtension class is shown here. We have introduced a PickingPolicy attribute to demonstrate how data in an Extension can be initialized through the lifecycle (a discussion on how policies may be used by processable Extensions can be found in Chapter 20).

```java
public class PickableExtension extends LMBOExtension {

    // Override of initialize from LMBOExtension
    public void initialize(LifecycleManagedBusinessObject businessObject,
                           Object[] creationParms) {

        // Set the LifecycleManagedBusinessObject reference
        ivBusinessObject = businessObject;

        // Get the PickingPolicy from the creation parameters
        // and set the attribute
        ivPickingPolicy = (PickingPolicy)creationParms[0];
    }

    // Note that the pick method does not return any value,
    // giving it the potential to be called automatically
    // through the BusinessEntityLifecycle
    public void pick() {

        // Delegate implementation to the policy
        ivPickingPolicy.pick(ivBusinessObject);

        // Indicate that the method was called (for our example)
        System.out.println("pick() called");

        // Register the "Pick" event
        getLifecycle().registerEvent(ivBusinessObject,"Pick");
    }


    // Override of the getId method
    // It's OK for one ID to be shared by all instances of this class
    // because there will be not more than one PickableExtension
    // on any given OrderDetail
    public String getId() {

        return "PickableExtension";
    }

    // These methods must be overridden by ExtensibleItem
    // subclasses; they are described in Chapter 16
    public ReturnValue handleInvokeMethod(String methodName,
                                          Object[] parameterList) {

        // Object to hold result
        Object result = null;
        if (methodName.equals("pick")) {
            pick();
        }
```

```
        else {
            // At this point we know that the method
            // was not supported by this Extension,
            // so return a ReturnValue indicating this
            return new ReturnValue(null,false);
        }

        // If we get here, a method was called,
        // so put the result in a ReturnValue,
        // indicate that the method was invoked,
        // and return the result to the caller
        return new ReturnValue(result,true);
    }

    public boolean supportsMethod(String methodName) {
        if (methodName.equals("pick")) {
            return true;
        }
        else {
            return false;
        }
    }

    // A policy used in picking that is set when
    // the PickableExtension is created
    public PickingPolicy ivPickingPolicy = null;
}
```

Here are the StateTransition, ExtensionCreation, and MethodInvocation classes that encapsulate the actions of a state transition within a BusinessEntityLifecycle:

```
public class StateTransition {

  public void apply(LifecycleManagedBusinessObject businessObject) {

    // Handle Extension removals first
    Enumeration removalEnum = ivExtensionsToRemove.elements();
    while (removalEnum.hasMoreElements()) {
        businessObject.removeExtensionBy(
            (String)removalEnum.nextElement());
    }

    // . . . then do Extension additions
    Enumeration creationEnum = ivExtensionCreations.elements();
    while (creationEnum.hasMoreElements()) {
        ((ExtensionCreation)creationEnum.nextElement()).
            apply(businessObject);
    }

    // . . . and finally method invocations
    Enumeration methodsEnum = ivMethodInvocations.elements();
```

```
        while (methodsEnum.hasMoreElements()) {
            ((MethodInvocation)methodsEnum.nextElement()).
                apply(businessObject);
        }
    }

    public void addExtensionToRemove(String extensionId) {

        ivExtensionsToRemove.addElement(extensionId);
    }

    public void addExtensionCreation(ExtensionCreation extCreation) {

        ivExtensionCreations.addElement(extCreation);
    }

    public void addMethodInvocation(MethodInvocation methInv) {

        ivMethodInvocations.addElement(methInv);
    }

    public Vector ivExtensionsToRemove = new Vector();
    public Vector ivExtensionCreations = new Vector();
    public Vector ivMethodInvocations = new Vector();
}

public class ExtensionCreation {

    ExtensionCreation(Class extensionClass,
                    Object[] creationParms) {

        ivExtensionClass = extensionClass;
        ivCreationParms = creationParms;
    }

    public void apply(LifecycleManagedBusinessObject businessObject) {

        LMBOExtension extension = null;

        // We use the given class to generically create
        // an instance of the extension, we assume that the
        // new Extension is an instance of LMBOExtension
        try {
          extension = (LMBOExtension)ivExtensionClass.newInstance();
        } catch(Exception ex) { ex.printStackTrace(); }

        // We then use the generic initialize method to
        // initialize the new Extension instance
        extension.initialize(businessObject,ivCreationParms);

        // Now add the Extension to the businessObject
        businessObject.addExtension(extension);
    }
```

```
      public Class ivExtensionClass = null;
      public Object[] ivCreationParms = null;
}

public class MethodInvocation {

   MethodInvocation(String methodName,
                    Object[] parms) {

        ivMethodName = methodName;
        ivParms = parms;
   }

   public void apply(LifecycleManagedBusinessObject businessObject) {

        // Invoke the method through invokeMethod;
        // note that the return value will not be kept, so
        // methods called through the lifecycle should
        // generally not have return values
        businessObject.invokeMethod(ivMethodName,ivParms);
   }


   public Object[] ivParms = null;
   public String ivMethodName = null;
}
```

Here's the BusinessEntityLifecycle class itself. This example shows a very simple implementation of the lifecycle's transition map using a ConditionSetKey class that allows only direct comparisons of Condition sets.

```
public class BusinessEntityLifecycle {

  public void registerEvent(
     LifecycleManagedBusinessObject businessObject,
     String eventId) {

     // Retrieve the matching Condition (if any) from the Condition map
     Condition condition = (Condition)(ivConditionMap.get(eventId));

     // If a Condition was retrieved, add it to the business object's
     // Condition set
     if (condition != null) businessObject.addCondition(condition);
  }

  public void processConditionChange(
     LifecycleManagedBusinessObject businessObject) {

     // First build a ConditionSetKey from the Conditions of the
     // LifecycleManagedBusinessObject
```

```
        ConditionSetKey key =
            new ConditionSetKey(businessObject.getConditionSet(),
                                businessObject.getLastChangedCondition());

        // Next, use the key to find a StateTransition
        StateTransition transition =
            (StateTransition)(ivTransitionMap.get(key));

        // Finally, apply the StateTransition (if one is found)
        if (transition != null) transition.apply(businessObject);
    }

    // Maintenance method to add an entry to the Conditions map
    void addConditionBy(String eventId, Condition condition) {

        ivConditionMap.put(eventId,condition);
    }

    // Maintenance method to add an entry to the transition map
    void addStateTransitionBy(ConditionSetKey key,
                              StateTransition stateTransition) {

        ivTransitionMap.put(key,stateTransition);
    }

    // A mapping of event IDs to Conditions
    public Hashtable ivConditionMap = new Hashtable();

    // A simple mapping of ConditionSetKeys to StateTransitions
    public Hashtable ivTransitionMap = new Hashtable();
}
```

Now we configure a BusinessEntityLifecycle instance for use with our OrderDetail. We'll set up this BusinessEntityLifecycle to invoke the picking process automatically on an OrderDetail when the plan method completes:

```
// Set up a sample BusinessEntityLifecycle that will allow
// the planning process to trigger the picking process automatically
BusinessEntityLifecycle
    orderDetailLifecycle = new BusinessEntityLifecycle();

// Set up the map of EventIds to Conditions to recognize
// the "Plan" EventId and map it to the "Planned" Condition
Condition plannedCondition = new Condition("Planned");
orderDetailLifecycle.addConditionBy("Plan",plannedCondition);

// Now add an entry to the transition map that will
// automate the picking process after planning has completed.
// We do this by adding a StateTransition that will be
// triggered by the occurrence of the "Planned" Condition.
```

```
// First we build up the StateTransition
StateTransition plannedStateTransition = new StateTransition();

// Next we create an ExtensionCreation object
// that will be used by the lifecycle to create the
// PickableExtension and add it to the OrderDetail

// Get the class for the PickableExtension
Class pickableClass =
Class.forName("LifecycleSample.PickableExtension");

// The PickableExtension needs a PickingPolicy when it is created,
// so create a parameter array with a PickingPolicy instance in it
Object[] creationParms = new Object[1];
creationParms[0] = pickingPolicy;

// Create the ExtensionCreation object
ExtensionCreation pickableExtensionCreation =
    new ExtensionCreation(pickableClass,creationParms);

// Add the ExtensionCreation object to the StateTransition
plannedStateTransition.addExtensionCreation(pickableExtensionCreation);

// Now create a MethodInvocation object that will
// invoke the pick method; because there are no
// parameters for the pick method, we pass an empty array
MethodInvocation pickMethodInvocation =
    new MethodInvocation("pick",new Object[0]);

// Add the MethodInvocation object to the StateTransition
plannedStateTransition.addMethodInvocation(pickMethodInvocation);

// Now build a key that will allow the StateTransition to be
// selected when the "Planned" Condition is added to the
// OrderDetail

Vector conditionSet = new Vector(1);

// For this example we will assume that "Planned"
// will be the only Condition present when it is
// added to the OrderDetail's Condition set
conditionSet.addElement(plannedCondition);

// Create the key, using our "Planned" Condition
// as the last-changed Condition
ConditionSetKey key = new ConditionSetKey(conditionSet,
                                          plannedCondition);


// Finally, add our StateTransition to the
// transition map
```

```
orderDetailLifecycle.addStateTransitionBy(key,
                                          plannedStateTransition);
```

Finally, we create an OrderDetail instance that uses the BusinessEntityLifecycle we just configured:

```
// Create an instance of OrderDetail with no Extensions
OrderDetail orderDetail = new OrderDetail(orderDetailLifecycle);

// For this example we will manually create and add the
// PlannableExtension
PlannableExtension plannableExt = new PlannableExtension(orderDetail);
orderDetail.addExtension(plannableExt);


// Now call the plan method on the OrderDetail,
// thereby causing the lifecycle to automatically add
// the PickableExtension and call the pick method
System.out.println("Calling plan()");
orderDetail.invokeMethod("plan",null);
```

Known Uses

The Business Entity Lifecycle pattern is used within the SanFrancisco framework in the Order Management and Accounts Payable/Accounts Receivable Core Business Processes.

Within the Order Management package, the classes Order, OrderPriceDetail, OrderRequestedDetail, OrderPlanningDetail, and many other OrderDetail-type classes are implemented as a type of LifecycleManagedBusinessObject. The business entity lifecycle behavior of these objects is quite similar to that of the order details used in our example.

Within the Accounts Payable/Accounts Receivable package, the class CollectionDocument is implemented as a LifecycleManagedBusinessObject.

Use of the Business Entity Lifecycle pattern in these situations allows the SanFrancisco framework to include useful implementations of the OrderDetail and CollectionDocument classes (and their Extension classes) while leaving the specific configuration of their BusinessEntityLifecycles up to the users of the framework.

Related Patterns

- **Extensible Item.** LifecycleManagedBusinessObjects are specialized ExtensibleItems (see Chapter 16).

- **Memento.** The set of Conditions that represent the lifecycle state of a business object can be thought of as a memento (as defined in *Design Patterns*).

- **Builder.** ExtensionCreation objects can be thought of as builders (as defined in *Design Patterns*) of specific Extension subclass instances.

- **Command.** StateTransition objects are a type of command (as defined in *Design Patterns*) in that they encapsulate a set of actions to perform against a LifecycleManagedBusinessObject.

- **Key/Keyable.** One possible implementation of the BusinessEntityLifecycle's transition map involves using ConditionSetKeys implemented as SpecificationKeys (see Chapter 11).

19

Hierarchy Information

Intent

Provide a mechanism for capturing and defining hierarchical process structure and common lifecycle behavior for instances of a business entity that share a specific usage type.

Motivation

In Chapter 18 we discussed how the Business Entity Lifecycle pattern could be used to enable and invoke a series of processes on a business object. In our discussion we assumed that the results of these processes could be captured in the form of new information added to the target business object. This linear progression of process execution is useful in many situations, but it may be too restrictive in others.

Consider the planning process for a remote sales OrderDetail in the Food Warehouse application: The purpose of the planning process is to decide the location from which the given quantity of the given product is to be picked. In some situations, it may not be possible to pick the entire quantity from a single lot or warehouse. In this case, multiple planning details are needed to hold each specific location and the amount of the total requested quantity that should be picked from that location (see Figure 19.1). Since these planning details hold the information that is vital to the picking process, the planning details themselves (rather than the order detail) will be targets of the picking process, making them lifecycle-managed objects in their own right.

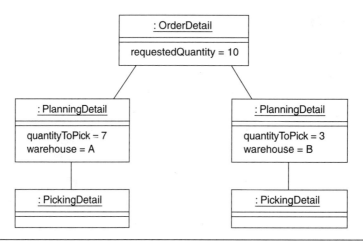

Figure 19.1. Processing Detail Hierarchy for an OrderDetail

Processes such as planning that produce multiple details introduce a hierarchical structure to the business entity to which they are applied. The resulting details are logically children of the detail from which they were produced. We can model this hierarchical structure by introducing a type of LifecycleManagedBusinessObject that contains parent and child references. We'll call this class HierarchicalLifecycleManagedBusinessObject.

Chapter 20 describes how hierarchical processes such as planning and picking can be arbitrarily arranged to support different usage variations of a certain business entity. For example, the different sales order types in the Food Warehouse application vary by the specific set of applicable processes and how those processes are arranged. Although the Business Entity Lifecycle pattern can be used to define which processes may be enabled on a single LifecycleManagedBusinessObject and the order in which they are performed, it does not provide a mechanism for describing the organizational structure of multiple hierarchical processes.

For example, if the planning process produces PlanningDetails that are themselves LifecycleManagedBusinessObjects, what BusinessEntityLifecycle instance should be used by the PlanningDetails? Because the BusinessEntityLifecycle used for a PlanningDetail in one order type may be different from the one used in another order type, we cannot hard-code this knowledge into the planning process. To make it easier to create different order types, we need a means of capturing the BusinessEntityLifecycle instance that is to be used for details at each specific level of a LifecycleManagedBusinessObject process hierarchy.

The solution is the introduction of a HierarchyInformation class that holds structural and behavioral information for each position of a HierarchicalLifecycleManagedBusinessObject hierarchy. HierarchyInformation objects contain a

BusinessEntityLifecycle instance for use with HierarchicalLifecycleManaged-BusinessObjects at that position in the hierarchy. HierarchyInformation objects also contain a collection of child HierarchyInformation objects, allowing them to be arranged into hierarchies that will determine the process structure for a given usage variation of a business object. The child collection is a map that is keyed by the process ID of the process that will create the details at the next position in the hierarchy (later in the chapter we'll discuss why we use a map).

HierarchicalLifecycleManagedBusinessObjects at a given hierarchy position reference a shared HierarchyInformation object that contains information for that position (see Figure 19.2). They use their associated HierarchyInformation object to set their BusinessEntityLifecycle reference. Processes invoked on a HierarchicalLifecycleManagedBusinessObject use the associated Hierarchy-Information object to find the child HierarchyInformation object to associate with the child processing details that they create.

We'll use the Food Warehouse remote sales order detail process hierarchy to demonstrate the use of the Hierarchy Information pattern: Let's assume that remote sales order details use a hierarchical planning process. Before the first remote sales OrderDetail object is created, we will create a HierarchyInformation object for use with remote sales OrderDetails. This HierarchyInformation object will hold the BusinessEntityLifecycle instance to be used with remote sales OrderDetails, as well as a single child HierarchyInformation object. The child HierarchyInformation object will represent the PlanningDetail position in the order detail hierarchy and will hold the BusinessEntityLifecycle instance to be used with PlanningDetail objects in this hierarchy. The child HierarchyInformation object will have a key of "Planning" in the parent HierarchyInformation object's

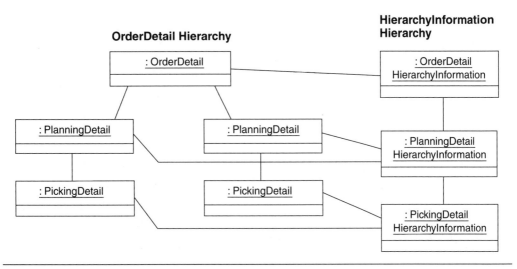

Figure 19.2. OrderDetail Hierarchy with HierarchyInformation

child map. OrderDetails and PlanningDetails are implemented as Hierarchical-LifecycleManagedBusinessObjects.

When a remote sales OrderDetail is created, it is given its designated HierarchyInformation object, from which it gets its BusinessEntityLifecycle. When the planning process is performed on the OrderDetail, it retrieves the child HierarchyInformation object by using a key of "Planning." As the planning process creates PlanningDetails, it associates them with the child HierarchyInformation object and then sets them as children of the OrderDetail object. To enable a hierarchical picking process on the PlanningDetails, we would simply add a HierarchyInformation object for use with PickingDetails as a child of the PlanningDetail HierarchyInformation object .

The primary reason for using a key to retrieve child HierarchyInformation objects is to allow multiple processes to be enabled at a given hierarchy position. For example, PickingDetails may support both a shipping and a quality control process. To allow this combination of processes, the HierarchyInformation object used for PickingDetails would have two child HierarchyInformation objects—one for ShippingDetails and one for QualityControlDetails (see Figure 19.3).

Up to this point, we have described a mechanism for allowing processes on a HierarchicalLifecycleManagedBusinessObject to locate HierarchyInformation objects for their child details, but one problem remains: How do we find the correct HierarchyInformation object for the top HierarchicalLifecycleManaged-BusinessObject in a hierarchy (e.g., an Order)? We solve this problem by recognizing that creation of the top-level object is itself a business process. What's missing, then, is an object to support this creation process. To address this need, we have introduced a HierarchyInstantiator class.

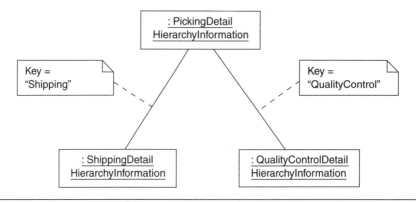

Figure 19.3. HierarchyInformation for PickingDetail

The only responsibility of a HierarchyInstantiator object is to support top-level creation processes. These creation processes (or "creatables") are represented as processable Extensions, as described in Chapter 20. A HierarchyInstantiator object does not exhibit lifecycle behavior, nor does it have children; it acts only as an invocation and anchor point for the creation processes. For this reason the HierarchyInstantiator class is simply a type of ExtensibleItem, rather than a HierarchicalLifecycleManagedBusinessObject. Like a HierarchicalLifecycle-ManagedBusinessObject, however, HierarchyInstantiator objects need access to a collection of child HierarchyInformation objects that correspond to the top-level business objects that can be created from the HierarchyInstantiator's processes. However, a HierarchyInstantiator object does not need access to a BusinessEntityLifecycle. We handle this situation by factoring out a base class for HierarchyInformation that contains the child collection but does not contain a BusinessEntityLifecycle. We call this class HierarchyInformationBase. The HierarchyInformation class extends HierarchyInformationBase and adds the BusinessEntityLifecycle attribute. HierarchyInstantiator objects contain a reference to a HierarchyInformationBase object. Generally, a single HierarchyInstantiator object is used as the creation point for groupings of related hierarchical business objects (e.g., all Order variations would be enabled on one HierarchyInstantiator object). Figure 19.4 shows the roles of the HierarchyInstantiator and HierarchyInformationBase objects in an Order structure.

The pattern we have described here allows us to build up hierarchies of HierarchyInformation objects that define the structure and behavior of their associated business object hierarchies. In many cases, entire branches of these hierarchies (subhierarchies) may be reused. For example, consider a supplementary charge process that creates charge details associated with various order details (e.g., processing fees for OrderDetails, or packaging fees for ShippingDetails). Supplementary charge details themselves will be the subject of an invoicing process. The HierarchyInformation objects used by supplementary charge details and their subsequent invoicing details form a subhierarchy that can be reused at different points within a HierarchyInformation hierarchy for a specific order type (see Figure 19.5) or shared across different order type hierarchies.

The Hierarchy Information pattern provides a foundation on which to implement hierarchical domain processes on business objects. Chapter 20 provides additional detail on how these processes can be designed and implemented.

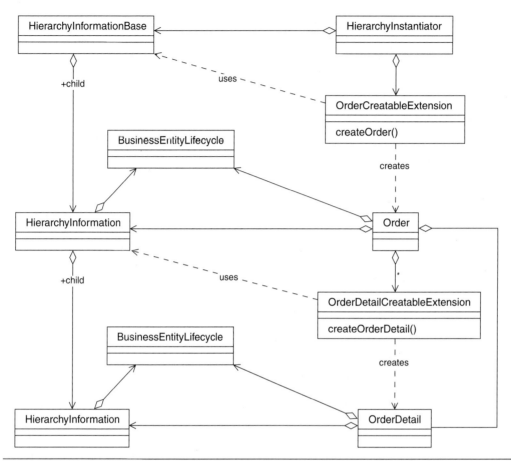

Figure 19.4. Classes Involved in Creating the First Two Levels of an Order Hierarchy

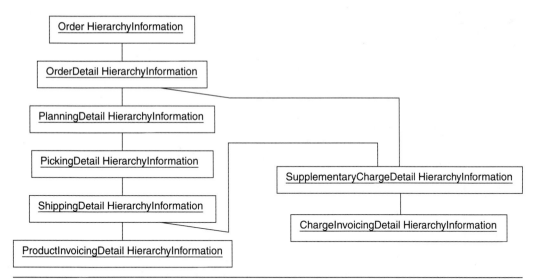

Figure 19.5. HierarchyInformation Hierarchy for a Remote Sales Order Showing Reuse of a Subhierarchy

Applicability

Consider using the Hierarchy Information pattern when any of the following criteria apply:

- A hierarchical domain process structure must be implemented for a business object such as an Order.

- You are modeling a set of lifecycle-based entities that are hierarchical in nature. An example would be a hierarchy of components in a manufacturing system.

Structure

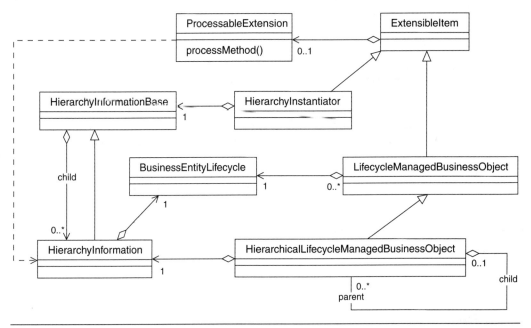

Figure 19.6. Hierarchy Information Structure

Participants

- **HierarchyInformation.** An object that holds structural information for a given position in a business object hierarchy. This information consists at minimum of a BusinessEntityLifecycle (see Chapter 18) to be used for business objects at the corresponding hierarchy position, and a keyed collection of HierarchyInformation children that hold information for the next position in the hierarchy. Often HierarchyInformation objects also hold business information for their associated business objects, such as configured attributes and business policies. HierarchyInformation objects are arranged in hierarchies that form the templates for the business object hierarchies associated with them.

- **HierarchicalLifecycleManagedBusinessObject** (Order, OrderDetail, PlanningDetail). A business object that is used to represent hierarchical lifecycle-based business objects, such as the processing details produced by the execution of hierarchical processes. Such an object is a type of LifecycleManagedBusinessObject that incorporates parent and child linkages, allowing the objects to be arranged in object hierarchies. HierarchicalLifecycleManagedBusinessObjects contain a reference to a

HierarchyInformation object from which they retrieve their Business-EntityLifecycle.

- **HierarchyInformationBase.** An object that is used as the root of a HierarchyInformation object hierarchy. Unlike a HierarchyInformation object, a HierarchyInformationBase object does not contain a reference to a BusinessEntityLifecycle.

- **HierarchyInstantiator.** An object that is used as a common invocation and anchor point for processes that create top-level hierarchical business objects. These creation processes are represented as Extensions on a HierarchyInstantiator object.

- **ProcessableExtension** (PlannableExtension, PickableExtension). A class that represents an Extension class that enables a domain process on its target business object.

- **ExtensibleItem.** A base class for business object classes that exhibit dynamic behavioral change. See Chapter 16 for additional details.

- **LifecycleManagedBusinessObject.** A base class for business objects that exhibit lifecycle behavior. See Chapter 18 for additional details.

- **BusinessEntityLifecycle.** A class that contains the lifecycle information for its associated LifecycleManagedBusinessObjects. See Chapter 18 for additional details.

Collaborations

- HierarchicalLifecycleManagedBusinessObjects use their associated HierarchyInformation to retrieve their BusinessEntityLifecycle.

- A ProcessableExtension uses the HierarchyInformation object associated with its target business object (either a HierarchicalLifecycleManaged-BusinessObject or a HierarchyInstantiator object) in the implementation of its processMethod method (e.g., "plan," "pick," "ship") to find the appropriate child HierarchyInformation object for the processing details it creates.

Consequences

The Hierarchy Information pattern has the following benefits and drawbacks:

Benefits

- **Decoupling of Hierarchy Levels.** By encapsulating the information necessary to create a business object at a given position in a hierarchy, the

Hierarchy Information pattern allows hierarchical domain processes to be implemented without specific knowledge of the business entity lifecycles of their child details.

- **Runtime configuration.** Hierarchies of HierarchyInformation objects act as metadata for their associated business entity hierarchies, storing the hierarchy structure as well as the lifecycle behavior for business objects at each position in the hierarchy. For most business processes, this metadata extends into business information, such as configurable attributes and business policies associated with the business process. This information can be easily maintained at runtime, allowing new business object hierarchies to be defined (e.g., new hierarchies could be defined for new order types), as well as existing hierarchies to be changed or enhanced (e.g., a quality control process could be introduced into an existing order type).

- **Support for decoupled processes.** The Hierarchy Information pattern serves as an enabling mechanism for implementing decoupled hierarchical domain processes, as described in Chapter 20.

Drawbacks

- **Standard drawbacks of the Business Entity Lifecycle pattern.** Given that the Hierarchy Information pattern builds on the Business Entity Lifecycle pattern, the drawbacks of the latter should be considered (see Chapter 18).

- **Increased complexity.** Introducing hierarchy behavior to LifecycleManaged-BusinessObjects, as is necessary to represent hierarchical, lifecycle-based business entities, inevitably increases the complexity of the business object implementation.

- **Configuration errors at runtime.** Care must be taken to ensure the validity of the configuration of a HierarchyInformation hierarchy and the BusinessEntityLifecycle objects it contains to avoid the possibility of runtime errors as associated business object hierarchies are created.

Implementation

Consider the following implementation issues for the Hierarchy Information pattern:

- **Use of subclasses.** In the Hierarchy Information pattern, domain-specific subclasses of the HierarchyInformation class often are useful. These domain-specific subclasses may contain fixed attributes and behaviors that must be supported consistently by all HierarchicalLifecycleManaged-

BusinessObjects associated with that HierarchyInformation object. For example, a subclass of HierarchyInformation that is dedicated for use with PickingDetails may hold policies that are used in the implementation of PickingDetail methods. These policies may vary with different instances of the PickingDetail HierarchyInformation subclass, depending on the HierarchyInformation hierarchy in which they are placed (e.g., a remote sales order hierarchy or a direct sales order hierarchy). Business attributes held by a HierarchyInformation subclass instance are typically accessed via wire-through methods from the business objects associated with the HierarchyInformation object.

- **Use of a common interface for accessing children.** In the SanFrancisco framework implementation of this pattern, we introduced a common Java interface implemented by both the HierarchicalLifecycleManaged-BusinessObject and the HierarchyInstantiator classes. The interface introduces a getChildHierarchyInformationBy method that allows a process on either a HierarchicalLifecycleManagedBusinessObject or a Hierarchy-Instantiator object to access a child HierarchyInformation object using the same interface and method. This approach is useful if you plan to implement creation processes that could be executed on either a Hierarch-yInstantiator or a HierarchicalLifecycleManagedBusinessObject instance.

- **Use of hierarchical method delegation.** When implementing the HierarchicalLifecycleManagedBusinessObject class, you may choose to introduce drill-up and drill-down variations of the invokeMethod method as described in Chapter 17. The drill-up method allows a user to retrieve information from a business object in a hierarchy that exists in another business object at a higher level. For instance, a user can retrieve the customer name or total requested quantity from a PickingDetail, even if that information resides in the ancestor Order or OrderDetail objects.

Sample Code

Here's the HierarchyInformationBase class. Note that the BusinessEntityLifecycle reference is not introduced here, because it is not required by the Hierarchy-Instantiator objects that will reference objects of this class.

```
public class HierarchyInformationBase {

    // Retrieve a child HierarchyInformation by ID
    HierarchyInformation getChildHierarchyInformationBy(String id) {
        return (HierarchyInformation)(ivChildren.get(id));
    }
```

```
    // Add a child HierarchyInformation with the given key
    public void addChildHierarchyInformationBy(String id,
                                    HierarchyInformation child) {
        ivChildren.put(id,child);
    }

    // This is our map of child HierarchyInformation objects
    // keyed by String IDs
    public Hashtable ivChildren = new Hashtable();
}
```

The HierarchyInformation class is implemented as a subclass of Hierarchy-
InformationBase:

```
public class HierarchyInformation extends HierarchyInformationBase {

    // Constructor. All HierarchyInformation objects must
    // have a parent and a lifecycle.
    public HierarchyInformation(HierarchyInformationBase parent,
                            String id,
                            BusinessEntityLifecycle lifecycle) {

        parent.addChildHierarchyInformationBy(id,this);
        ivLifecycle = lifecycle;
    }

    public BusinessEntityLifecycle getLifecycle() {
        return ivLifecycle;
    }

    // This is the lifecycle to be used with business objects
    // at this level of the hierarchy
    public BusinessEntityLifecycle ivLifecycle = null;
}
```

Here's a simple implementation of the HierarchicalLifecycleManaged-
BusinessObject class that does not support hierarchical method delegation (described in Chapter 17). We have introduced the getChildHierarchyInformationBy
method so that processes can easily retrieve the appropriate child Hierarchy-
Information object for their processing details.

```
public abstract class HierarchicalLifecycleManagedBusinessObject
                        extends LifecycleManagedBusinessObject {

    // The setParent method is used to set up parent-child linkages
    public void setParent(
        HierarchicalLifecycleManagedBusinessObject parent) {
        ivParent = parent;
        parent.setChild(this);
    }
```

```
    // Add the child to the children collection
    public void setChild(
        HierarchicalLifecycleManagedBusinessObject child) {
        ivChildren.addElement(child);
    }

    // Retrieve a child HierarchyInformation by ID
    public HierarchyInformation
        getChildHierarchyInformationBy(String hierInfoId) {
        return ivHierarchyInformation.getChildHierarchyInformationBy(
            hierInfoId);
    }

    // The hierarchical parent
    public HierarchicalLifecycleManagedBusinessObject ivParent = null;

    // A collection of children
    public Vector ivChildren = new Vector();

    // Reference to the HierarchyInformation for this level
    public HierarchyInformation ivHierarchyInformation = null;
}
```

Finally, here's the HierarchyInstantiator class. HierarchyInstantiator objects have little fixed behavior because their sole purpose is to support creation process Extensions.

```
public class HierarchyInstantiator extends ExtensibleItem {

    // Constructor
    public HierarchyInstantiator(
        HierarchyInformationBase hierarchyInfo) {
        ivHierarchyInformation = hierarchyInfo;
    }

    // Retrieve a child HierarchyInformation by ID
    public HierarchyInformation
        getChildHierarchyInformationBy(String hierInfoId) {
        return ivHierarchyInformation.getChildHierarchyInformationBy(
            hierInfoId);
    }

    // These methods must be overridden by ExtensibleItem
    // subclasses; they are described in Chapter 16
    public ReturnValue handleInvokeMethod(String methodName,
                                          Object[] parameterList) {
        // The HierarchyInstantiator class does not introduce
        // any methods that can be called through invokeMethod,
        // so return a ReturnValue indicating this
        return new ReturnValue(null,false);
    }
```

```
public boolean supportsMethod(String methodName) {
    return false;
}

// Reference to the HierarchyInformation for this level
public HierarchyInformationBase ivHierarchyInformation = null;
}
```

Known Uses

The Hierarchy Information pattern is used in the implementation of all order types and hierarchical order processes provided in the SanFrancisco Order Management Core Business Process.

Related Patterns

- **Business Entity Lifecycle.** HierarchicalLifecycleManagedBusinessObjects are a type of LifecycleManagedBusinessObject (see Chapter 18).

- **Decoupled Processes.** The Hierarchy Information pattern serves as an enabling mechanism for implementation of the hierarchical variation of the Decoupled Processes pattern (see Chapter 20).

- **Hierarchical Extensible Item.** The HierarchicalLifecycleManaged-BusinessObject class may optionally support hierarchical method delegation as described in Chapter 17.

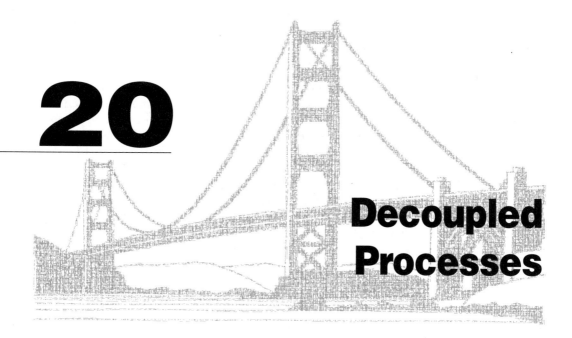

20

Decoupled Processes

Intent

Represent applicable business processes for a given business entity in a self-contained and reusable form, allowing the processes to be arranged in arbitrary orderings for specific types and uses of the business entity.

Motivation

Certain lifecycle-based business entities such as order details can be thought of as being process oriented, meaning that their lifecycles are defined primarily by series of domain processes performed on the business entity. For example, the remote sales order details of Food Warehouse undergo planning, picking, shipping, and invoicing processes during their lifetimes. Specific processes may be combined in different ways, depending on the business rules for the specific type of business entity on which they are acting. For example, in an FW remote sales order, invoicing is preceded by shipping, whereas in a direct sales order, invoicing is preceded by picking (see Figure 18.3 in Chapter 18).

Although their inclusion and ordering may vary, individual processes (e.g., planning, picking, or quality control) are often quite similar or even identical, regardless of the specific type of business entity on which they act. For this reason, each process should be able to run without direct knowledge of other processes occurring before, after, or at the same time. Likewise, the information resulting from a process should not be directly aware of the information preceding or following it from prior or subsequent processing, respectively.

As we have already implied, many domain processes are sequential by nature (e.g., the output from one process is used as the input to one or more subsequent processes). Put another way, the objective of many domain processes is to produce information (i.e., the results of processing), which may then be further processed (i.e., the information becomes *processable*). For example, the output from the picking process is information about when, where, and who picked the requested quantity of the requested product. In a remote sales order detail, this picking information (along with information from previous processes) becomes the input for the shipping process (i.e., the information becomes shippable).

By separating and encapsulating the processable aspects of the information produced by a process from the processing information itself (e.g., by allowing picking information to be produced without the picking process knowing that the information is to be shippable, and allowing the shipping process to be enabled without knowing that the data on which it is to act was produced by the picking process), we can decouple the next processing step (or steps) from the information used as input to that step. Thus, different processables representing various processes (e.g., shippable, invoiceable) can be combined with a processing result (e.g., picking result, shipping result) to make that processing result processable in different ways. The combination of the processable and processing-result parts of a given process form a package that can be mixed and matched with other related process packages on a given business object. Figure 20.1 shows two such process packages.

The Business Entity Lifecycle pattern (see Chapter 18) provides a foundation on which this decoupling can be built. Using the Business Entity Lifecycle

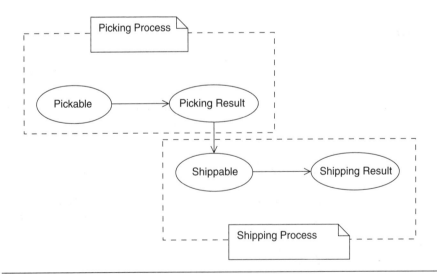

Figure 20.1. Decoupled Processes

pattern, we can represent processables and processing results as Extensions added to a LifecycleManagedBusinessObject such as an OrderDetail. The associated BusinessEntityLifecycle can be used to control the ordering of processes for a business object by adding processable Extensions at appropriate stages in the object's lifecycle. Generally the addition of a processable Extension will be triggered by the completion of another process. When the process method on the processable Extension is invoked (e.g., the pick method on a PickableExtension), an associated processing-result Extension (e.g., a PickingResultExtension) will be created and added to the LifecycleManagedBusinessObject to store the results of the process.

The processing-result Extension will generally enable methods on the LifecycleManagedBusinessObject to allow users and future processes to access the resulting information from the process. An interface can be associated with the processable Extension (see the discussion of interfaces in Chapter 16) that typically declares the process method, as well as accessor methods for data that the given process requires from previous processes. Using the picking process as an example, a Pickable interface would be provided that declares a pick method and a getRequestedQuantity method (see Figure 20.2). Since only the pick method will be implemented by the PickableExtension, the declaration of getRequestedQuantity on the Pickable interface formalizes the requirement that any LifecycleManagedBusinessObject that is to be pickable must provide a requested quantity that is accessible to the picking process.

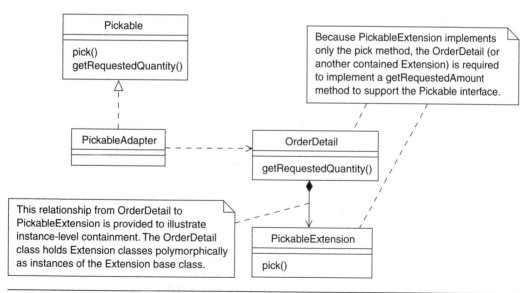

Figure 20.2. Formalizing Interface Requirements for a Process

With this approach, the package for a given process will consist of the following:

- A processable Extension class
- A processable interface and adapter class
- A processing-result Extension class

We can enable the process package on a LifecycleManagedBusinessObject by simply making the necessary configuration changes to its associated BusinessEntityLifecycle.

The picking and invoicing processes on a Food Warehouse direct sales order detail are examples of processes that can be decoupled using the Decoupled Processes pattern, allowing them to be reused with other types of order details. In this pattern the picking process would be represented as a package consisting of a PickableExtension class, a Pickable interface and adapter class, and a PickingResultExtension class (see Figure 20.3). The PickableExtension class

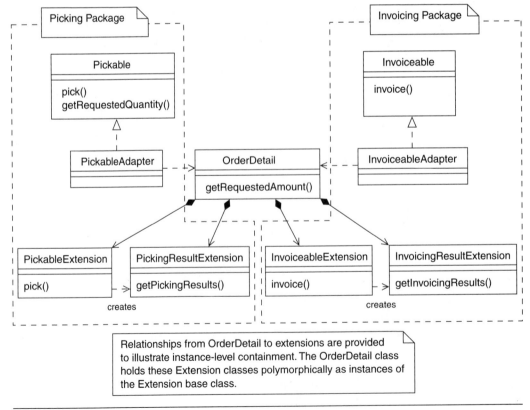

Figure 20.3. Decoupled Picking and Invoicing Processes

would enable a pick method on the OrderDetail object and allow it to be cast to a Pickable (via its adapter). When the pick method is invoked, the Pickable-Extension creates an instance of the PickingResultExtension class and adds it to the OrderDetail.

Invoicing would be represented in a similar fashion, by use of an InvoiceableExtension class, an Invoiceable interface and adapter class, and an InvoicingResultExtension class. The BusinessEntityLifecycle associated with direct sales OrderDetails would be configured to add an InvoiceableExtension to the OrderDetail object upon completion of the pick method. We could reuse the picking and invoicing process packages with a remote sales OrderDetail by using a separate BusinessEntityLifecycle that enables a shipping process upon completion of the pick method and adds the InvoiceableExtension only upon completion of the shipping process.

Decoupling Hierarchical Processes

By representing the results of a process as a processing-result Extension added to the target business object, we have assumed that the result of the process is a modification of the target business object itself. Although this assumption is applicable in many cases, in some situations execution of a process on a certain business object results in the creation of one or more child business objects that represent distinct pieces of information resulting from the process.

Consider the planning process for an OrderDetail in a company with multiple warehouses: A single warehouse may not be able to supply the entire quantity of a requested product. In this case, the planning process on the OrderDetail needs to create two separate PlanningDetail objects, each with a different source warehouse and plannable quantity (see Figure 20.4). These PlanningDetails are

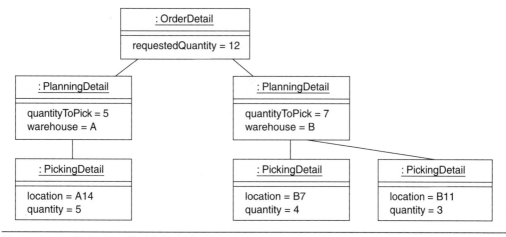

Figure 20.4. OrderDetail with Multiple Planning and Picking Details

considered children of the OrderDetail within the order hierarchy. Once created, the next process (picking) will be enabled on the PlanningDetails rather than on the OrderDetail object. The picking process might in turn partition PlanningDetails further by assigning specific stock locations from which to pick the planned goods.

This nonlinear progression of processing results produces a hierarchy of processing-detail objects, each controlled by a BusinessEntityLifecycle object. We can implement this variation of the Decoupled Processes pattern in a straightforward fashion by using the Hierarchy Information pattern (see Chapter 19). In this case the package for a given process consists of the following:

- A processable Extension class
- A processable interface and adapter class
- A processing-detail HierarchicalLifecycleManagedBusinessObject class

We can enable the process package on a HierarchicalLifecycleManaged-BusinessObject by making the necessary configuration changes to its associated BusinessEntityLifecycle and adding the HierarchyInformation object for the child processing-detail objects to the HierarchyInformation object associated with the target HierarchicalLifecycleManagedBusinessObject.

Applicability

Consider using the Decoupled Processes pattern when any of the following criteria apply:

- The business entity being modeled supports multiple, sequential, or parallel domain processes.
- These domain processes and their ordering may vary by the context in which the business entity is used, or the domain processes may be reused by another, similar business entity.
- Order structures or similar business entities whose business entity lifecycles are concerned primarily with the execution of a series of processes against the business entity need to be implemented.

Structure

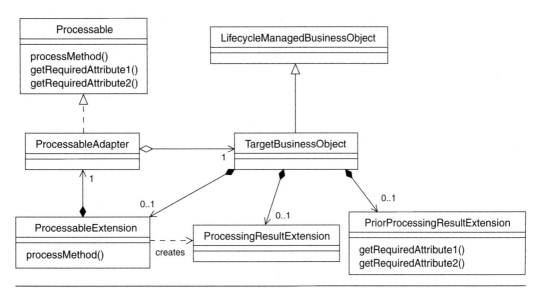

Figure 20.5. Decoupled Processes Pattern: Nonhierarchical Variation

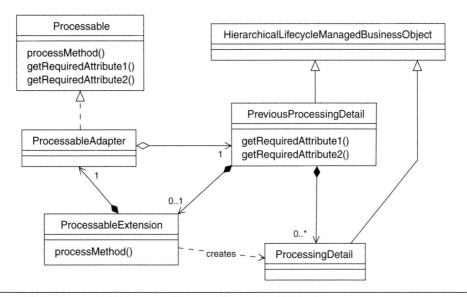

Figure 20.6. Decoupled Processes Pattern: Hierarchical Variation

Participants

- **ProcessableExtension** (PickableExtension). An Extension class responsible for enabling its associated process on the LifecycleManagedBusinessObject to which it is added. ProcessableExtension declares and implements a process method (e.g., pick) that performs the process and stores the processing results in either a ProcessingResultExtension (nonhierarchy case) or one or more ProcessingDetails (hierarchy case) that it creates.

- **Processable** (Pickable). A Java interface that declares a process method (e.g., pick), as well as accessor methods for data that the given process requires from previous processes.

- **ProcessableAdapter** (PickableAdapter). An adapter class that adapts the processable interface to the LifecycleManagedBusinessObject (the use of adapters with ExtensibleItem-type business objects is described in Chapter 16).

- **ProcessingResultExtension** (PickingResultExtension). An Extension class that is used in the nonhierarchical variation of the Decoupled Processes pattern. The ProcessingResultExtension is created by the ProcessableExtension during execution of the process method and holds information resulting from the process. The ProcessingResultExtension enables methods on the LifecycleManagedBusinessObject that can be used for accessing this resulting information. These methods may be used to support processable interfaces of future processes.

- **PriorProcessingResultExtension** (PlanningResultExtension). A ProcessingResultExtension produced by the previous process performed on the TargetBusinessObject.

- **LifecycleManagedBusinessObject.** A base class for business objects exhibiting lifecycle behavior. See Chapter 18 for additional details.

- **TargetBusinessObject** (OrderDetail). A specific subclass of the LifecycleManagedBusinessObject whose instances are the target of the process performed by the ProcessableExtension.

- **ProcessingDetail** (PickingDetail). A HierarchicalLifecycleManagedBusinessObject class that is used in the hierarchical variation of the Decoupled Processes pattern. ProcessingDetails are created by the ProcessableExtension during execution of the process method and hold distinct pieces of information resulting from the process. ProcessingDetails may themselves be targets of additional decoupled processes. ProcessingDetails may contain ProcessingResultExtensions or may directly support the business information (i.e., attributes) resulting from processing.

- **HierarchicalLifecycleManagedBusinessObject.** A base class for Lifecycle-ManagedBusinessObjects that can be placed in a hierarchy. See Chapter 19 for additional details.

- **PreviousProcessingDetail** (PlanningDetail). A specific subclass of the HierarchicalLifecycleManagedBusinessObject whose instances were produced by a previous process and are the target of the process performed by the ProcessableExtension.

Collaborations

- ProcessableAdapter objects delegate method calls to their associated LifecycleManagedBusinessObjects or HierarchicalLifecycleManaged-BusinessObjects through the invokeMethod method.

- ProcessableExtensions use their associated LifecycleManagedBusiness-Objects or HierarchicalLifecycleManagedBusinessObjects to obtain information necessary to implement their process methods.

- In the nonhierarchical variation of the pattern, ProcessableExtensions create ProcessingResultExtensions to hold the results from processing and add them to their associated LifecycleManagedBusinessObjects.

- In the hierarchical variation of the pattern, ProcessableExtensions create ProcessingDetail objects and add them as children to the Hierarchical-LifecycleManagedBusinessObjects associated with the ProcessableExtensions.

- In the hierarchical variation of the pattern, ProcessableExtensions use the HierarchyInformation objects associated with their HierarchicalLifecycle-ManagedBusinessObjects to find the appropriate child Hierarchy-Information objects for the ProcessingDetails they create.

Consequences

The Decoupled Processes pattern has the following tradeoffs, benefits, and drawbacks:

Tradeoffs

- **Hierarchical versus nonhierarchical variation.** Once you have decided to implement a business process with the Decoupled Processes pattern, you must then decide whether the nonhierarchical or hierarchical variation of the pattern is more suitable for the process you are modeling. This decision should be based on the nature of the output of your process. If the process produces multiple, distinct groupings of information (i.e., processing details) on which subsequent processes may be *separately* invoked, the hierarchical variation is the correct (and only) choice. If this is not the case, the nonhierarchical variation should be used because it has less overhead in terms of performance and size.

Benefits

- **Flexible ordering of processes.** The Decoupled Processes pattern allows sequential and parallel domain processes to be selected and ordered as necessary for the context in which a business object is used.

- **Reuse of processes.** Processes represented as decoupled process packages can potentially be reused with different business objects of a similar nature.

- **Addition of new processes.** We can add additional decoupled process packages to existing business object types by simply reconfiguring the associated BusinessEntityLifecycles, and, in the hierarchical case, the associated HierarchyInformation objects, to incorporate the new processes.

Drawbacks

- **Standard drawbacks of the Business Entity Lifecycle and Hierarchy Information patterns.** Given that this pattern is dependent on the Business Entity Lifecycle pattern (see Chapter 18) and, in its hierarchical variation, on the Hierarchy Information pattern (see Chapter 19), the drawbacks and tradeoffs of those patterns apply here.

- **Dependent processes.** Not all domain processes can be fully decoupled or arbitrarily arranged. For example, the picking process on an OrderDetail cannot precede the planning process, because the purpose of planning is to create information that can be used in picking. In addition, it may not be possible to introduce an elaborate picking process on an OrderDetail type that does not have a planning process. It is important to realize that although the Decoupled Processes pattern helps eliminate unnecessary, artificial dependencies between processes, it cannot eliminate those that are inherent to the domain processes being represented.

Implementation

Consider the following implementation issues for the Decoupled Processes pattern:

- **Use of a policy.** It may be useful to place the domain logic for execution of a process in a policy (see Chapter 7) that is used by the processable Extension, thereby allowing the process algorithm to be altered without changes having to be made to other classes in the process package. With this approach, the processable Extension delegates implementation of the process method to the policy. The processable adapter is passed as input to the policy. The policy uses the processable adapter to retrieve information necessary for completing the process. In the nonhierarchical case, this policy could be held either directly by the processable Extension, or by another easily accessible business object that provides context (e.g., Company). In the hierarchical case, the policy could be placed on the HierarchyInformation object associated with the processing details produced by the process, thereby allowing the HierarchyInformation object to have additional behavioral control over the creation of its associated processing details.

- **Repetitive processes.** Some processes may be invoked multiple times against a single target business object. For example, the pick method may be called on an OrderDetail each time a portion of the total requested quantity is physically picked. Each subsequent call to the pick method would pass a picked quantity indicating which portion of the total had just been picked. This case lends itself to the hierarchical variation of the pattern, which allows a separate PickingDetail to be created for each call to the pick method.

- **Processes without processing details.** In some situations the result of executing a certain domain process may be limited to changing the state of the target business object itself. For example, the confirmation process on a PlanningDetail may simply change a "confirmed" flag held directly as an attribute on the PlanningDetail class. The flag would be set to false when the PlanningDetail was created. A ConfirmableExtension would be provided that introduces a confirm method. This method would set the "confirmed" flag on the PlanningDetail to true. In this particular case, the process package consists only of the Confirmable interface and adapter class and the ConfirmableExtension class (see Figure 20.7).

- **Creatable processes.** The creation of business objects that are not normally considered process details, such as Orders and OrderDetails, can be thought of as a creation process. Like other domain processes, the creation process can be represented with the hierarchical variation of the Decoupled

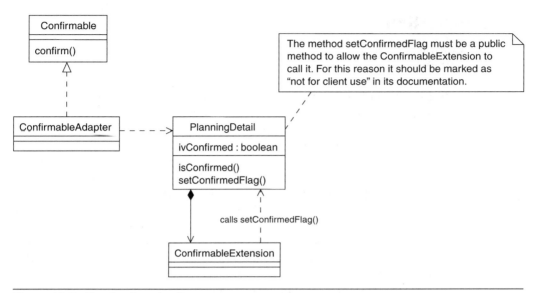

Figure 20.7. The Confirmation Process

Processes pattern. In accordance with the pattern, a "creatable" interface and Extension is introduced that simply creates a business object (e.g., Order or OrderDetail) in its process method. Creatable processes for top-level business objects (e.g., Orders) should be enabled on HierarchyInstantiator objects as described in Chapter 19.

Sample Code

We'll start by showing a nonhierarchical picking process package. Here's the Pickable interface:

```
public interface Pickable {

    // This is the process method
    public abstract void pick(Employee responsibleEmployee,
                              Date pickingDate);

    // This method is introduced to ensure that any
    // object that is pickable must make available
    // a requested quantity for the picking process to use
    public abstract int getRequestedQuantity();
}
```

Here's the PickableAdapter:

```
public class PickableAdapter implements Pickable {

    // Constructor
    public PickableAdapter(
        LifecycleManagedBusinessObject businessObject) {
        ivBusinessObject = businessObject;
    }


    public void pick(Employee responsibleEmployee,
                     Date pickingDate) {
        // Delegate the method call to the associated OrderDetail;
        // this call will eventually be handled by the PickableExtension
        Object[] parms = new Object[2];
        parms[0] = responsibleEmployee;
        parms[1] = pickingDate;
        ivBusinessObject.invokeMethod("pick",parms);
    }

    public int getRequestedQuantity() {

        // Delegate the method call to the associated OrderDetail;
        // the OrderDetail itself or another Extension
        // is expected to handle this call
        Integer requestedQuantity =
            (Integer)(ivBusinessObject.
                invokeMethod("getRequestedQuantity",null));
        return requestedQuantity.intValue();
    }


    LifecycleManagedBusinessObject ivBusinessObject = null;
}
```

Here's the PickableExtension:

```
public class PickableExtension extends LMBOExtension {

    // Override of initialize from LMBOExtension
    public void initialize(LifecycleManagedBusinessObject
                           businessObject,
                           Object[] creationParms) {

        // Set the LifecycleManagedBusinessObject reference
        ivBusinessObject = businessObject;

        // Set the ExtensibleItem class adapter attribute
        ivAdapter = new PickableAdapter(businessObject);
    }
```

```
// The process method
public void pick(Employee responsibleEmployee,
                 Date pickingDate) {

    // We can use the contained adapter to get the
    // requested quantity from the OrderDetail
    int requestedQuantity =
        ((Pickable)ivAdapter).getRequestedQuantity();

    // Business logic for the picking process goes here

    // Create an instance of PickingResultExtension
    // to store the results
    PickingResultExtension resultExtension =
        new PickingResultExtension(ivBusinessObject,
                                   responsibleEmployee,
                                   pickingDate);

    // Add the Extension instance to the business object
    ivBusinessObject.addExtension(resultExtension);

    // Register the "Pick" event
    getLifecycle().registerEvent(ivBusinessObject,"Pick");
}


// Override of the getId method
// It's OK for one ID to be shared by all instances
// of this class, since there will be not more than one
// PickableExtension on any given OrderDetail
public String getId() {

    return "PickableExtension";
}

// Override of abstract ExtensibleItem methods
// (see Chapter 16)
public ReturnValue handleInvokeMethod(String methodName,
                                      Object[] parameterList) {

    // Object to hold result
    Object result = null;
    if (methodName.equals("pick")) {
        pick((Employee)parameterList[0],
             (Date)parameterList[1]);
    }
    else {
        // At this point we know that the method
        // was not supported by this Extension,
        // so return a ReturnValue indicating this
        return new ReturnValue(null,false);
    }
```

```
        // If we get here, a method was called,
        // so put the result in a ReturnValue,
        // indicate that the method was invoked,
        // and return the result to the caller
            return new ReturnValue(result,true);
    }

    public boolean supportsMethod(String methodName) {
        if (methodName.equals("pick")) {
            return true;
        }
        else {
            return false;
        }
    }
}
```

Here's the PickingResultExtension:

```
public class PickingResultExtension extends LMBOExtension {

    // A constructor is provided to allow PickableExtensions
    // to create PickingResultExtensions directly
    public PickingResultExtension(
        LifecycleManagedBusinessObject businessObject,
        Employee responsibleEmployee,
        Date pickingDate) {

        ivBusinessObject = businessObject;
        ivResponsibleEmployee = responsibleEmployee;
        ivPickingDate = pickingDate;
    }

    public Employee getEmployeeResponsibleForPicking() {

        return ivResponsibleEmployee;
    }

    public Date getPickingDate() {

        return ivPickingDate;
    }

    // Override of the getId method
    // It's OK for one ID to be shared by all instances
    // of this class, since there will be not more than one
    // PickingResultExtension on any given OrderDetail
    public String getId() {

        return "PickingResultExtension";
    }
```

```java
// Override of abstract ExtensibleItem methods
// (see Chapter 16)
public ReturnValue handleInvokeMethod(String methodName,
                                      Object[] parameterList) {

    // Object to hold result
    Object result = null;
    if (methodName.equals("getEmployeeResponsibleForPicking")) {
        result = getEmployeeResponsibleForPicking();
    }
    else if (methodName.equals("getPickingDate")) {
        result = getPickingDate();
    }
    else {
        // At this point we know that the method
        // was not supported by this Extension,
        // so return a ReturnValue indicating this
        return new ReturnValue(null,false);
    }

    // If we get here, a method was called,
    // so put the result in a ReturnValue,
    // indicate that the method was invoked,
    // and return the result to the caller
    return new ReturnValue(result,true);
}

public boolean supportsMethod(String methodName) {
    if (methodName.equals("getEmployeeResponsibleForPicking")) {
        return true;
    }
    if (methodName.equals("getPickingDate")) {
        return true;
    }
    return false;
}

// Override of initialize from LMBOExtension;
// since PickingResultExtensions will be created
// directly by PickableExtensions rather than by the
// BusinessEntityLifecycle, this method will not be used
public void initialize(LifecycleManagedBusinessObject
                       businessObject,
                       Object[] creationParms) {

    // Set the LifecycleManagedBusinessObject reference
    ivBusinessObject = businessObject;

    ivResponsibleEmployee = (Employee)creationParms[0];
    ivPickingDate = (Date)creationParms[1];

}
```

```
    protected Employee ivResponsibleEmployee = null;
    protected Date ivPickingDate = null;
}
```

Now we'll use the planning process for an OrderDetail to demonstrate the hierarchical variation of the Decoupled Processes pattern. The planning process is best represented through the hierarchical approach when multiple warehouses are involved. This approach allows separate PlanningDetails to be created for each warehouse. This example also uses a PlanningPolicy as described earlier in the "Implementation" section.

Again, we'll start with the processable interface. Note that the interface declares a createPlanningDetail method for use by the PlanningPolicy, thereby simplifying the policy implementation by freeing it of dependencies on the specific representation of the Plannable object.

```
public interface Plannable {

    // This is our process method
    public abstract void plan();

    // These methods are introduced to ensure that any
    // object that is plannable makes available
    // a requested quantity and requested delivery date
    // for the planning process to use
    public abstract int getRequestedQuantity();
    public abstract Date getRequestedDeliveryDate();

    // This method is used by the planning policy to create
    // instances of PlanningDetails that will be children
    // of the target Plannable object
    public abstract void createPlanningDetail(Warehouse warehouse,
                                              int plannedQuantity);
}
```

The PlannableAdapter is implemented in standard fashion, so we'll skip to the PlannableExtension. Note the delegation of the planning process to the PlanningPolicy object:

```
public class PlannableExtension extends LMBOExtension {

    // Override of initialize from LMBOExtension
    public void initialize(
        LifecycleManagedBusinessObject businessObject,
        Object[] creationParms) {

        // Set the LifecycleManagedBusinessObject reference
        ivBusinessObject = businessObject;

        ivPlanningPolicy = (PlanningPolicy)(creationParms[0]);
```

```
        // Set the ExtensibleItem class adapter attribute
        ivAdapter = new PlannableAdapter((OrderDetail)businessObject);
    }


    public void plan() {

        // Delegate the planning process to the PlanningPolicy
        // Pass the adapter to represent this plannable business object
        ivPlanningPolicy.plan((Plannable)ivAdapter);

        // Register the "Plan" event
        getLifecycle().registerEvent(ivBusinessObject,"Plan");
    }


    // This method is used by the planning policy to create
    // instances of PlanningDetails that will be children
    // of the target Plannable object
    public void createPlanningDetail(Warehouse warehouse,
                                     int plannedQuantity) {

        // Create the PlanningDetail attached as a child to
        // this business object. Pass this business object as parent
        // and "PlanningDetail" as HierarchyInformation ID
        new PlanningDetail(
                (HierarchicalLifecycleManagedBusinessObject)
                    ivBusinessObject,
                "PlanningDetail",
                warehouse,
                plannedQuantity);
    }


    // Override of the getId method
    // It's OK for one ID to be shared by all instances
    // of this class, since there will be not more than one
    // PlannableExtension on any given OrderDetail
    public String getId() {

        return "PlannableExtension";
    }

    // Override of abstract ExtensibleItem methods
    // (see Chapter 16)
    public ReturnValue handleInvokeMethod(String methodName,
                                          Object[] parameterList) {

        // Object to hold result
        Object result = null;
        if (methodName.equals("plan")) {
            plan();
```

```
        } else if (methodName.equals("createPlanningDetail")) {
            createPlanningDetail((Warehouse)parameterList[0],
                                ((Integer)parameterList[1]).intValue());
        }
        else {
            // At this point we know that the method
            // was not supported by this Extension,
            // so return a ReturnValue indicating this
            return new ReturnValue(null,false);
        }

        // If we get here, a method was called,
        // so put the result in a ReturnValue,
        // indicate that the method was invoked,
        // and return the result to the caller
        return new ReturnValue(result,true);
    }

    public boolean supportsMethod(String methodName) {
        if ((methodName.equals("plan")) ||
            (methodName.equals("createPlanningDetail"))) {
            return true;
        }
        else {
            return false;
        }
    }

    PlanningPolicy ivPlanningPolicy = null;
}
```

Here's an example of a concrete PlanningPolicy subclass:

```
public class PlanningPolicyDefault extends PlanningPolicy {

    public void plan(Plannable plannable) {

        // Retrieve the information necessary to perform
        // the planning process from the given Plannable object
        int requestedQuantity = plannable.getRequestedQuantity();
        Date requestedDeliveryDate = plannable.getRequestedDeliveryDate();

        // Planning process logic goes here

        // Here's a sample callback to the Plannable
        // object to create a PlanningDetail
        plannable.createPlanningDetail(chosenWarehouse,chosenQuantity);

    }
}
```

Finally, here's the PlanningDetail implemented as a HierarchicalLifecycle-ManagedBusinessObject (see Chapter 19 for further information):

```
public class PlanningDetail extends
    HierarchicalLifecycleManagedBusinessObject {

    // Constructor. By taking the ID of the HierarchyInformation as
    // parameter, we allow the creator of the PlanningDetail to
    // determine which HierarchyInformation child is appropriate,
    // thereby allowing for different HierarchyInformation objects to be
    // used for PlanningDetails within a single business object
    // hierarchy.
    public PlanningDetail(
        HierarchicalLifecycleManagedBusinessObject parent,
        String hierarchyInformationId,
        Warehouse warehouse,
        int plannedQuantity) {

        // Set the HierarchyInformation reference
        ivHierarchyInformation =
            parent.getChildHierarchyInformationBy(
                hierarchyInformationId);

        // . . . and the BusinessEntityLifecycle
        ivLifecycle = ivHierarchyInformation.getLifecycle();

        // Set up parent-child linkage
        setParent(parent);

        // Set attributes from planning process
        ivWarehouse = warehouse;
        ivPlannedQuantity = plannedQuantity;
    }

    public Warehouse getWarehouse() {
        return ivWarehouse;
    }

    public int getPlannedQuantity() {
        return ivPlannedQuantity;
    }

    // Override of abstract ExtensibleItem methods
    // (see Chapter 16)
    public ReturnValue handleInvokeMethod(String methodName,
                                          Object[] parameterList) {

        // object to hold result
        Object result = null;
        if (methodName.equals("getWarehouse")) {
            result = getWarehouse();
        }
```

```
            else if (methodName.equals("getPlannedQuantity")) {
                result = new Integer(getPlannedQuantity());
            }
            else {
                // At this point we know that the method
                // was not supported by this Extension,
                // so return a ReturnValue indicating this
                return new ReturnValue(null,false);
            }

            // If we get here, a method was called,
            // so put the result in a ReturnValue,
            // indicate that the method was invoked,
            // and return the result to the caller
             return new ReturnValue(result,true);
        }

    public boolean supportsMethod(String methodName) {
        if (methodName.equals("getWarehouse")) {
            return true;
        }
        if (methodName.equals("getPlannedQuantity")) {
            return true;
        }
        return false;
    }

    public Warehouse ivWarehouse = null;
    public int ivPlannedQuantity = 0;
}
```

Known Uses

The Decoupled Processes pattern is used to represent all order processes in the SanFrancisco Order Management Core Business Process. With this pattern we can provide many different types of sales, purchase, and quotation orders by reusing a common set of order process packages. The order processes implemented with the Decoupled Processes pattern include the following:

- Planning
- Picking
- Shipping
- Receiving
- Invoicing
- Acknowledgment
- Quality control

Related Patterns

- **Business Entity Lifecycle.** The Business Entity Lifecycle pattern (see Chapter 18) is an integral part of implementation of the Decoupled Processes pattern. Processes are represented as Extensions that are in part created and enabled by a BusinessEntityLifecycle.

- **Hierarchy Information.** The hierarchical variation of the Decoupled Processes pattern is implemented using HierarchicalLifecycleManaged-BusinessObjects (see Chapter 19).

- **Simple Policy.** In the Decoupled Processes pattern, a policy may be used to encapsulate the process algorithm (see Chapter 7).

A

UML Nomenclature

This book uses Universal Modeling Language as the means to express designs. Many excellent books, such as Fowler, Scott, and Booch's *UML Distilled*, provide detailed descriptions of UML and its use in object-oriented analysis and design. As a quick reference, however, we describe here the highlights of UML nomenclature as used in design diagrams.

UML Notation

UML notation uses rectangles to define both packages[1] and classes. The visual distinction between the two is that a package has a smaller rectangle on top and a class has two horizontal lines within it that connect to the vertical sides. The class name is located above the two horizontal lines, any exposed attributes are located between the two lines, and any exposed methods are located below the two lines. An italicized class name indicates that the class is an abstract class. See Figure A.1 for package and class notation.

Class relationships are a key part of object-oriented design diagrams. Various combinations of diamonds, solid and dashed lines, and open and closed arrows are used to depict a dependency, association (aggregation or composition), or generalization relationship between two classes (see Figure A.2):

- **Dependency** is depicted by a dashed line with an open arrow.

---

1. Packages in UML nomenclature are referred to by SanFrancisco as categories.

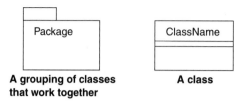

A grouping of classes
that work together   A class

Figure A.1. Package and Class Notation

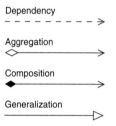

Figure A.2. Object-Oriented Design Diagram Notation

- **Aggregation** is indicated by an open diamond (at one end) connected to a solid line that is then connected to an open arrow.[2] The diamond end indicates the container class; the arrow end indicates the contained class.

- **Generalization** is represented by a solid line and a triangle arrow, where the arrow is adjacent to the base class.

- **Composition** is represented by the same configuration used for aggregation, except that the diamond is solid. As in aggregation, the diamond end indicates the container class and the arrow end indicates the contained class.

Table A.1 explains cardinality[3] as it applies to association relationships.

Objects and Collaboration Diagrams

One way to portray message flow between object instances within UML is to use a collaboration diagram. Within a collaboration diagram, object instances are shown as labeled rectangles, with messages (method calls) between objects shown in text and associated with a short arrow indicating the direction of the message. Each message is numbered, and the numbers indicate an ordered sequence in which the messages are executed.

---

2. The presence of an open arrow indicates navigability in only the direction of the arrow. The absence of an open arrow indicates navigability in either direction.

3. Cardinality is defined as the number of elements possible in a relationship.

Table A.1. Cardinality

Explanation	Class Relationship
An instance of class A is always associated with one instance of class B	◇————1——→
An instance of class A is always associated with one or more instances of class B	◇————1..*——→
An instance of class A is associated with zero or one instance of class B	◇————0..1——→
An instance of class A is associated with zero, one, or more instances of class B	◇————0..*——→

B

Project SanFrancisco

History

In March 1995, the SanFrancisco project was started at the IBM site in Rochester, Minnesota, by a group of object-oriented technologists and a consortium of business partners. The first phase focused on four key and well-defined domains (Distribution, Logistics, General Ledger, and Accounts Payable/Accounts Receivable). Together, domain experts and the object-oriented technologists started to define the core business activities (processes) within each of these domains. This work was carried out at various business partner sites in Sweden, Norway, and England. A larger business partner community reviewed the results of this analysis at various points in the process. While the domain content was being defined, the overall SanFrancisco technical architecture was also being defined.

In September 1995, development teams were put into place in Rochester, Minnesota, and Böblingen, Germany, to create the first release of the product. In July 1997, the first release of the product was made available. This release included the Foundation layer, many of the Common Business Objects, and the General Ledger framework. In May 1998, the second release included many enhancements to the first release, as well as the addition of the Order Management and Warehouse Management base functions. In December 1998, the third release included more function to support the existing frameworks and the addition of the Accounts Payable/Accounts Receivable framework. June 1999 brought a fourth release, with major enhancements to product performance and fully deployable versions of all business components.

Mission

The mission of the SanFrancisco Project is as follows:

1. **To provide a platform-independent base for building business applications.** The SanFrancisco team selected Java as the development language as a way of gaining platform independence. SanFrancisco's Foundation layer builds on Java to present a common interface for the services and APIs necessary to build fully functional business applications.

2. **To abstract out highly reusable business objects.** Various business objects are needed by many different domains. By identifying these common business objects, SanFrancisco increased the ability to reuse code, one of the primary objectives of object orientation, and enhanced interoperability between the application frameworks. We distilled these business objects to their generally common attributes and mechanisms. This distilling process took into account not only the use of these classes in various domains, but also diverse international and cultural considerations.

3. **To provide the core capabilities within specific domains.** Each application domain contains a set of processes that are typically present regardless of the particulars of the business. These processes are supported by numerous business objects that are recognizable to any domain expert. The combination of domain-specific Core Business Processes and their associated business objects is the essence of the SanFrancisco Application Business Components. SanFrancisco provides most of the essential functions within a particular business domain, and it provides those functions consistently across domains. By providing the core functions of each business domain in the form of an application framework, SanFrancisco allows application providers to focus on the differentiating factors for their particular implementations of the business application, spending less time and effort in creating their complete applications.

Architecture

SanFrancisco is composed of three integrated layers, which together support a flexible framework-based environment for developing platform-independent, distributed and object-oriented business applications. The three layers are as follows:

- Foundation
- Common Business Objects
- Core Business Processes

Application designers may build their applications using just the Foundation layer, the Foundation and the Common Business Objects layers together, or all three (using the Core Business Processes for one or more specific domains).[1]

Platform-Independent Base (Foundation)

By choosing Java as its implementation language, the designers of SanFrancisco took a major step toward cross-platform portability. However, modern business applications require more capabilities than just portability. An enterprise-strength business application needs capabilities like dynamic query and consistent internationalization support across all systems used by the application. The SanFrancisco Foundation layer provides the "plumbing" for the other layers and hides the complexity of the technical environment from the application developers. It offers a wide variety of features, including the following:

- Masking the platform-specific needs from the application layer, by providing common cross-platform functions
- Including critical APIs for services like security and transactions
- Providing consistent behavior and common methods for the administration of applications
- Providing the basis for managing distributed objects
- Persisting business data, through standard approaches such as relational database tables, for later use and providing a means to access those business objects

The Foundation layer provides the basis for a distributed application architecture that supports the division of application processing across various systems, greatly enhancing application performance and scalability.

Reusable Business Objects (Common Business Objects)

SanFrancisco's Common Business Objects (CBOs) include many business objects that can be found in multiple domains. These business objects provide the essential functions needed in those domains. For example, Currency is a CBO because almost every business application deals with the concept of money, in the form of prices, costs, revenue, assets, and so on. Because international businesses span multiple countries using various currencies, SanFrancisco's currency values can be easily converted from one currency to another and can be

---

1. For a detailed treatment of the SanFrancisco frameworks, see *SanFrancisco Component Framework: An Introduction*, by Monday, Carey, and Dangler.

formatted for output according to the proper currency symbols and numeric representation rules of a particular country. Other examples of CBOs include calendars of various types and internationalized address support. Many business applications rely on a natural calendar for scheduling a wide variety of business activities and events. Businesses rely on personal and business addresses to deliver information, products, and services.

Domain-Specific Capabilities (Core Business Processes)

When domain experts describe their business domains, they talk in terms of the business processes and business objects that make up those domains. The SanFrancisco team worked with various domain experts to determine the generally common business processes within each domain. This task is more difficult than it sounds because a business domain can be very diverse, supporting companies in a wide variety of businesses and countries.

Even though each company has unique considerations, a core set of processes, when abstracted to the proper level, remains relatively consistent within a business domain. These core processes are what SanFrancisco provides in the form of application frameworks. SanFrancisco's Core Business Processes rely on both the Foundation and the Common Business Objects layers, adding their own objects and capabilities. Each Core Business Process is a rudimentary application in its own right. If user interfaces were provided, a business could perform many of its basic day-to-day activities with the application frameworks provided by SanFrancisco.

The CD-ROM

Installing the Software That Accompanies the Book

Contained on the back cover of this book is a copy of the SanFrancisco Release 1 Version 3 Evaluation Edition CD. This evaluation edition is not the currently released edition of SanFrancisco, but it is the final version of the Evaluation Edition. Later SanFrancisco business component framework releases add more function and have substantial performance improvements.

The CD contains a substantial amount of documentation on the SanFrancisco business component framework as well as running samples and source code for many of the samples.

Before installing the software, read the following documents (available on the CD):

1. The SanFrancisco Evaluation Kit (V1R3): Getting Started redbook. The redbook is from IBM and guides you from the installation of the CD all the way through using several samples. It is available in the directory \SF_Redbook\sg24-5182-01. The file name is sg245182.pdf. You will need an Acrobat Reader to read the PDF file. You can download Acrobat Reader at http://www.adobe.com/. Ensure that you have at least the 3.01 version of Acrobat Reader.

2. Read the installation instructions available in the root directory of the CD. The file name is Install.htm. Load the file into a Web browser for reading.

If you are ready to install the software, keep in mind that when running SanFrancisco, you are running a complete server-side framework. You must adhere to the minimum requirements for installation:

- Processor Speed: Pentium 200 MHz
- Main Memory: 128 MB RAM
- Available Disk Space: 100 MB (substantially more if you choose to install all of the documentation, and even more if you install the documentation in multiple languages)
- Display Resolution: 1024x768, 256 colors

Finally, each version of SanFrancisco is tested with specific versions of the Java Development Kit (JDK). The JDK that was tested with this version of SanFrancisco is JDK 1.1.6. This JDK and the accompanying JIT compiler are also available on the CD. We strongly recommend that you install the Java version that is available on the CD.

For more information on future evaluation editions or for additional documentation on SanFrancisco, see the IBM SanFrancisco Web site: http://www.software.ibm.com/ad/sanfrancisco

CD-ROM Warranty

Addison Wesley Longman, Inc. warrants the enclosed disc to be free of defects in materials and faulty workmanship under normal use for a period of ninety days after purchase. If a defect is discovered in the disc during this warranty period, a replacement disc can be obtained at no charge by sending the defective disc, postage prepaid, with proof of purchase to:

Editorial Department
Computer and Engineering Publishing Group
Addison-Wesley
One Jacob Way
Reading, Massachusetts 01867-3999

After the ninety-day period, a replacement disc will be sent upon receipt of the defective disc and a check or money order for $10.00, payable to Addison Wesley Longman, Inc.

Addison Wesley Longman, Inc. makes no warranty or representation, either expressed or implied, with respect to this software, its quality, performance, merchantability, or fitness for a particular purpose. In no event will Addison Wesley Longman, Inc., its distributors, or dealers be liable for direct, indirect, special, incidental, or consequential damages arising out of the use or inability to use the software. The exclusion of implied warranties is not permitted in some states. Therefore, the above exclusion may not apply to you. This warranty provides you with specific legal rights. There may be other rights that you may have that vary from state to state. The contents of this CD-ROM are intended for personal use only.

More information and updates are available at: http://www.awl.com/cseng/titles/0-201-61644-0

Bibliography

Booch, Grady. 1994. *Object-Oriented Analysis and Design with Applications*, 2nd ed. Addison-Wesley, Reading, MA.

Cline, Marshall, Greg Lomow, and Mike Girou. 1999. *C++ FAQs,* 2nd ed. Addison-Wesley, Reading, MA.

Fowler, Martin. 1997. *Analysis Patterns: Reusable Object Models.* Addison-Wesley, Reading, MA.

Fowler, Martin, Kendall Scott, and Grady Booch. 1999. *UML Distilled.* Addison-Wesley, Menlo Park, CA.

Gamma, Erich, Richard Helm, Ralph Johnson, and John Vlissides. 1995. *Design Patterns: Elements of Reusable Object-Oriented Software.* Addison-Wesley, Reading, MA.

Jacobson, Ivar, Magnus Christerson, Patrik Jonsson, and Gunnar Overgaard. 1992. *Object-Oriented Software Engineering: A Use Case Driven Approach.* Addison-Wesley, Reading, MA.

Johnson, Maynard, Randy Baxter, and Tore Dahl. 1999. *SanFrancisco Life Cycle Programming Techniques.* Addison-Wesley, Menlo Park, CA.

Monday, Paul, James Carey, and Mary Dangler. 2000. *SanFrancisco Component Framework: An Introduction.* Addison-Wesley, Reading, MA.

Index